ELIZABETH WILSON has been a mental-health worker, a university lecturer and a feminist campaigner, was on the board of Liberty, is currently a school governor, a Trustee of the London Library and was until recently Visiting Professor at the University of the Arts, London. She is the author of a number of books on fashion and urban culture, including *Adorned in Dreams: Fashion and Modernity* (1985, 2003), *Bohemians: The Glamorous Outcasts* (2000), and *Cultural Passions* (2013). She is also the author of three crime novels published by Serpent's Tail: *The Twilight Hour*, *War Damage* and *The Girl in Berlin*, and is working on a fourth. She lives with her partner in London.

LOVE GAME

A HISTORY OF TENNIS, FROM VICTORIAN PASTIME TO GLOBAL PHENOMENON

Elizabeth Wilson

A complete catalogue record for this book can
be obtained from the British Library on request

The right of Elizabeth Wilson to be identified as the author of this
work has been asserted by her in accordance with the Copyright,
Designs and Patents Act 1988

First published in 2014 by Serpent's Tail,
an imprint of Profile Books Ltd
3A Exmouth House
Pine Street
London EC1R 0JH
www.serpentstail.com

ISBN 978 1 84668 910 9
eISBN 978 1 84765 878 4

Designed and typeset by sue@lambledesign.demon.co.uk

Printed by Clays, Bungay, Suffolk

10 9 8 7 6 5 4 3 2 1

FSC
Mixed Sources
Product group from well-managed
forests and other controlled sources
Cert no. SGS-COC-2061
www.fsc.org
© 1996 Forest Stewardship Council

This is for fellow fan Paulo, and for Mark and Angie,
for putting up with us

Tennis is like sex … Thrusting across the net – the ball is just a medium, a messenger of love and loathing all rolled up in one … Listen to the language! … *sweet spot, throat* of the racquet. *Dish* and *shank, stab* and *slice* … and *penetrate* – it's pornographic … *Approach* and *hold, break, break back, stroke* … and *connect* – it's romantic.

Lionel Shriver: *Double Fault*

CONTENTS

PART THREE: THAT'S ENTERTAINMENT

1

The game of love

'BY THE TIME I WAS THIRTEEN I was madly in love. It was a blinding, choking, loyal love, filled with devotion and dedication. Obvious to all, it was understood only by a few.'[1]

The object of Ricardo Pancho Gonzales' affection was his tennis racquet. He even took it to bed with him. A Mexican–American from a humble background, he was to have a troubled, passionate relationship with the game. The scar on his cheek gave his Latin looks a dangerous edge; he was no stereotype of the languid, white-clad player. Nor was he alone in falling in love with a game.

The placid Dan Maskell, who also came from a working-class family, but was a far different character from the fiery Mexican, started as a ball boy, and 'thus began a love affair with lawn tennis that has never faded'.[2] The British pre-war star, Fred Perry, felt the same. Indeed, in no other sport than tennis has the relationship of players and spectators, the game and its followers, been so often discussed in terms of romantic love. Even hard-bitten journalists fell for tennis. A. L. Laney, a sports writer between the wars, entitled his autobiography *Covering the Court: A Fifty Year Love Affair with the Game of Tennis*, and confessed: 'I had fallen in love with tennis and this book is the account of that love affair'. He loved the players too. The first time he saw the early American star, Little Bill Johnston, he immediately fell in love with him, 'completely and without reservation'. He had previously 'worshipped from afar' the Californian, Maurice McLoughlin, a ferocious serve-volleyer who won the United States National tournament in 1912 and 1913, when he also reached the challenge round at Wimbledon. But Laney's passion for Little Bill was different from his hero worship of McLoughlin. It was love, and 'once I had fallen, little else seemed to matter so much as seeing him again and seeing him win. Many had this same experience and the younger they were the more they were smitten.'³ And in the twenty-first century, it was not uncommon for a manly voice to shout from the stands, 'I love you Roger,' when Federer was playing.

'Love', the word, is at the centre of tennis. It is embedded in the unique and eccentric tennis scoring system. Love meaning nothing – zero. Playing for love. That it was, uniquely, a sport in which women and men played together made it a 'love game' in a social and romantic sense. Yet the feminine element in tennis was always controversial. As was that troublesome 'love'. It was not a manly word. When a friend introduced the seventies American star, Chrissie Evert, to her future husband, the handsome British player, John 'Legs' Lloyd, she was immediately attracted. As he left, he said, 'Lovely to meet you.' Chrissie turned in dismay to her friend: 'Oh no! He's gay!'⁴ Such was the association of love with effeminacy, at least in the American mind.

The love of which Laney wrote and Gonzales spoke was akin to what the ancient Greeks termed *agape*: an intense admiration and more: something spiritual and almost religious. Yet the rhythm of tennis was also erotic. The cleanly struck shots that streamed off the racquet, the ball exploding off the court and the body's leap from gravity and time – these were inspirational. The player pressed with stroke after stroke and built to the final unanswerable shot and this was repeated in game after game, climax and anti-climax building ever higher, all leading to the point of no return. For player and spectator alike the game provided no guaranteed orgasmic moment, no certainty of a win. The game enacted an unpredictable dialectics of desire – and the spectator's desire is focused on the player.

The tennis star is subjected to intense scrutiny. Tennis matches can last for hours and during them the spectators' gaze is relentlessly trained on the player's body, movements and moods, as happens in no other sport, certainly not to the same extent. (The attention paid to footballer David Beckham is the exception rather than the rule.) This is even more the case in the age of the close-up, the replay and the slow-mo. These place the tennis player alongside the film star as an icon of glamour and beauty.

The erotic body of the player is deployed in a sport discussed in terms of artistry; the performer whose body is her instrument is considered a creative genius. Sports writer Frank Deford questioned whether a sportsperson could be an artist in the full sense of the word. A sporting performance, he thought, might be beautiful, but a great athlete was more like some natural wonder – a flower, a waterfall or a snow-capped mountain.

This is clearly wrong. To suggest that an athlete is some kind of natural phenomenon is to ignore the hard work and intense dedication that goes into the development of any outstanding performer. There is nothing 'natural' about becoming the best tennis player (or the best dancer) in the world. To an inborn gift of eye-hand coordination the player must bring the capacity to devote herself to endless repetitive practice of the same movement. To that must be added the 'feel' outstanding players have for their game. This, it has been suggested, is 'an affinity for translating thought into action'. Players 'see' the visual field in a manner differently from those less gifted and this enables them to discern subtle patterns unrecognised by others. Chess masters, artists and athletes have this special awareness. They can break down their field of operation into clusters of patterns and, often without conscious thought, translate them into movement. This is a form of creative expression in which the athlete's body is the instrument. Her split-second movements are those of an artist and may indeed display originality amounting to genius.[5]

There is the further uncertainty whether the performance arts require *creative* genius in the way that, say, composing music is said to do: whether the cellist Rostropovich – the performer who brings music to life – is a genius on the same level as Beethoven or Shostakovich, who created that music. It is problematic to rate a bodily performance by comparison with a 'work' created out of random words or sounds.

The performance of a dancer is as ephemeral as that of an athlete. The difference is that dance is, by long tradition, acknowledged as art, supported by music, narrative and *mise en scène*. The athlete lacks such supports, but, like the dancer, creates through movement. You could even argue that tennis is more creative than dance, since the dancer usually follows choreography designed in advance, whereas the tennis player must always improvise.

Tennis appears to be closer to dance than to any other performance form (with the possible exception of figure skating). The great 1920s champion Bill Tilden excelled at dancing and skating and on court his movement was astonishingly graceful. His fleet-footedness was legendary: the Spanish player Manuel Alonso thought it was like seeing Nijinsky dance across the stage. He perfected the art of taking a little half-step just before he turned, enabling him to make a perfect stroke with perfect spin.

Tilden himself certainly believed he was an artist. He quoted his friend, the opera singer Mary Garden, as providing him with the concept of athlete as artist. 'You're a tennis artist and artists always know better than anyone else when they're right. If you believe in a certain way to play, you play that way no matter what anyone else tells you. Once you lose faith in your own artistic judgement, you're lost. Win or lose, right or wrong, be true to your art.'[6]

Helen Wills Moody, eight times Wimbledon champion, agreed that tennis was 'in its way an art. Tennis encourages the player to express himself and his personality,' she wrote. 'Into his game he puts something of his personality so that his play becomes a unique expression.'[7]

Gianni Clerici, the Italian historian of tennis, endorsed this view: 'I had always thought of tennis, from the very moment of my childhood when I chose it as my game, as something different. I sensed that there was another way of looking at the sport: as a work of art.'[8]

Tennis, art or not, is unquestionably a sport, if sport is defined as a competitive game involving physical exertion. It is the tension between art and sport that makes it so special, but, unique as it is, tennis has always existed and evolved within the wider culture of sport. Sport has played a central and increasing role in international culture from the mid-nineteenth century onward, until in today's globalised world it dominates. It offers the panaceas religion was once thought to provide. It combines spectacle and warfare, nationalism and obsession, passion without consequences.

Tennis, while seeming to summon just such allegiances and devotions, has never quite fitted into this picture. The Victorian game was invented by sportsmen who were also sports writers, but it was played at garden parties. Its social elaboration does not sit easily with the common idea of sport. In particular, it challenges the sporting ethos. The tennis match may seem at one level like a duel or a fight, but it is also a dance, with its own elaborate courtesies, and its rhythm of pauses, etiquette and protocol; and it takes place within the wider ritual of the tournament, an expansive social environment distinct from the football stadium or boxing ring. In this, it is closer to an opera or music festival than a sport – going to Wimbledon is more like a day at the opera at Glyndebourne than an afternoon of football at the Emirates stadium.

Those in charge of tennis have, however, especially since the Second World War, endeavoured to fit it ever more closely into the pattern of other sports. Tennis was, and is, less dangerous than some sports: boxing, say, motor racing, cycling and skiing. Nor is it a contact sport. But the sport's promoters have increasingly emphasised physical exertion and the pugilistic aspects of the game, rather than elegance and beauty.

This has been within a world in which the sporting ethos is so dominant and so little challenged that the attempt to locate tennis at least partly outside it may seem eccentric or downright perverse, but this is necessary if the eccentricity and richness of the game itself is to be fully understood. The contemporary conventional sporting perspective is itself a kind of tunnel vision; a more expansive, cultural viewpoint may provide a better appreciation of the 'game of love'.

To approach tennis with 'love' may be dangerous if, as Oscar Wilde wrote, 'each man kills the thing he loves' – whether because that love is too obsessive or too critical. Many critics, as we shall see, believed that 'love' in tennis was dangerous – that the very fact of this word being used in the scoring system rendered it unmanly. But love is also a hopeful word, a word of celebration; and in the end, the point of writing about tennis is to celebrate the beauty, the glamour and the joy of this unique game.

PART ONE

A LEISURED CLASS

Healthy excitement and scientific play

I N MARCH 1874 THE LONDON *Court Journal* reported news of a new game, likely to replace the croquet of which everyone had tired. 'Sphairistike or lawn tennis' was just the thing for those in search of 'novelty', and, continued the report, 'it has been tested at several country houses, and has been found full of healthy excitement, besides being capable of much scientific play'. The game was for sale as a box set, 'not much larger than a double gun case' and 'contained bats and balls and a portable court'. Thus was the birth of lawn tennis announced to a public ready to fall for the charms of a game that, from its birth combined thrills, social cachet and commercial possibilities.

A confident upper class and an expanding bourgeoisie with money and leisure to spare were refashioning social, cultural and educational life in the 1870s. Britain had just passed the apex of its industrial if not imperial power, but was still the wealthiest country in the world. The stifling grip of the evangelical Victorian Sunday was weakening. Aspiring urban artisans and white-collar workers were beginning to have a little leisure and a little money to spend. Various publics from different social groups and classes demanded new forms of entertainment to replace the old rural folk traditions – or in some cases to reconstruct them along modern lines. Sport, whether played or watched, was one among a number of pleasurable entertainments offered to the growing town-dwelling public. Venues new and old, such as the Lyceum and the Egyptian Hall in Piccadilly, not to mention the music halls and eventually the cinemas, brought all sorts of novel shows and spectacles to this public, ranging from spiritualist séances to the conjuring tricks of Maskelyne and Devant.

Lawn tennis seemed designed, as was hinted by the words 'country houses', for an elegant and exclusive section of society. It quickly became fashionable and it provided an alluring social occasion. It was the new version of an ancient game, a game so old that no one knew how it got its name of 'tennis'. Popular in the Middle Ages and the Renaissance, it had lost favour by the eighteenth century, but with the growth and reorganisation of sports in the Victorian period was revived in a form distinct enough to be classed as new. It was at first viewed as a pastime or craze rather than a sport, displacing other games played on social occasions rather than as competitive events.

Croquet, for example, provided an opportunity for upper- and upper-middle-class society to get a little open-air exercise in an environment in which men and women mingled. But, as Lieutenant Colonel Osborn, an early devotee of tennis, wrote in 1881, croquet had become 'a tyranny', because it vested all power in the captain of each team, his 'subordinates' having 'no volition of their own ... compelled to [play] exclusively to suit [his] convenience'. By the 1870s an open-air version of badminton, originally introduced from India, was replacing croquet, but the shuttlecock proved uncontrollable in even the slightest breeze. Another craze was 'rinking' – roller skating on indoor asphalt courts to the accompaniment of band music. This, Colonel Osborn said, was boring and monotonous and often led to falls and injuries. Yet for a while people were 'quite demented' with it.

Histories of sport have usually classified lawn tennis retrospectively as yet another new sport of the later Victorian period. To link it, as Osborn did, with these other 'crazes' places it more accurately as a hybrid that bridged the sporting culture then developing and the burgeoning world of entertainment in the rapidly expanding cities. In the sixteenth and seventeenth centuries, especially in France, theatrical performances had often been held on tennis courts, and there is a connection between tennis and theatre too often unrecognised.[1]

Osborn felt that lawn tennis, unlike croquet and rinking, was likely to endure. It was more versatile and more exciting. Above all, it provided an idyllic social occasion:

> The scene should be laid on a well kept garden lawn. There should be a bright warm sun overhead ... Near at hand, under the cool shadow of a tree, there should be strawberries and cream, iced claret mug, and a few spectators, who do not want to play but are lovers of the game ...[2]

Lawn tennis was never to equal the popularity of cricket and football. Yet it represents more accurately than any other spectacle the hugely significant changes in society at the moment of its birth. Tennis was perfectly fitted to captivate the increasingly secular world of the late nineteenth century.

Not least, lawn tennis differed from the other sports so rapidly developing in that period because, uniquely, men and women shared the pitch, playing in partnerships usually of two on each side of the net. It arose as the suffrage movement, underway since the 1850s, was widening its demands to include education as well as the vote and property rights, and generally a greater public role and a widening of opportunities for women. The playing of sport was to the fore as girls' schools and university colleges were founded. Advances in medical science were leading to a changed view of the importance of exercise for bodily (and indeed spiritual) health for women as well as men; dress reform societies waged war against restrictive female fashions.

There was a corresponding relaxation in the irksome taboos restricting social intercourse between men and women. Chaperones and corsets were still the order of the day, but the very

growth of a consumer society dedicated to commercial entertainment acted to dissolve ancient prejudices that were often
embedded in religious dogma.

Tennis was destined to flourish in the novel space of the
suburban garden lawn, which was a 'tamed' version of the countryside just as the new sporting culture was a tamed version of
previously rough and unregulated activities. In the 1860s Major
T. H. Gem and Mr J. B. Perera had marked out an Edgbaston
lawn as a tennis court and in 1872 the first lawn tennis club was
founded at nearby Leamington Manor House Hotel.

These developments anticipated 'sphairistike' (the classical
Greek name was soon abandoned) and its patenter, Major Copton
Wingfield. Descended from an ancient landed family that had
fallen into decline and relative poverty, Wingfield hoped the boxed
lawn tennis set would revive his fortunes and used his aristocratic
connections to publicise it in society magazines such as the *Court
Journal* and *Vanity Fair*. *The Field*, bible of the English gentleman
at home and abroad, became interested and within a few months
lawn tennis was launched as the latest fashionable craze.

Wingfield's claim to be the inventor of lawn tennis, calling
his boxed set 'The Major's Game of Tennis', likewise his tale
of its invention at a country house party in Wales in December
1873, lending it social cachet, were more than a little shaky. Nor
did he ever benefit financially from his initiative as he seems to
have hoped. Assailed with family problems – the early deaths of
his three sons and the chronic mental illness of his wife – he did
not renew his patent. Nevertheless, it is significant that it was a
commercial venture, and so anticipated the marketing of tennis,
as of all sports.

In 1868 the All England Croquet Club had been founded at
the offices of *The Field* magazine. J. H. Walsh, editor of *The Field*
and Henry Jones, a regular contributor, were journalists as well
as sportsmen (Jones was also a doctor), and sports journalism
from the beginning shaped the public perception of lawn tennis –
and indeed, amplified the importance and popularity of all sports.

Harry Gem, one of the founders of the modern game, made this
sketch of the first game played in Leamington Spa

Walsh and Jones found a site for their club the following year at
Wimbledon. By that time croquet was rapidly losing its popularity and in a letter that appeared in the same issue of *The Field*
that first publicised Major Wingfield's new game, J. Hinde Hale, a
committee member of the club, suggested that lawn tennis might
be the thing to replace croquet on its 'now deserted grounds'.[3]

So rapid was the advance of lawn tennis that in 1877 the All
England Club staged its first tournament there. By this time a
new set of rules had been established. The MCC (the Maryle-
bone Cricket Club), as the most important official body over-
seeing any sport, had been asked to reconcile the differences in
the rules between the game played by Gem and Perera and that
of Wingfield. A sub-committee opted for the rectangular court,
rather than the hourglass-shaped one of Wingfield's game, and,
even more significantly – and against the recommendations of
the MCC – adopted the traditional tennis system of scoring
rather than the cumulative method used in the game of rackets
(and most other sports). So, within a decade, first the MCC and
then, decisively, the All England Croquet Club, had taken control
of the game.

In its early years military men and more unexpectedly the clergy were among the keenest promoters and players of the game. Perhaps this only shows how central these professions then were within the upper-middle classes, as compared to their marginal or niche status in the twenty-first century. Colonel Osborn concluded his eulogy on tennis with the statement that, 'if all these conditions are present, an afternoon spent at lawn tennis is a highly Christian and beneficent pastime'. It 'produces a feeling of benevolence towards the human race generally. It causes its votaries to regard the world and all that it contains with that charity that hides a multitude of sins' (surely a rather ambiguous remark). He speculated that this was why it was 'so extensively patronised by the clergy'. Perhaps it was partly because their vicarage lawns were ideally suited to the game, but also because 'lawn tennis on a Sunday afternoon is very superior to sermons'.

Tennis was by no means confined to the vicarage, however. It was associated with secular aesthetes when the new 'aesthetic' suburb of Bedford Park in West London was completed in the late 1870s, attracting affluent residents of artistic bent, patrons of the Aesthetic Movement. This movement was organised round the Grosvenor Galleries in central London. Its adherents promoted the idea of beauty in all things. Many had radical social leanings, but their effete posing was subjected to merciless caricature. That Oscar Wilde was a fervent adherent was later fatally to stigmatise their philosophy.

A tennis club was quickly established in Bedford Park and, shockingly, its members played tennis on Sundays, behaviour that aroused immense local disapproval. There were petitions and irate letters to the *Acton, Chiswick and Turnham Green Gazette*, whose editorial on 28 May 1880 stated: 'If lawn tennis on Sundays is right at the Bedford Park Club, may it not be claimed that billiards, bagatelle, bowls and even skittles would be proper at the surrounding public houses ... That is the legitimate outcome of such reasoning and surely every Englishman would deprecate such an influx of Sunday amusements.' In other words, the sight of their social betters larking about on a tennis court on the Sabbath was sure to incite the lower orders to rowdy, dissolute and ungodly behaviour.[4] Certainly the presence of alcohol, women vigorously disporting themselves and cautious flirtation flouted traditional Victorian moral ideals.

Yet tennis-loving vicars played a most progressive role in promoting tennis for women. The first woman Wimbledon champion, Maud Watson, remembered that her father, a broad-minded vicar, had allowed her and her sisters to play in a match at Hurlingham club: 'People thought it was scandalous that he should let us play in public! We enjoyed it though!'[5] The father of the seven-times Wimbledon ladies champion, Dorothea Lambert Chambers, was another vicar who encouraged his daughter to excel at the game.

'Wimbledon' soon became a well-attended social fixture, attracting large crowds to watch the first real stars of the game, the Renshaw brothers. This was a tournament reserved for amateur (male) players, entering as individuals, not in a team, nor, as in so many other sports, as representatives of a school, county, community or nation. As singles play gained over doubles, individualism was further cemented into the sport. At the same time the championships announced themselves as a social event in the London 'season', thus maintaining the society associations that set the game apart.

Just as each player represented only himself, so the spectators were taking part in a different kind of spectacle, quite unlike cricket or football matches, where group loyalties were to the fore. The fashionable Wimbledon crowd came to see individual players, just as they would attend the theatre to see an opera or music-hall singer, a star who attracted allegiance entirely by virtue of their style of play and expertise and, increasingly, by their force of personality. It was true that the most famous sportsman of the late Victorian period, Dr W. G. Grace, the cricketer, appealed to his fans by virtue of his personality and his play, but cricket – as, for that matter, football – was far more closely connected to local and national loyalties than was the case with tennis.

In the meantime, tennis was rapidly developing a distinctive style of play. In the early years of the Wimbledon championships most entrants were essentially players of the ancient game of real tennis, bringing to the lawns their slow ground strokes, played with massive 'cut' or slice. The first champion, Spencer W. Gore, believed that the new game lacked variety and was too monotonous to last. He overcame this and outwitted his opponents by inventing the volley, but the next year he in turn was defeated by Frank Hadow, who discovered that the lob could defeat the volleyer. It was Hadow, too, who abandoned the underspun strokes of the real tennis players in favour of the flat, fast and hard stroke.

The return of the safety-first, monotonous ground-stroke game played by Hadow lasted only until the arrival of William and Ernest Renshaw. They took the sport seriously, analysing their own game and that of other players in continual efforts to improve. They even set out courts in the South of France where they could practise all year round. Their development of the over-arm serve and the smash startled and enraptured spectators and enraged opponents. William Renshaw, the better player of the two, dominated the sport for most of the1880s and set it on its path to international popularity.

Lawn tennis clubs proliferated, but by the early 1890s the rapid rise of the game had tailed off. Now the latest craze was the bicycle, which offered more adventurous ways for girls to meet boys. In 1895 the Wimbledon championships made a loss of £33, then a serious sum of money. The departure of the Renshaw brothers had left a void and it was not until the arrival of a new set of brothers, Reggie and Laurie Doherty, that the game regained its popularity, demonstrating how particularly important individual personalities were to this sport.[6]

With the waning of its popularity in fashionable circles, lawn tennis was saved by two developments. It became popular in the new suburbs and it spread like wildfire internationally. Women were increasingly interested in the game and beginning to play it seriously. This met with opposition from those who (unlike Maud Watson's father) felt that while it might be permissible for women and girls to play in the privacy of the country house park or the suburban vicarage garden, it was indecent for them to play in public.

The Irish nevertheless introduced a women's event in Dublin in 1879 and in 1884 Wimbledon followed suit. There, at the age of nineteen, Maud Watson defeated her sister to win the inaugural championship.

Tennis did not remain for long exclusive to Britain. The circumstances favouring its success were also present in France, and indeed across Europe and in the United States and Australia. France was in the grip of Anglomania at the end of the nineteenth century and the new game was soon being played all over the country, but especially on the Riviera.

The wealth of French landed estates was dwindling by the beginning of the twentieth century; industrialists, businessmen and members of the professions benefited from a new spirit of enterprise and the belle époque saw republicanism finally firmly established, together with an economic upturn and a cultural flowering. Tennis was associated with exclusive clubs and precisely expressed the aspirations of the bourgeoisie. Leon de Janzé reported that only 300 of the 800 members of the Société Sportive de l'Ile de Puteau, one of the chicest Paris clubs at the turn of the century, actually played tennis. Many attended purely for the social life, for tea, dinner and dancing.[7] Tennis player Coco Gentien described women playing in huge hats. Their skirts swept the ground, only occasionally allowing a glimpse of a foot shod in a white leather shoe with a heel.[8]

Everyone was becoming more athletic. 'The members of polite society,' wrote one French journalist, 'are all turning into athletes, those, that is, who play lawn tennis. It is just being recognised that the latter is a sport. Until now it was held to be an innocent pastime for anaemic men and pale young ladies ... as easy-going as lotto or whist.' Not any longer. 'Rigour, skill and stamina' were now essential.

The game was brought to the United States when a Miss Mary Outerbridge saw it played in Bermuda and brought a boxed set home with her. The first game of tennis in America was probably played on a court that her brother, A. Emilius Outerbridge, helped her lay out on the lawns of the Staten Island Cricket and Baseball Club. Harry Stevens, whose mother, Mrs Paran Stevens, was a dedicated social climber and who was himself courting the writer, Edith Wharton, at the time, also brought tennis equipment from England, where he'd been studying. He had a court laid out in Newport on the lawn of his mother's mansion on Bellevue Avenue.

The game spread rapidly. In Boston James Dwight and his cousin Frederick Sears Jr set up the first court in the Boston area at the resort of Nahant. J Arthur Beebe, son-in-law of a prominent Nahant 'resorter', William Appleton, had brought back a Wingfield set from London and the court was laid out on the Appletons' lawn. 1876 saw the first tournament played there, but at this point the squash and rackets scoring system was used.

Tennis started in Philadelphia in a similar way, that is, among private families. At this time, as in England, there were wide differences in equipment and rules. After one tournament in which this became clearly problematic, Dwight, Sears and Clarence Clark, who had pioneered the game in Philadelphia, agreed that some sort of regulation was needed.

In 1881 a convention in New York saw the founding of the US National Lawn Tennis Association and the meeting also agreed that the first official championships (men's) would be held in August at the newly built Newport Casino. Newport thus became the first fashionable centre of the game.[9]

As in England, the game was at first restricted to the Social Register and the WASPs of the eastern seaboard, but gradually tennis spread across the continent and California pioneered more democratic participation. Maurice McCloughlin learned his tennis on the public courts at Golden Gate Park in San Francisco and was the first tennis player from 'the other side of the tracks' to become national US champion.

Lawn tennis became popular in the Antipodes, and there too it was first played by the colonial aristocracy. Such was the success of their new players that in 1907 the Australian Norman Brookes won the singles, the mixed doubles and, with Anthony Wilding from New Zealand, the men's doubles at Wimbledon. In 1908 the pair defeated the United States in the recently inaugurated Davis Cup.

The Davis Cup was the brainchild of the American, Dwight Davis. Anthony Wilding believed that this event, played by teams of players from different nations in both singles and doubles, had 'done more to advance lawn tennis as a popular pastime and to raise it to its present high standard than any other agency'. The Australasian win (played in Australia) had, he believed, put paid to the idea that 'lawn tennis was a mild pastime requiring a little skill but none of the athletic qualities essential in cricket'. The beaten American pair, Beals Wright and R. B. Alexander, played in a number of Australian tournaments and 'the bare fact that men of such attractive personality were connected with lawn tennis did much to advance the game in popular favour'.[10] The Davis Cup was intended to develop tennis as a team game and enhance its appeal by invoking nationalism, but even here it was the individual personalities that attracted spectators to the game. Yet while it popularised the game, its social exclusivity remained, and into the twenty-first century membership of a tennis club was often more than a matter of the fee, but also involved being recommended and knowing the 'right people'.

Real tennis and the scoring system

THE ANCIENT GAME FROM WHICH lawn tennis was adapted had been played at least since the early Middle Ages. Its roots lay in spectacle. The origins of ball games are 'shrouded in mystery' according to the German historian, Heiner Gillmeister, who believes they emerged out of the ceremonies that took place at weddings, when a show was put on that would be memorable to all those present. At aristocratic nuptials these would be courtly tournaments and jousts. The tournament was a stylised version of armed combat, a festive version of or preamble to it, at which knights displayed their skills before an audience that included the ladies of the court. Echoes of this still linger at the modern Spanish bullfight. Gillmeister speculates that these tournaments originally took place in front of the castle portcullis, a grid that became in tennis a grille at one end of the court. This would also explain the tennis term 'dedans' or 'within', the passage of arms being between those outside and those within the fortification.[1]

At a more humble level tennis may have developed out of the manic and often violent football of the common people, the difference being that the ball was hit with the hand, not the foot, hence its early name, *jeu de paume*, game of the palm. It appears to have originated in France or the Netherlands, but a similar game was recorded around the same period in many parts of Europe and even in the Mayan civilisation in Latin America. As it developed in Europe, the ball came to be hit with a gloved rather than a bare hand and finally, by the sixteenth century, the gloved hand had been replaced by a racquet.

The terms 'real tennis' and 'royal tennis' (in the USA 'court tennis') were only adopted in the 1870s to distinguish the traditional game from the newfangled 'lawn' version. 'Real' was conflated or confused with 'royal' and this term seems to have been based on the fallacy that originally only kings and princes played the game. Henry VIII certainly did play tennis and was indeed fanatically devoted to the game. It was widely played in the courts of Europe and the famous 'tennis court oath' that kick-started the French Revolution in 1789 took place in the tennis court at Versailles.

Such evidence as exists suggests that the game was more widely played by plebeian citizens than later generations realised. An early version of the *jeu de paume* probably evolved from other team games and was played in the street. It was also popular with monks. They were forbidden to participate in the rough football of the times, but a ball game where the ball was hit with the hand was more suited to the confines of the cloister. It is therefore plausible to suggest that the real tennis court developed from the medieval monastic cloister with its gothic arches and slanting roof and gallery onto which the ball must first be served, a design maintained to this day in real tennis, but one of the many complications abandoned by the Victorian military men who developed the modern game.

Gillmeister cites a court case in the city of Exeter in the southwest of England that relates to a dispute about the game. In 1447 the Dean and Chapter of the cathedral attempted to close the cathedral cloisters and adjacent open area on account of the noise and damage caused by young people of the town playing tennis there, especially during religious services. Gillmeister also mentions examples of it being played in the street and by larger teams. Gambling was closely associated with tennis, as with all sports.

An alternative theory has it developing in the streets of northern Italian towns at the same period. Medieval shop fronts often had a sloping roof to protect the goods laid out below and the style developed of hitting the ball up onto the roof, known as a 'pentys' (later, penthouse) to begin the point.[2]

Whatever its origins, tennis became something of a craze during the Renaissance, when the first professional players – women as well as men – appeared. In France their incorporation into the *Communauté des Maitres Paumiers-Racuertiers* elevated the status of tennis 'from a mere game to an art, like horsemanship or fencing', argues one of today's real tennis players.[3]

The ancient game featured regularly in the literature and art of the Middle Ages and the Renaissance. Tennis seems to have been more frequently illustrated and written about than the other games, such as cricket and football, that were played in these early times, partly, perhaps, because of its special association with court life and the aristocracy.

The many images of tennis from the thirteenth century onwards assisted Gillmeister in tracing the development of the game, for example, when the racquet began to be regularly used, the height and arrangement of the net and even styles of play. He shows its particular hold on the artistic imagination and how it had a special relationship to courtly literature and to a conception of the ideal human being. It appeared as a recommended part of a young man's education, contributing to a 'civilising process', teaching good manners and appropriate behaviour, as well as providing a suitable form of bodily exercise, so long as it was not taken to excess – although Charles V dismissed it as one of the games that did 'nothing to teach the manly art of bearing arms'. Its appearance in the medieval romance literature added to its glamour and eroticism, for it was associated, long before the Victorian garden party, with dalliance as well as sporting vigour and courage in combat. It was also considered an intellectual game and known as 'chess in motion', so it is easy 'to see why such a game should so have fascinated the intellectuals of the Middle Ages – who were the monks'.[4] Indeed, one writer thought 'the art of the racquet the most appropriate sport for the man of letters'.[5]

The most unusual aspect of the sport was its peculiar scoring system. This, as we saw earlier, was retained for lawn tennis against the advice of the MCC and like much else about the *jeu de paume* its origins are mysterious.

In the first place, tennis was and is unlike most sports in that a game has no fixed duration. There is no such thing as a 'draw'; the game has to continue until one player (or pair) is victorious. As Clerici wrote: 'Its method of scoring had no limits and, theoretically at least, could last for days on end and not even come to an end then.' (In 2010 a match at Wimbledon between the Frenchman Nicolas Mahut and American John Isner did continue over three days and more than eleven hours, ending when Isner prevailed 70-68 in the final set.)

The scoring of most sports is cumulative – the side or individual with most points wins. In some sports one additional point or goal is sufficient; in others, table tennis, for example, the winner must gain a margin of at least two.

None of this applies to tennis. It bears some resemblance to snooker in that the match is divided into smaller sections, in snooker known as 'frames', and in tennis as 'sets'. A set like a match is equally of indeterminate duration. The first player to reach six games wins the set, but must win by a margin of two games. A score of 6–5 is therefore not a winning margin; the set will then have to go to at least 7–5.

There are further subdivisions within each game. A game is scored not by simple addition, but by an elaborate system using arcane language. Both players start at zero, which is called 'love'. The game then progresses to fifteen – thirty – forty. If both players reach forty, this then becomes 'deuce' (*à deux* in French, although today the usual French term is *égalité*). Once deuce is reached a player must win two more consecutive points to win the game.

Critics have argued that this system is 'unfair' because it is possible for a player to win a match having won fewer points than his opponent. (One such critic was Charles Lenglen, father of Suzanne Lenglen, the 1920s tennis star.) It has also been criticised for being too bafflingly elaborate. It was at first considered beyond the intelligence of a woman to grasp it. Why the sub-committee of the MCC chose the 'real tennis' system against the wishes of the committee is not recorded. The serendipitous result, however, was that, together with the indeterminate length of a match, it creates a game and a spectacle that is more dramatic and that contains more possibility of changes of fortune than almost any other sport.

The system permits mini-crises at crucial points in the course of a match and the enhanced possibility of dramatic reversals. Of course, a sudden change in fortune is possible in most sports, but there is no other that sees ebbs and flows on the same scale. For example, with three minutes left to play, it is unlikely that a football team leading by a margin of three goals will lose the match. The outcome is clear before the end of play. Even if the losing team scores, say, two more goals, that does not nullify the lead. In tennis, by contrast, a lead can be nullified: when a one-set lead becomes set all, for example; or within a single game when break points (15–40) disappear and the score moves back to deuce.

The Indian player, Vijay Amritraj, argued that the beauty of the system was that in tennis you can craft a victory from almost certain defeat. Describing a match in which he was match point down against one of the greatest of all players, Rod Laver (the score was 6–7, 5–6, 0–40), he wrote: 'In tennis you can take it by stages. Every game won is a staging post back from the desert: one more step back towards the oasis where you can look your opponent in the eye again on something like level terms. I saved the three match points and just kept playing point by point – the old cliché that is the best one in the book. Point by point and somehow I won seven straight games for victory.'[6]

This was also what happened in one of the most famous matches at the beginning of the open era, in 1969. The match was between the ageing Gonzales and the Puerto Rican Charlie Pasarell, who played for the US. Gonzales had turned pro too young to achieve what he might have done as an amateur and was now forty-one years old, but still a formidable and, some felt, terrifying player. Pasarell had been briefly America's number one ranked player, but had never gone beyond the quarter finals at any major tournament. On the other hand, for the previous two years at Wimbledon he had brought drama to the Centre Court in incredible five-set matches. This third year surpassed even those.

The first set alone went to 11–9 in Pasarell's favour. The light was fading and rain began to fall, but the referee, Captain Mike Gibson, refused to halt the match before the end of the second set, which Gonzales lost 1–6. When play resumed the next day he was thus already in an apparently losing position, needing to win the three remaining sets. He ground out the third set, winning it by 16–14 when Pasarell double faulted twice in one game; and then won the fourth set more easily, 6–3. But in the fifth set the moment came when he was at 4–5 and 0–40 down. That meant three match points for Pasarell. After seven deuces Gonzales won that game to reach 5–all. The situation was repeated at 5–6. Pasarell reached match point, for the third time, now on his own serve, at 8–7, but he lobbed, the ball landed out and that was the end of Pasarell, who lost the next eleven points. Gonzales won the match 11–9 in the final set.[7]

The nail-biting tension and hysterical excitement of such a match can never be recaptured in print, but it illustrates the superior dramatic potential of tennis. The indeterminate length of the game heightens the tension and allows for several changes in momentum over the course of a match. The scoring system requires an additional skill from the player, because in tennis not all points are equal. The best players will vary the intensity of play according to the importance of the moment, will know how to up the tempo when needed, will judge when to play safe and when to go for broke. As in opera, the building of momentum results in crescendo – lull – crescendo – climax, an experience for both player and spectator that is not quite like the experience of watching other sports.

There have been many suggestions as to the origins of 'tennis', 'love' and the system based on multiples of three. In the 1920s A. E. Crawley suggested that love, fifteen, thirty, forty, deuce, advantage related to the clock, divided into four quarters (with 45 reduced to 40), by which the monks kept the score. This, though, is speculative and no one really knows. Gillmeister dismissed virtually all these theories.

The word 'tennis' itself may have come from the French 'tenez', spoken as the server prepared to play. The term 'love' is also mysterious, although possibly it had something to do with the universal practice in earlier times of betting on matches ('for love or money'). That one word has caused more controversy than any other aspect of the game, but these linguistic mysteries only add to the romance of tennis.

In spite of recurring grumbles about the scoring system, the only serious change to have taken place was the introduction of the tie-break, first used at the US Open in 1970. This was a modification of the rule whereby a set could only be won when one player went two games ahead. Although the final set 70–68 score in the 2010 Wimbledon match between Mahut and Isner was unique, before the introduction of the tie-break, sets did fairly often go beyond the 6–all point at which the tie-break is now introduced. While lengthy matches might be exciting, they could also be monotonous, as well as exhausting for the players. The tie-break broke the stalemate that could occur. The first player to reach seven points wins the set, but still has to win by a margin of two points.

The tie-break was invented by Jimmy Van Alen, who presided over the Newport Casino and Tennis Club, Rhode Island, where the very first tournaments in America were played and where he also founded the Tennis Hall of Fame, opened in 1954. Van Alen was one of the upper-class amateurs who directed the sport in the amateur era. Amritraj described him as 'a New England aristocrat who still dressed like his ancestors must have done at garden parties at the turn of the century'. But in introducing the tie-break he was an unlikely innovator. He had wanted to go further and abolish the two-point-lead rule and have a single nine-point tie-breaker, but the more conservative form prevailed and soon became universal. The only tournaments to retain a no-tie-break final set were the three major tournaments, Wimbledon, Australia and France (the US Open does have a tie-break final set).

The Pasarell–Gonzales match illustrated the lengths to which a match could go. Even in an era in which rallies were much shorter, it lasted over three hours. Then and recently, when matches have become longer, the tie-break was popular and produced its own additional twist of excitement.

The poetic tennis scoring system was more than a nostalgic gesture to its medieval origins; it did perhaps symbolise its courtly and monastic past. More importantly it recreated in the modern game its aesthetic possibilities and creativity. It was – and is – also intensely contemporary – indeed postmodern – in its eclectic elaboration and a reminder of the wonderful eccentricity of the game and indeed of so many of its players, at least in its early years. It remained a powerful exception to the tendencies towards uniformity that were increasingly to encroach on the game in the late twentieth century.

4

The growth of a sporting culture

I N EIGHTEENTH-CENTURY RURAL ENGLAND, landowners and
the gentry had happily played cricket, organised fights and gone
hare-coursing in company with agricultural workers and artisans.
There was no social threat from their subordinates. Britain was
relatively stable politically and was becoming more democratic.
Sports, even if unruly, suggest Norbert Elias and Eric Dunning,[1]
represented a 'civilised' advance in that their contests symbolised
the resolution of conflict by means of rules and conventions that
all respected, rather than by violence.

As Britain became an urban industrial society, there was a
dramatic increase in playing and watching or following sport.
Certain traditional sports, especially the more bloodthirsty ones,
such as cock fighting and bear baiting, went into decline, in some
cases actively suppressed, while others, such as bowls and hockey,
developed a higher profile. The ancient sports of cricket and
football continued, but in less anarchic, more regulated forms.
Meanwhile new sports entered the arena.

Many reasons have been suggested for the explosion in
organised sports.[2] There were economic reasons, from gambling
(though this was much disapproved of and many attempts
were made to suppress it) to the production and marketing of

equipment and accessories and the organisation of commercial matches and other events. For some sportsmen it was the
entry into better paid employment, although few sportsmen
became wealthy. The growth of sports also fed into the growing
newspaper industry, where popular journalism and its reporting
of sports events in turn amplified their popularity.

An important factor was economic and industrial advance in
itself. This led to the development of new technologies that were
swiftly applied to sports, some of which changed beyond recognition. The mere availability of this new technology, however, does
not explain why it was applied so eagerly to so many sports.

Nor does it explain why sports and related activities were
so popular, nor why they acquired virtues not previously attrib-
uted to them. Some have suggested that sports were a form
of social control, an opium of the people, distracting them
from political struggle, but others claim that sports provided
needed respite from lives of toil. Physical exercise was healthy,
and health was increasingly a preoccupation with advances in
medical knowledge and fears about the noxious environment
of industrial cities. Many looked to sports to create workers fit
for the factories and fields or, if necessary, for war. Aside from
these functional explanations were others that emphasised the
psychological and even spiritual benefits of sport. On an individual level they might provide a kind of catharsis, that is, a form
of excitement ending in emotional resolution. They were held to
promote community solidarity. Organised team sports in particular fostered local, community and national pride, the latter of
growing importance as other nations, especially Germany and
the United States, began to challenge Britain's economic and
imperial pre-eminence.

More mundanely, the slowly diminishing working day
resulted in more leisure time and workers craved pleasure and
excitement to fill it. This, the simplest explanation, that sports
provided pure pleasure and excitement, again at a premium in the
lives of working men, may be the most convincing of all. Taking

part in sports was enjoyable; so was being part of the crowd at a match, a race or a tournament. It was *fun*.

Before the seventeenth century ordinary women had taken part in sports, including hunting, alongside men, as well as having sports of their own, such as skipping and racing; there were even women pugilists. They also joined the crowds that gathered at contests as onlookers. The Puritans, disliking all forms of playful activity, were particularly down on female participation. As Dennis Brailsford points out, play lost its openness and innocence and, like sex, 'moved uncertainly into a hinterland between the claims of purity and the frequent actuality of prurience in its male promoters and spectators';[3] in other words, the puritanical wish to remove women from display had the opposite effect from that intended.

By the nineteenth century women had largely withdrawn as the doctrine of women's place being in the home took hold. Upper-class women rode to hounds and practised archery, but vigorous exercise for leisured women, even walking, developed seriously only in the second half of the nineteenth century. As education for women including healthy exercise developed, middle-class women became more active and at the end of the century took to the bicycle (an expensive piece of equipment) with alacrity, but poorer women remained excluded and in spite of girls playing hockey, tennis and golf, which caused mockery in the pages of *Punch* and other periodicals, sport remained a predominantly masculine activity.

As such it developed a new and uplifting ideology, a form of justification that removed it from the sphere of play. For the word 'sport' had in earlier times been used to refer to erotic dalliance. In the seventeenth century it had even been considered devilish, not because 'of a general disapproval of pleasure, but more specifi- cally because sport suggested idle, profitless and fundamentally unserious action'.[4]

Pleasure remained an awkward concept for the high-minded Victorians. From the start of the nineteenth century an increasingly influential Evangelical movement had sought to reform manners and morals. For example, the Society for the Suppression of Vice was waging a war against pornography as early as 1802. To the most committed Evangelicals, almost all pleasurable activities and spectacles were sinful: cards, blood sports, novel reading, dancing, drink and, perhaps above all, the theatre. Even tea and coffee were viewed with suspicion. The bosom of the family was the only safe place to be; and through their emphasis on a particular form of family life they were at least partly responsible for the belief in 'the natural differences and complementary roles of men and women' taking hold throughout middle-class society.[5]

Evangelical Christianity was not universally accepted and ran counter to other trends in British society, but for several decades the movement was able to wage successful war against pleasure. Sunday observance cast a pall. There were even attempts to close the London parks on the Sabbath. The All England Club did not have Sunday play until 1889 – and to this day a relic of Sunday observance results in no play on the 'middle Sunday' of Wimbledon (and indeed play on the final Sunday was only introduced in 1982).

Yet sport was able to develop and expand, even in this stifling moral climate, because virtues were claimed for it. Key to the promotion of sport were the public (that is private) schools that educated the sons of various elite groups. The confident and rising middle class did not, as in France, evict a decadent aristocracy. Instead, the aristocracy was assimilated and an important agent in this was the public school.

In Georgian England there already existed a porous 'genteel' class including the lesser landed gentry, merchants, clerics, business and professional men; the term 'gentleman' developed as an inclusive one to cover subtle variations in status. The nineteenth-century boys' boarding school strengthened and institutionalised the ideal of the 'gentleman' and, significantly, cemented it with the elevation of sporting activity to a moral principle.

Thomas Arnold, headmaster of Rugby School from 1828 to

1841, was a key figure in the development of the public school ethos. He was a passionate Christian and dedicated to imprinting Christian spiritual and moral ideals on his pupils. One of these, Thomas Hughes, was deeply influenced by Arnold and idealised his beliefs in the bestselling novel, *Tom Brown's Schooldays*. Arnold himself had never shown the slightest interest in sport, but Hughes made the educational, spiritual and moral value of sport central to his book. His friend, the Christian socialist, Charles Kingsley, developed similar ideas in his novels *Westward Ho!* and *Alton Locke*. A journalist coined the term 'muscular Christianity' to describe the new importance these writers ascribed to sport and the moral and religious connotations it had suddenly acquired; muscular Christianity became effectively the label for an ideology or a new vision of the virtuous life: an exclusively masculine one.

The ideal expressed the view that a healthy mind and soul should be housed in a healthy body. Sports, especially rugby and cricket, were invaluable. They fostered comradely spirit as well as physical fitness and courage, and they preserved the 'boyish-ness' of the youth in the man. This was the essential ideal for the builders of the Empire, which the British liked to believe was a moral and civilising crusade.

Games and sport rather than 'education and bookishness' were now considered the appropriate means of developing manly men fit both to protect the weak and to promote the patriotic ideals of Empire. Sport was a healthy alternative to the hellish secular temples of debauchery and degeneracy, the theatre and the public house. Even more importantly, organised sports taught certain moral values: fair play, courage in the face of physical pain, the acceptance of loss and disappointment when losing, strict adherence to rules – the 'stiff upper lip', in other words.

This form of evangelicalism was in part a response to the Catholic-leaning, 'High Church' Oxford Movement.[6] In the 1830s this had sought to revive the ritualism and devotional traditions of the pre-reformation Church, but to many evangelicals, the clerics in the Oxford Movement appeared tainted with 'effeminacy', their love of robes and ceremonial redolent of 'unmanliness'. Kingsley felt that its adherents betrayed 'an element of foppery – even in dress and manner; a fastidious, maundering, die-away effeminacy, which is mistaken for purity and refinement'. In 1865 the magazine *Punch*, ever the voice of the red-blooded Victorian bourgeois family man, published 'Parsons in Petticoats', whose author derided High Church parsons who 'are very fond of dressing like ladies. They are much addicted to wearing vestments in smart and gay colours, and variously trimmed and embroidered.'

The Movement may well have attracted some adherents who, consciously or unconsciously, were drawn to their own sex. Sexual attraction between men had always been classified as a sin and had resulted in draconian sentences and persecution (in England sodomy was punishable by death until 1861), but it may have caused a particular kind of moral panic in Victorian England. This was due to a changed understanding of homosexual desire. No longer was it simply a sin to which anyone might succumb; now homosexuality became a medical and psychological category and the homosexual came to be seen as a different kind of person in thrall to a form of degeneracy that ought to be eradicated.

Sport, then, was an antidote to effeminacy and involved a special kind of manliness. It was no longer frivolous, but earnest; even a kind of moral work rather than time-wasting play. Lawn tennis challenged this. It was revolutionary in having women and men participate together, actually playing on the same arena and hitting the ball at one another. Even golf and croquet did not pit men against women in the same way.

Inevitably how women dressed for tennis became an immediate focus. It is a common assumption that 'sport' and 'fashion' are polar opposites. In fact, costume historian James Laver believed that all fashionable wear, especially men's wear, had, at least since the eighteenth century, originated in sportswear. Beau Brummell had inaugurated a revolution in men's dress soon after 1800. He had banished colour, embroidery, lace, high heels, powdered hair, jewellery and even make-up for men, replacing them with sober blacks and neutrals, white linen and leather boots, costumes based on the riding clothes worn in the countryside. (A century later Chanel's minimalist style for women was inspired partly by the British woman's riding habit.)

The renunciation of flashy display was consistent with the muscular Christianity expressed in the nineteenth-century sporting ideal. It was no longer considered manly to follow fashion – although this was a case of massive disavowal since, in practice, men cared greatly about their appearance and were the authors of most of the many rules about what constituted correct dress in any and every social situation. Fashion nonetheless became more definitely a feminine domain (and by the early and mid-twentieth century was also associated with designers whose sexuality was uncertain or dissonant and usually concealed).

That tennis was at first primarily a social occasion is indicated by the fact that women who participated in the early years of the game wore fashionable day dress. In the late 1870s and 1880s, this had reached a summit of elaboration, with bustles – heavy drapes of material caught up at the back over a wire cage concealed beneath layers of petticoats – tight bodices and constricting sleeves. Underneath this mountain of material lay hidden the corsets without which many women would have felt indecent. Teddy Tinling claimed that his friend Elizabeth Ryan – who did not remove the whalebone from her own corsets until the 1920s – said the corsets lying over the dressing-room fender after a match were not a pretty sight, 'because some of them were bloodstained'. The stiff material and boning must have cut into or scratched the players' bodies.

Women were subject to a classic double bind: mocked for wearing such ridiculously fashionable clothes, but condemned as unfeminine when they wore clothes more suitable for play. Yet at this period fashionable dress was itself under attack. Middle-class women were becoming more active, demanding attractive garments suitable for walking and for public life in the cities. In

Britain, the Rational Dress Society, formed in 1881, stated in its founding documents that it 'protests against the introduction of any fashion in dress that either deforms the figure, impedes the movement of the body or in any way tends to injure health'. It aimed to promote styles of dress 'based on considerations of health, comfort and beauty'. As the feminist and bicyclist, Lady Harberton, pointed out, the question of restrictive dress for women came to the fore at this time partly because women had already won a number of battles in the fight for emancipation: 'Now that women are being gradually allowed to take their place in Society as rational beings and are no longer looked upon as mere toys and slaves; and now that their livelihood is becoming more and more to be considered their own affair, the question of dress assumes proportions which it did not use to have.'

Lottie Dod, who first won Wimbledon at the age of fifteen in 1887 (and on four subsequent occasions) and was never beaten, always spoke up in favour of the right of women players to dress in a manner that did not impede their tennis. She took to wearing a cap after the kerchief that at first had kept her hair in order flew off during a match, owing to her violent volleying. She was admired for her on-court outfits; on one occasion she was described as wearing a dark blue skirt and rust-coloured blouse with embroidered collar and cuffs. White at this early period was by no means universal.

As in so many other spheres of life, tradition was the sediment of actions and choices that had seemed initially merely pragmatic. When lawn tennis began there were no rules concerning dress. White gained popularity because it was more practical. It showed sweat stains less than colours did, and absorbed less heat, and so was cooler to wear when playing in hot sunlight. Contrary to what some commentators have maintained, there seems no evidence that white was chosen for reasons of snobbery – it easily got dirty and only those could wear it who could afford continual washing and cleaning. This is more likely to have been part of the myth of the 'sissy', 'snobby' game.

The presence of women, whatever they wore, remained controversial and it may have been partly for this reason that it was not, or rarely, played at the public schools. Writing in 1924, George Hillyard, an important figure in tennis in the late nineteenth and early twentieth centuries, pleaded for it to be included. But it never was in any consistent way. Hillyard had no real explanation for this, other than that it was not a team game, but then as he pointed out, neither were rackets or squash, which were played at public schools.[7]

In 1902 there appeared a player who perfectly embodied the manly sporting ideal. The New Zealander, Anthony Wilding, whose parents had emigrated from Herefordshire four years before his birth in 1883, arrived at Trinity College, Cambridge, to study law. He was an outstanding tennis player, but was struck by the fact that no one at Cambridge took it seriously. The undergraduates referred to it as 'pat ball' or, in the Oxbridge slang of the time, as 'patters' – and this view was widespread.[8] Tennis was not seen as a manly sport, and the *Daily Telegraph*, for example, had been known to refer to it as a 'harmless and amusing vagary', akin to a 'gypsy van holiday' or a 'slumming crusade' – its social positioning somehow associated with its moral ambiguity.

This did not deter Wilding who felt that 'pat ball' no longer adequately described the game. There had been a complete change from the tennis played thirty years previously and the style of 'gently lobbing the ball over the net into the middle of the court' was now 'as extinct as the moa', two of the most marked alterations being increased pace and volleying.

He also thought that 'the modern tendency in lawn tennis is to make the game faster; it may not be such an accurate style as that adopted by the giants of yesterday, but strenuous it is'.

Wilding was a paradoxical figure as a tennis player. His Australian doubles partner, Norman Brookes, noted that Wilding took 'infinite pains' to develop the technical side of his game and to train scientifically. In this way he reproduced the specialism and the ideals of scientific efficiency and continual improvement that were at the heart of industrial society – and were to shape tennis, as all sports. His biographers claim that after him 'athletes rather than aesthetes dominated the game' and he himself likened tennis to boxing in terms of the physical effort involved (a comparison that was to return a century later).

That Wilding was killed in the trenches at Neuve-Chapelle in 1915 further established him as a heroic figure. After his death, A. Wallis Myers wrote a eulogy to his friend, trying to account for his extraordinary popularity: 'He was not a scholar. He cared nothing for politics; he hated war. Of books, music and the fine arts he had but cursory knowledge.' Myers could only explain Wilding's appeal as due to 'personal magnetism' and to the fact that while 'physically and mentally he became a man; spiritually he was a boy to the end'. So as Wallis Myers described him, he perfectly embodied the *Tom Brown's Schooldays* ideal.[9]

Yet Wilding loved the deeply glamorous side of tennis, light years removed from the public school ethos. He frankly admitted that he preferred the tournaments in the south of France to those in rainy England. The weather was much better and the tournaments themselves were more fun and less drearily businesslike. There were also the better restaurants and the casinos and other entertainments. Play continued on Sundays; and finally, matches were better organised, with a proper 'order of play', whereas in England players had to hang about – sheltering under the trees if, as often happened, it was raining – not knowing when they would be called. The Monte Carlo tournament in particular was run on a lavish scale, there was 'free admission to the grounds and the whole business, like the motor boat races and pigeon shooting [was] an auxiliary to the casino'.

Wilding was an Adonis of the court and this brought him a devoted fan following. After Norman Brookes defeated him in the Wimbledon final of 1914 – he'd won the title the four previous years – Mrs Brookes, seated in the audience, recalled that 'the emotion of the ladies round me on Tony Wilding's defeat was embarrassing, in fact some actually wept; and when an excited autograph hunter rushed on the court and Tony bent his back for Norman to rest the book upon it, a sigh of anguish went up'.[10]

Wilding was a pivotal figure just at the outbreak of the First World War. After it had ended, the Riviera he had loved would become the setting for tennis at its most glamorous and worldly.

5

On the Riviera

ONCE THE RIVIERA HAD BEEN a jagged line of beaches, with nothing between the turquoise sea and the Basses Alpes but umbrella pines, olive groves and fishing villages. The local peasants did not notice that it was a sleeping paradise waiting to be transformed until an English milord, Lord Brougham (a former British Lord Chancellor), was detained in the village of Cannes in 1834 and fell in love with the climate and scenery, so different from what he referred to as the 'land of fog' he had left behind. He built a villa and made Cannes his permanent home, where friends visited him, returning to Britain with tales of the warm south, with the result that it soon became fashionable for the English leisured classes to winter there. They were shortly followed by their European counterparts.

The Englishness of Nice was underlined by the erection of Protestant churches and the colonisers brought their strict Victorian manners and morality with them. The visitors spent winters in the South for their health and to recuperate. The South of the northern imagination was, says Mary Blume, a land of the recovery of innocence and simplicity.[1] Yet these were travellers of a new type. Their wealth came typically from investment; many were *rentiers*, gentlemen (and ladies) of *leisure*. As art historian Kenneth Clark was to comment of his own parents, 'they were known as the idle rich … some may have been richer, but none were idler'.[2]

Leisure was itself a new concept. It represented 'spare time' – empty time that needed to be filled. Travel was no longer religious – a pilgrimage; nor was it part of the grand tour – an educational enterprise aimed at widening the minds of the young aristocrat. It was the pursuit of health, yes, but also of pleasure and excitement. The development of tourism expressed a thirst for experience and novelty for their own sake.

The vision persisted of the Mediterranean coast as an innocent and idyllic retreat, an ideal spot for the simple life to be lived. Yet when the French poet, Stéphen Liégeard, named it the Côte d'Azur in the 1880s he had already tinged it with sophistication.[3] The innocence and isolation of the villages and olive groves were gradually displaced as villas and hotels appeared on the cliffs and promontories and, as gardens encroached on former farmland, its ambience began to change. Lines of exotic plants – cypresses, mimosa, eucalyptus and above all the palm tree – created a different, more stylised, slightly unreal landscape. Tourism was creating a new location: the Riviera. The lower corniche road was built and in 1864, the railway arrived in Nice, which became the earliest tourist economy city. By the 1870s its foreign inhabitants numbered 25,000. The development of the Mediterranean coast was in full swing.

In 1866 François Blanc undertook the construction of the Monte Carlo casino. He had been found guilty of stock market fraud in France in 1837, but was a brilliant financier according to Lord Brougham, and this was borne out by his success in the principality of Monaco. He had already run the casino at the German spa town of Bad Homburg and now created a complete gambling city with lavish hotels built on the lines of the heavily ornate establishments found in inland spas. Gambling was forbidden in France, so the principality had a monopoly. In 1875 the visit of the Prince and Princess of Wales to Monte Carlo set the seal of social glamour upon it and the whole Côte d'Azur.

The belief that a sojourn beside the Mediterranean was good for the health promoted the development of physical recreations.

Two of the earliest British tennis stars, the Renshaw brothers, had several courts laid down at a Cannes hotel with a surface known as *terre battue*, made of crushed bricks and shards of pottery from a nearby atelier. Soon other hotels followed suit and tennis tournaments sprang up along the littoral. Cannes became the Mecca of continental tennis.

Norman Brookes' teenage wife Mabel described this life with wide-eyed wonder on her first visit from Australia shortly before the First World War. The English still predominated then, 'adding a solid background of more famous names and much money' to the exotic social whirl. The Casino was the focal point of night life; the restaurant, band, dance floor and even the gigolos were superb. 'Soft lights, tangos, hot house flowers, the wide glassed windows facing the Med., Greek syndicate gamblers, kings, Russian grand dukes, demi-mondaines, rich merchants, some smart French types from Paris, crowded a bejewelled scene.' There was also the beautiful scenery: 'Tumbling gardens of spring flowers down on to the coast, aeroplanes circling in a vivid sky and Nice half-hidden below ... the white wisteria cloying the air' and not least the intoxicating presence of cohorts of titled British beauties, the celebrities of their day, familiar from their photographs in glossy magazines.[4]

Charles Lenglen was one of those who took his family to spend the winter on the Riviera at the turn of the twentieth century. A small *rentier*, who had inherited a horse-drawn bus company from his father, he quickly noticed the unusual athletic ability of his only child, Suzanne, born in 1898. By the age of ten she was skilled at diabolo, a game played with a top suspended and thrown up with a string. Playing the game on the front at Nice, she soon drew crowds of tourists with her astonishing dexterity.

The Lenglen family, however, was no troupe of wandering performers. Lenglen *père* was soon inscribed at the fashionable Nice Tennis Club and it was not long before Suzanne had been admitted as a member of this club, which normally debarred children.

Charles trained his daughter himself, developing her game in two crucial ways. He placed squares and eventually small coins on the court and had her practise her ground strokes until she could unfailingly direct the ball to any point on the court. Secondly, finding the normal women's game too slow and stately, he studied the men's game and taught Suzanne to play like a man, with power, drive, placement and speed. Such was her talent that the adult male club members were happy to hit with her.

Charles no doubt also noticed that even before the First World War tennis players enjoyed a privileged place in Riviera society. Dressed in flawless white, they mingled with the grand dukes, the courtesans, the financiers and the English aristocracy, like angels floating above the sumptuous worldly procession, as in a Renaissance painting. The craze for tennis that had already gripped France was beginning to establish the tennis player as a kind of celebrity – and in any case many of the players were already rich or titled or both. In the Mediterranean sunshine the decorous fun of the Edwardian lawn tennis tea party took on a more sophisticated élan.

Suzanne had already won a major tournament in Paris before the outbreak of war in 1914 and had suffered her last singles defeat – to Marguerite Broquedis. This was also the year in which she met and started to play with the American, Elizabeth Ryan, creating a doubles partnership that would never be beaten. Formal tennis tournaments were in abeyance during the First World War, but Lenglen continued to develop her game. Ballet or Greek dance lessons – or both – further enhanced her wonderful movement. Then, once the United States entered the war in 1917, the Riviera began to see wounded American soldiers who arrived to convalesce. As they recuperated tennis fever was renewed. This was perhaps the moment the Americans discovered the Riviera – several years before the arrival of Dick and Nicole Diver, the protagonists of Scott Fitzgerald's Riviera novel, *Tender is the Night* – but their presence was only one aspect of the change that overtook the Côte d'Azur after 1918. It was not unrelated to the cultural changes that made the emergence of 'Suzanne Lenglen', the international celebrity, possible.

In the period of fast-developing capitalism in the 1920s, tennis represented all the characteristics of that burgeoning consumer society. It was an age of sensations and what A. L. Laney termed 'ballyhoo'. It was individualism and competition – capitalism – in the purest form. Team sports were also competitive, yet 'the team' had originally represented the collective effort of the British as they built the Empire. The tennis star emerging after 1918 was more akin to a film star. Film brought the beauty and personality of the acting stars incredibly close; they were as if accessible. The tennis player too was a similar figure, with the addition of heroism in that she or he was pitted against a single adversary. Rivalry, the clash of personality and the intricacies of each individual were under the microscope.

In the 1920s tennis was also the most international of all sports. The Davis Cup had helped to create this situation, but more important was its status as an elite game and the favourite of international café society. As such it projected a glamour absent from other mass spectator sports then developing. At the same time it was part of the enhanced sporting culture that had emerged in part out of the war.

Suzanne's close friend, Antoine 'Coco' Gentien ('a delightful socialite playboy' according to Teddy Tinling), quoted the prophecy of a friend: 'A sea of blood is about to engulf Europe and everything we have loved will drown in it. As soon as men have stopped killing each other they will persist in their love of combat and sport will replace more refined pleasures.'[5] This was exactly what happened. The nationalism intensified by war could be channelled in this new direction.

The war, moreover, had brought physical prowess and endurance to the fore. Medical and scientific advances led to a new understanding of the importance of bodily health and strength; and sport, which already had a place in the construction of the physically and morally healthy body, mind and soul

– and body politic – before 1914, became still more important. 'Healthy recreation' was the new watchword. For the expanding middle classes tennis became an alluring leisure activity, for both players and spectators. But more than that, the belief that sport promoted character and morality, while now less openly religious (or rather, Christian) became if anything more pervasive.

At the same time pleasure was not dead, for a new emphasis on entertainment, pleasure and self-development offset the mood of post-war disillusionment and spectator sports were central to this. Alongside the development of sport came sports journalism – part of the wider development of the popular and tabloid press, whose agenda was sensationalism and excitement. After the privations, dangers and anxieties of war – and also its singular purposelessness: the loss of millions of lives in return for the unsatisfactory and unsustainable Treaty of Versailles – citizens sought forgetfulness in hedonism and the spectacle of sport seemed to promise a fair contest, excitement and partisanship without the reality of death. As Fred Perry observed in the 1930s, 'Then as now ordinary people were more interested in Amelia Earhart's flying from Honolulu to California in 18½ hrs and in Donald Campbell's landspeed record of 301 mph than in Hitler or Baldwin.'

The Riviera was the most glittering theatre for the new sporting culture, but, suggests Mary Blume, the North/South dichotomy took on a new and more ambiguous meaning. From signifying the recovery of innocence, the South (particularly the south of France) now suggested licence, excess and decadence. The writer Somerset Maugham, who lived there, referred to it as a 'sunny place for shady people'.[6] Even in the 1870s some of the most famous courtesans of the day – Liane de Pougy, la Belle Otero and Cora Pearl (aka Emma Crunch from south London) – had made it their playground, or hunting ground, and the idea of escape to an enchanted land could easily modulate into the lure of forbidden adventure and abandonment of conventions.

The gambling that was at the heart of the Riviera's success

was a pointer to its moral uncertainty. The ideal of erotic and personal freedom also suggested by the Riviera could equally shade into self-destructive futility. The recognition of beauty and grace, the search for new experiences at all costs was the goal: 'not the fruit of experience but experience itself, is the end', as the nineteenth-century high priest of the Aesthetic Movement, Walter Pater, had expressed it. But this lust for experience and the exquisite aesthetic discrimination that supposedly accompanied it could lead, as in the case of Dick and Nicole Diver, to the collapse of moral discrimination. Too much freedom, too much 'spare time', too much *leisure*, led to a downward spiral of flirtations, love affairs, drugs and even insanity.

Tennis and tennis tournaments were central to the social round. Competitive matches were scheduled early enough in the day for players and spectators to seek relief afterwards from the midday heat in the cool of the hotel bars or dining rooms. Then, after the siesta, there might be another tennis match, and later *thé dansants* and gambling at the casinos. It was usually the men who gambled while their wives and mistresses danced with the *danseurs mondains*. These were not gigolos, but genuine dancing partners.

The Riviera was as much a magnet for artists as for tennis and golf players. From 1883 the Calais–Nice–Rome express, with its lavish sleeping cars, had plied the route from north to south. In 1922 this became the *Train Bleu* and such was its fame and aura that it gave the title not only to Agatha Christie's *Mystery of the Blue Train* ('At the tennis one meets everyone,' says Hercule Poirot in the course of solving this particular puzzle), but of Diaghilev's ballet, *Le Train Bleu*, created for the youthful dancer, Anton Dolin. Jean Cocteau had seen Dolin performing complicated acrobatics in a theatre corridor and this had given him the idea of a ballet revolving round the athletic hero of a seaside resort. What Diaghilev couldn't understand was why Dolin chose to spend his spare time in Monte Carlo playing tennis or having picnics, rather than improving his mind by listening to the conversation of Picasso and Stravinsky.[7]

Le Train Bleu had been anticipated by an earlier ballet, *Jeux*, originally commissioned by Diaghilev in 1912 to a score by Debussy as a vehicle for his star, Nijinsky. It revolved round a game of tennis played by two men and a girl – although Diaghilev had wanted all three protagonists to be men. It wasn't well received and was not revived. (A century later a new version, or recreation, was given its world premiere at the Royal Opera House in London. Based on a fragment of choreography by the late Kenneth Macmillan, it explored the themes of flirtation, games and rivalries and success-fully represented the movements of tennis in balletic form, emphasising the similarities between the two.)

Le Train Bleu, with sets by Picasso, was created in 1924 by Bronislava Nijinska (Nijinsky's sister) to celebrate the sporting and beach culture of the Riviera and also the Olympic Games, played in Paris that year. The ballet captures with utter vivacity the total physical and sporting élan and exuberance of the Côte d'Azur. In essence a traditional one-act ballet with pas de deux, solos and ensembles, it is nevertheless an example of 'lifestyle modernism' according to dance historian Lynn Garafola.[8] It concerns the game of love as a muscle man, a swimmer, a golfer and a tennis player flirt on the beach, costumed for the most part in the ultra-simple one-piece costumes of vests and abbreviated shorts of the 1920s, apart from the golfer in plus fours and check sweater and the tennis player clad in the style of Helen Wills, complete with white eye shade. The choreography mimics the golfer's drive; the tennis player's solos show how close to dance tennis can be.

This ballet was costumed by Chanel, herself a devotee of the Côte d'Azur lifestyle, to which her minimalist fashions were perfectly adapted. Her style, claimed Cecil Beaton, had created a completely new type of woman and of female beauty. Its archetype was a Spanish duchess:

> who appeared wearing a short white tunic with a deep
> scooped neckline and a skirt that stretched barely to the

knees ... sunburn stockings with white satin shoes whose
Spanish spike heels were fully six inches high. Her hair, bril-
liantined to a satin brilliance, was drawn back as tightly as a
bullfighter's ... [Her] complexion matched her stockings, for
she was burned by the sun to a deep shade of iodine. Two
enormous rows of pearl teeth were bared in a white, vital
grin, complementing the half a dozen rows of pearls ... that
hung about her neck.[9]

The new Riviera lifestyle started from the revolutionary assumption that the Riviera was the perfect resort, not for the winter,
as it once had been, but in the heat of the summer. At first the
gesture of arriving at the littoral just as the season was ending,
of staying in deserted hotels – your wealth having prevailed on
the proprietor to keep it open instead of, as usual, closing it – of
lounging on empty beaches or of pursuing your art uninterrupted
by the bustle of Paris or New York, was the most radical gesture,
denoting a new way of life, a new aesthetic, a new freedom of
the body. The photographer and painter Jacques Henri Lartigue
felt that the guests at the hotel where he was staying were 'dreary
and miserable' in their stuffy urban outfits. Worse still, they were
old, 'even the young ones'. By contrast he had glimpsed a young
woman in a white dress, 'bareheaded and laughing beneath the
sun', accompanied by a young man in a sweater and espadrilles,
'which go better with the landscape and the sunlight than the
creaking leather boots of the gentlemen who are afraid of the
sun'.[10]

    In other words the Côte d'Azur now did more than provide
a respite from the formal way of life; it challenged it. This was a
better way to *be*. It was also intoxicating: swimming in the trans-
parent sea, Lartigue felt overwhelmed by the light and completely
transported out of himself.

    On her first visit in 1926 Helen Wills, Lenglen's young rival
and later to become eight times Wimbledon singles champion,
felt that the Riviera was already past its best. To her it seemed 'not

quite real, it was like a dream in which things were happening with the extravagance of grand opera and the effect of a musical comedy. It had just about reached the point where it had had its day ... but its winter following had not yet entirely deserted it.'

What most startled her was this glimpse of 'a world new to me where the main object was pleasure'. There seemed nothing to do but to seek ways of passing the time pleasurably. 'This came as a surprise to me, as such a thing had not occurred to me before.' Her life hitherto had consisted almost entirely of serious study and serious tennis in the exclusive but sedate surroundings of Berkeley, California. Now, however, 'it began to dawn on me that people were interesting and sometimes amusing'. She described the glitzy Les Ambassadeurs where the bands played tangos and fox trots, you could see the yachts in the harbour from the long windows and the interior glittered with light. Best of all were the exotic human beings who peopled this strange environment, for example, a 'dramatic looking lady with tired eyes, and a series of halo hats in different colours, who used to arrive in a large yellow Hispano-Suiza with chauffeur and footman. She could dance only with gigolos, except on weekends, when her protector, a manufacturer, would come from Paris.' Helen Wills added with provincial innocence, 'I had vaguely imagined such people existed only on the screen. Certainly there were none in Berkeley, California.' [11]

The post-war Riviera was louder and faster and some felt more vulgar than in its Edwardian heyday, but it had not lost its glamour. And tennis played there continued to have great prestige. The English influence was waning, but still dominated the sport. One travel writer of the period described the La Festa club at Monte Carlo, 'in the capable hands of Mr William G. Henley, the secretary of the Federation Monégasque de Lawn-Tennis, who used to be the British Consul for these parts. Write to him at La Festa ... If you are respectable, no difficulty will be made about your becoming a member. Subscriptions cost very little; a member can introduce guests.'

In 1927 a new centre, La Festa Country Club at St Roman, was built. There it seemed the players were magnificently provided for. Dressing rooms were the last word in luxury. There were showers, a good bar and access to the beach and the sea. There was even a telephone in every cabin.

The Riviera tournaments marked the beginning of the international tennis season, their standing outshone only by Wimbledon, the French tournament at Roland Garros and the US National championships. Many aristocrats, including King Gustav of Sweden, still graced the courts and there was always a sprinkling of titles among the contestants: Baron de Morpurgo, Baron Kehrling and Baron Salm.

The administration remained under the control of the British: A. E. Madge, who officiated as referee and manager at the first Monte Carlo tournament in 1903 was still in charge more than twenty-five years later. (The administration of golf was also almost entirely British.)[12]

Other less salubrious influences were at play, for the Riviera tennis world in the 1920s exemplified what many felt were morally dubious aspects of the game, now in terms of money rather than sexual misconduct. After 1924 tennis had been disbarred from the Olympic Games on the grounds that it was not a genuinely amateur sport. It was clear that, unassisted, Charles Lenglen could not have supported his daughter's lifestyle. A great friend of Suzanne was the society hostess, Lady Wavertree, whose 'constant companion' was F. M. B. Fisher, an executive of the Dunlop company that produced racquets and balls and constituted an important presence on the Riviera. Also powerful and important were the three Burke brothers who ran the Carlton tennis club at Cannes and who were among Suzanne's closest friends.

In 1926 a historic match between Lenglen and Helen Wills attracted hordes of press correspondents. The cloud of journalists, desperate for stories as they hung about waiting for the match, began to probe the rather suspect financial basis of the scene. Searching questions were asked of players who appeared to have no visible means of support, yet who were staying in the best hotels. This included Helen Wills and her mother, although, to be fair, on their arrival they had booked into a simple *pension*, only to be whisked to the Carlton Hotel, where they were offered free hospitality for their whole stay. This they accepted, perhaps a little naively, having been told that it was the usual thing. Wills also accepted several outfits from Jean Patou, Lenglen's couturier.

There were protracted arguments between journalists and the Burke brothers about the price demanded for the rights to report the Wills–Lenglen encounter; and equally acrimonious ones between the Burkes and the newsreel companies. The whole ugly issue of profit was exposed to view, and the question, not fully answered, was raised: who profited from the huge sums generated by this extraordinary show?

So, says Teddy Tinling, 'the whole question of under-the-counter payments to "amateur" stars and the then dirty word "shamateurism", were first publicly aired in the discussions surrounding the Lenglen-Wills match.'[13] Tennis no less than other sports was vulnerable to corruption. Its sheen of glamour began to develop cracks, exposing a less than beautiful reality beneath the hedonistic surface. Jean Vigo's bitterly satirical film, *A Propos de Nice*, made in 1931, filmed the tourists promenading along the crowded front, still dressed for town in homburg hats, high heels, cloche hats and furs, and juxtaposed the poverty of a service class catering to the rich and idle: the laundries, the weary waiters, the slums behind the façade.

6

What's wrong with women?

IT WAS IRONIC THAT SUZANNE LENGLEN, a woman, should have become the first international tennis celebrity, given the controversy surrounding women's very presence on the court. Long before she stepped into the spotlight the men in charge of the game had thoroughly objected to a new generation of young women who had rebelled against the lives of passivity led by their mothers and were bent on a different existence. Lottie Dod wrote forcefully of the difficulties that faced women in the early years. She pointed to the curious inconsistency whereby tennis was regarded at one and the same time as 'only a lady's game', a 'pat ball' pastime unworthy of sporting men, yet equally 'quite beyond their powers' either to play it or to understand the scoring system. There was 'at one time a real danger', said Lottie Dod, 'lest men's and women's lawn tennis should be entirely separated, with different grounds, balls, and laws.'[1] True, a women's tournament was organised in Dublin in 1879, but it was not played on the usual courts in Fitzwilliam Square, as this was considered too public a venue. Nor were ladies admitted as members to the Fitzwilliam Lawn Tennis Club. When women's tournaments were initiated at Wimbledon in 1884, the doubles were played away from the main grounds.

It is difficult to understand these objections until one becomes fully aware of just how restricted the lives and movements of middle-class women were in the 1870s and 1880s. Many people, and not just men, felt it was not respectable for women to be seen playing actively in public at all. Women violated their own femininity in making violent movements, and seeming to perspire or be out of breath was unthinkable and even indecent, so strongly was femininity equated with passivity. This was one of the most inhibiting factors for female players: the convention that prevented young women from any vigorous display of movement. Lord Curzon, one-time viceroy of India and a government minister at this period, is notoriously said to have said of sexual intercourse that 'ladies don't move' and this prohibition on lively activity extended much more generally. Anything else was damaging to their femininity. There was also the question of fashionable dress, for, asked Lottie Dod in exasperation, how could women 'ever hope to play a sound game when their dresses impede the free movement of every limb? In many cases their very breathing is rendered difficult.'

She herself wore a white flannel cap on her dark, cropped hair, a skirt that stopped short of the ankles and showed black woollen stockings and black shoes. Her shirt was high collared, its sleeves long. This was for the period a radical outfit, especially the short hair, but she was able to get away with it because, being under sixteen, she was still regarded as a child.

Women's daywear became simplified in the 1890s with the introduction of the tailored coat and skirt outfit suitable for working women in the fast growing cities. The middle-class craze for the bicycle led to further attempts to promote practical women's clothing. Tennis wear followed suit.

Women's tennis dresses were simplified and more suitable for active play, with unboned collars, deeper than normal armholes and pleats stitched only at the top. By this time special shoes were also worn, with rubber soles and often canvas tops. Even so, when May Sutton became the first American woman to win Wimbledon at the age of seventeen in 1905, her outfit marked a further stage in informality as she daringly rolled up her sleeves,

"HULLO, GERTY! YOU'VE GOT
FRED'S HAT ON, AND HIS COVER
COAT?"
"YES. DON'T YOU LIKE IT?"
"WELL—IT MAKES YOU LOOK LIKE
A YOUNG MAN, YOU KNOW, AND
THAT'S SO EFFEMINATE!"

A satirical look at sporting fashions from *Punch* in 1891, one
of many comments on the bicycling and sports playing young
women of the time

revealing a bare forearm, and shortened her skirts – but was
refused permission to play until she had lowered the hems again.
Reminiscing in the early 1970s, her older sister, Violet, also a
tennis player, recalled that in their playing days they had worn:
'a long undershirt, pair of drawers, two petticoats, white linen
corset cover, duck shirt, shirtwaist, long white silk stockings and
a floppy hat.' She nevertheless believed that they had managed to
run faster than the girls she was still teaching in 1972.[2]

Mrs Sterry, another female champion from this period, artic-
ulated the very thing about women playing tennis that annoyed

the many correspondents to *The Field* magazine who wrote in to thunder their hostility to the idea of women playing. 'I am sure that the tournaments would not possess half their present attractions if men alone competed,' she wrote in 1903. Ladies, she added, must ensure that they went on court looking their best as 'all eyes are on them'.[3] It was precisely to this, of course, that the male opponents objected; they did not want their wives and daughters subjected to public gaze. Wallis Myers, however, an early aficionado of the game, agreed with her:

> The man who would attempt to divide the two forces and banish the fair sex from the chief arena into fields of their own can know little of the joy which their presence at tournaments gives to looker-on and player alike; he must know that most meetings only flourish by virtue of their social charms and that ladies are as essential to the well-being of a large open tournament as the committee or the much-abused umpires.[4]

Finding it impossible to exclude them entirely, the tennis authorities attempted to impose separate rules. For example, it was suggested that women might be allowed to hit the ball after it had bounced twice, might serve from the middle of the court and refuse any service they missed. In any case no gentleman should ever hit them a ball they couldn't reach.

By the turn of the twentieth century, nonetheless, women had won the day.

Herbert Chipp, the first secretary of the Lawn Tennis Association, was no advocate of the emancipation of women and yet in his *Recollections*, published in 1898, he recognised a fait accompli when he saw one:

> Among the manifold changes and consequent uprooting of prejudices which the latter half of the century has witnessed, nothing has been more characteristic of the new order of things than the active participation of women in its sports and pastimes ... the unblushing young women of the

day were daily joining in pursuits that their grandmothers would have regarded as unalloyed heathenism.[5]

He conceded however that times had changed and 'lawn tennis must claim a large share of the responsibility for the introduction of the new regime'. And although 'the athleticism of the *fin de siècle* woman appears sometimes too pronounced', he conceded that the changes 'must ultimately prove beneficial to the race at large – at all events physically. Whether the benefits will be as great morally is a question which only time can settle.' But he recognised that the new generation of women would not be 'worse mothers because, instead of leading sedentary lives, a great portion of their young years has been spent on the river, the tennis lawn, the hockey field and the golf links – ay, even on the now ubiquitous bicycle itself.'

Yet commentators and players alike continued to pour scorn on the women's game. A. L. Laney, writing after the First World War, had no time for it whatsoever. 'Few games played by women seem worth recalling,' he wrote. 'The dears are, on the whole, comparatively dull performers in sport and nearly always it is clashing personalities rather than skill or outstanding performance that make the occasion memorable. Unless something other than actual tennis has intervened to grace the occasion, you will search long through the history of the game to find matches suitable for embalming in the hackneyed superlatives of the sportswriter.' He described interminable matches characterised by purposeless hitting up and down the court by two girls, 'neither able to win when the chance comes, both forced to go on and on until one or the other finally loses.'[6]

Helen Jacobs, a rising star and later to become US Champion, writing of her final in the Riviera Beaulieu tournament in 1931 against a player of the old school, Mrs Satterthwaite,[7] described the latter as just such a player. Mrs Satterthwaite 'serves underhand, hits her forehand drive in the same manner in which she serves, and merely reverses the process for her backhand and ... seemed to take pride in creating records for the unbroken flight of the ball over the net. One of our rallies passed well beyond the hundred mark.' Jacobs was so discombobulated by her opponent's awful play that after the match had gone on for two and a half hours Mrs Satterthwaite won. 'For sheer endurance alone, she deserved the victory.'[8]

Yet this was not the only way women played tennis even before the First World War. Dorothea Lambert Chambers, who won Wimbledon seven times in the decade before 1914, wrote her own tennis manual, *Lawn Tennis for Ladies* and was no advocate for conventional 'ladylike' behaviour on court. On the contrary she insisted that women players should not remain 'absolutely immobile'. She advocated regular practice at tennis, movement about the court and an attention to the mental game as a way of developing confidence. Like later women players such as Suzanne Lenglen and Helen Wills, she developed her own game by playing against the best men at her tennis club and all the successful women players of these early years rejected the female 'pat ball' efforts of less committed and ambitious women.[9] Mrs Larcombe, a contemporary of Dorothea Lambert Chambers, made similar observations:

> The chief error among ladies is the tendency to develop one particular stroke at the expense of all others. This stroke as a rule is the forehand drive from the right corner across diagonally to the opposite corner … But … one stroke cannot be made to serve for all occasions. This cultivation of the forehand leads inevitably to a corresponding weakness in the backhand, a fault very hard to eradicate. In a doubles an active base-liner can 'run round' most balls that would otherwise come to the backhand, but in a singles it is practically impossible to defend a weak backhand.[10]

This affected their volleying, as 'one cannot have a weak backhand and be a volleyer'.

Lack of initiative was another female fault. They were 'so

content with the same old strokes, the same degree of proficiency'. The upshot was that ladies' tennis as a rule 'gives the spectator a sensation of dullness'. There was 'an absence of "headwork", of intention'. Women seemed unable and unwilling to change their game whereas Mrs Larcombe would have liked them to play an all-court game and try to improve their results.

Given that this was the dominant perception of the game, it should be no surprise that the appearance of Suzanne Lenglen at the first post-war Wimbledon caused a sensation. When she walked onto the Centre Court on 5 July 1919, she was more than just a new sporting figure. The French finalist wore a startlingly brief costume. Described as 'indecent' in parts of the press, it was a simple frock with short sleeves and a skirt reaching only to the calves, to reveal white stockings. On her head was a floppy hat. Yet, hailed as a revolutionary change in tennis dress for women, it was actually the result of a long and much slower process. The way in which the women of the western world gradually shed their clothes between 1914 and the 1920s was hastened by the war, but was evolutionary rather than revolutionary.

She nevertheless presented a startling contrast to her opponent, Dorothea Lambert Chambers, a seven-times champion and, at forty, twice Lenglen's age. She was dressed in an ankle-length Edwardian skirt, a shirt fastened at the neck and wrists and, although these of course were not visible, corsets.

An epic struggle ensued, enthralling to the sell-out crowd of 8,000. They had queued for hours to get in – and as they waited had sung an old war song adapted for the occasion: 'It's a Lenglen trail awinding'. King George V and Queen Mary, a keen follower of the game, were among the audience who watched a match that lasted for over two hours. Mrs Chambers twice held match point, but Lenglen won the third and deciding set 9–7. With her victory, she became symbolic of the new time.

The two women athletes who faced each other were at once cast as personifications of youth versus age, new versus old. It was the passage from the pre- to the post-war world. Dorothea

French star Mlle Broquedis, who anticipated Suzanne Lenglen,
playing in the 1912 Olympics

Chambers represented the Edwardian stuffiness of suburban
vicarage tennis. Suzanne, the 'goddess of tennis', said *The Times*,
was '*the* player for the Jazz age, gay, brittle and brilliant'. David
Gilbert has defended the older woman as a thoroughly modern
and forward-looking sportswoman. As we saw, she wrote her own
book on tennis, which advocated an active playing style. She won
Wimbledon seven times, both before and after having children.
She nearly defeated Lenglen, although she was twice her age.[11]

The growing popularity of sport generally, the craze for the
bicycle, the rise of the lower-middle class and the struggle for
women's emancipation, had all emerged before 1914. In their
various ways the *Belle Epoque* in France, the Progressive Era in
the United States and the Edwardian Indian summer in Britain
had carried within them the seeds of the 'Jazz Age'. Indeed,

within tennis itself, it was another Frenchwoman who took the first steps towards the modernisation of women's tennis: Marguerite Broquedis, who had already abandoned corsets. 'The first published tennis fashion columns in magazines, the first … special hairstyles for tennis, the first Olympic Gold Medal won for France by a woman, even the first suggestion that women's tennis should be beautiful, all derived from her,' wrote Teddy Tinling. Broquedis moreover, was much better-looking than Lenglen.[12]

Yet the 1919 Wimbledon final sent a message – about social change and about women's emancipation, about a new and different future in which fun would trump duty. Suzanne Lenglen benefited from changes that had been developing for over a decade; but like other players subsequently, she could be projected as a symbol. She was the 1920s goddess of modernity. She was brilliantly fixed – whether accurately or not – pinned like a butterfly to the gay and garish poster of the *années folles*.[13]

Change did not, however, necessarily mean straightforward progress. The bodily freedom Lenglen represented and expressed brought new problems for young women. Short skirts and short hair seemed radical, but in France and elsewhere the new, bobbed hairstyle, or, even more daring, the Eton crop, was controversial. The greater importance attached to looks and, already, the growing influence of Hollywood and the movies, meant that women had to spend more effort – and money – to achieve the new standards. Their bodies were more objectified; they were subject to greater scrutiny.[14]

Suzanne Lenglen attracted the sort of fervid admiration usually reserved for actresses and music-hall stars. Her fame seemed to bring to tennis the new consciousness of glamour and eroticism that by 1920 Hollywood was spreading across Europe and beyond. To this moment Lenglen was perfectly attuned, as if born to be the first international celebrity tennis star in the most international of all sports.

Her career also exemplified a life devoted to excess. Teddy Tinling recalls that years after Suzanne's 1919 triumph at

Wimbledon Mrs Lambert Chambers confided to him that she considered the outcome of the match to have been a tragedy – obviously for her, since it snatched from her the chance of an eighth Wimbledon championship; but even more seriously for Suzanne, because it gave her 'the taste of invincibility and a subsequent compulsion for it, which brought endless sacrifices and unnatural unhappiness, out of all proportion to the rewards of her fame'.[15]

Suzanne Lenglen and Henri Lacoste playing mixed doubles in 1925

Suzanne was not beautiful. Her face was heavy, with a prominent nose. She had dark, Mediterranean colouring and, often, deep rings beneath her eyes. It was her astonishing athletic, indeed balletic grace that held her audience entranced. And despite her lack of conventional good looks, she perfected a style of dressing that was copied everywhere, modelling outfits designed by the leading Paris couturier, Jean Patou, both on and off court. In particular, from 1920 onwards she replaced her linen hat with a length of silk georgette bound tightly round her newly bobbed hair in a bandeau and fastened with a diamond pin. Each bandeau in a different vivid colour – lemon, heliotrope, coral – matched the cardigan worn over her white dress, which soon was falling only to the knee, in line with the rapidly shortening fashionable skirts. She came onto court in a white ermine coat and fortified herself with nips of cognac or coffee between games. She participated fully in the social life of the Riviera, where tennis slotted seamlessly into the daily round of pleasure. She was an international celebrity sought by hostesses all over Europe and lived the luxurious lifestyle appropriate to her stardom.

From 1919 to 1926 Lenglen reigned as supreme tennis star and indeed supreme female athlete. Yet this life took its toll. Like a number of later female tennis stars, she was not only coached by her father, but was dominated by him. Theirs was a close bond, unhealthy perhaps insofar as it was predicated on Charles Lenglen's need to live out his own failed aspirations as an athlete through his daughter (a story that would be repeated many times in the tennis world). He bent her to his will with the threat of withdrawal of love. Both he and her mother were quick to criticise, and even success was greeted with admonitions to do more. After Suzanne won her first two major tournaments at the age of fifteen, her father simply said: 'Now you must win them all.' And it was reported that once when, rarely, Suzanne lost a set, Charles shouted, 'If you lose another game I'll disinherit you.' (Coco Gentien disputed these stories, attributing the last to the spite of Bill Tilden, who hated Lenglen.)

Suzanne herself was consumed by the fear of being unable to maintain her place at the summit. Illness became one method whereby she could escape when the strain became intolerable. It is not surprising in a sport so physical and so demanding on the player that the state of the body would become a preoccupation, even a neurotic one, but illness was also a psychological bolthole. On the occasions when Lenglen retired from a match the cause was more usually illness than injury. She was plagued by chest infections, contracted jaundice and was prone to other illnesses, but the strain was also a mental one. By 1926 the pressure was beginning to tell.

Her friend and admirer, Teddy Tinling, commented: 'Some say the tremendous exertions and the constant invincibility demanded of her by Papa Lenglen eventually reduced her to a frail, nervous wreck. Others think that early repressions by both her parents, who felt any normal life might impair her performance, were the real cause of her decline.' Certainly Tinling felt that when he knew her she 'seemed to spend her whole life on her toes, unable ever to relax'.[16] She had become temperamental and autocratic.

In 1924 she had withdrawn from Wimbledon with the after-effects of jaundice. In 1925 she won again and after a triumphant season undertook a 'Grand Tour', staying with European monarchs and heads of state. But in 1926 her career as an amateur player was to come to an abrupt and startling end.

7

A match out of Henry James

HELEN WILLS WAS TWENTY YEARS OLD. She had won the American championships for three successive years. She had been a finalist at Wimbledon in 1924, losing narrowly in three sets. (Suzanne did not play that year, withdrawing through illness.) Billed as the all-American girl, sporty, unsophisticated and natural, she provided the press with a dramatic contrast to the bird of paradise that was Lenglen.

In the spring of 1926 Wills announced that she would play the Riviera circuit of tournaments. She thus effectively threw down a gauntlet to Suzanne, perhaps without realising the extent to which this would plunge her into celebrity, for she and her mother, with whom she always travelled, were astounded to be greeted on their arrival in Paris by the leading French player, Jean Borotra, accompanied by the president of the French Tennis Federation.

In anticipation of the expected showdown journalists flocked to the Côte. Helen Wills was entered for several tournaments, but the contest did not happen at the first, the Hotel Metropole tournament, where Suzanne played (brilliantly) only in the doubles events; nor in the next, the Gallia, where she did not play at all, because Charles Lenglen was seriously ill. The tournament in the third week was in Nice, Suzanne's home turf, but this time it was Wills who did not take part. The Frenchwoman won five rounds without the loss of a single game.

By now the international press had ramped up the anticipated, but interminably postponed, encounter to apocalyptic proportions. Sport, a mixture of nationalism and heroism, had trumped politics and the Franco-American rivalry of the two women was front page news. In the American press Suzanne was cast as the evil vamp, the wicked European schemer out of a Hollywood movie, against the American Girl or the Girl from the Golden West, who represented everything pure and true about America and American womanhood. It had become a Henry James classic, the innocence of the New World pitted against the deceitfulness of old Europe.

Events moved to Cannes and the Carlton Hotel tournament. There, finally, the two women faced each other.[1]

The day of the final arrived. The club had been besieged since dawn, or even before, by huge crowds of fans, their excitement inflamed by the publicity that had raged for weeks. The pressmen, with nothing to report, had further and further ratcheted up expectations in a game of perpetual deferral, an endless tease. Now as the Train Bleu arrived packed with hopeful spectators and as the club officials were forced to form a flying wedge in order to storm the gates and get past the multitudes, extra banks of seats were still being built and every roof of every building surrounding the club had spectators clinging to it. The windows and balconies of the hotel itself were crammed. Finally as the hour approached, the glittering band of grand dukes, maharajahs, film stars, a phalanx of Bourbon royalty from Spain, the business tycoon Gordon Selfridge, accompanied by music-hall stars the Dolly Sisters, and the Duke of Westminster, took the seats of which they at least were assured.

Suzanne Lenglen arrived to the hysterical screams and waves of the fans. Helen Wills' arrival went almost unnoticed. Suzanne bowed, smiled, posed and waved, like the prima donna she was, but she had had a sleepless night after a huge argument with her sick father, who had forbidden her to play.

The match itself was not the walkover Lenglen's fans had

hoped for. She won the first set quite comfortably, 6–3, but then Wills began to up her game just as her opponent's strength seemed to be disastrously ebbing. Helen Wills' power game was beginning to undermine Lenglen's more artistic play, which depended on perfect movement. At 6–5, 40–15 Suzanne appeared nevertheless on the point of victory. A call of 'out' greeted Wills' next return shot and the contestants shook hands at the net. It was only several seconds later that an official managed to make himself heard above the hysterical cheering, to say that the call had been 'in' and that the 'out' had come from the crowd.

Suzanne was by now prostrate in her chair. She looked blank when she understood the decision, but, true to the sporting ethic she accepted the decision, rose to her feet and carried on. She lost the game: the score 6–6. She won the next and then at 7–6, 40–15, another match point, again Wills pulled her back to deuce. But this time Lenglen found her final ounce of strength and willpower and came through, defeating Wills 6–3, 8–6. Such was the chaos, the excitement, but also the exhaustion of Lenglen herself, who became completely hysterical, that the celebrations were cancelled and Lenglen ended the evening in a quiet restaurant in the port at Nice with Coco Gentien. (That is his account; others reported she had spent it with a woman friend.) Meanwhile Helen Wills was left alone and forgotten until a young man, Freddie Moody, came to her side to tell her how well she had played. They were married in 1929.

Naturally the tennis world expected the rivalry to be renewed, first at the French Open and then at Wimbledon. Helen Wills, however, was forced to withdraw from Paris with acute appendicitis and underwent an emergency operation.

That year Wimbledon celebrated its golden jubilee; fifty years of the event. Things went badly from the start. Suzanne was suffering from a sore arm. The draw for the tournament (then unseeded – seeding was only introduced in 1927) had turned up most of the top-ranked players on the Lenglen side of the draw. She drew the French Open finalist in her first singles match and

– much worse – her former doubles partner, Elizabeth Ryan and Ryan's new partner, in her first-round doubles match.

Next, a series of misunderstandings meant that when Queen Mary arrived to see the Frenchwoman play, Suzanne was unaware she was scheduled to play and was visiting her doctor. The situation was somehow smoothed over for the time being, but in their rage at this apparent insult to the reigning queen, the British press turned against the French star. A further blow was the loss of the doubles match after which Queen Mary appeared to ignore Lenglen as she left the court. (She later denied this – it was a misunderstanding, and she was pained that it had upset the French player.) Suzanne next returned to the Centre Court for her mixed-doubles match with Jean Borotra, but was heckled and booed by the spectators until the clowning Borotra defused the situation. On the following Monday she announced her withdrawal from all the events. She was to have been received at Court in July, but renounced that too and returned forthwith to France.

Shortly afterwards she accepted an offer from the American promoter, C. C. Pyle, to play a series of exhibition matches in the US. So she became the first big tennis star to turn professional. As in so many other ways, she was a pioneer, anticipating the future.

Her decision was more than controversial. The amateur status of the sporting star was in those days the foundation stone of all sport. The 'gentleman amateur' was hero. To play for money was unthinkable. The sportsman must be driven by pure love of the game and the game soared above commerce. This was the ideology that had originated in the British public-school system and spread across the world. Only amateur participation could provide the character-building that sports provided.

Yet this belief was never quite so dominant in the United States as in Britain. In the 1920s the American public was mad about sports. There was obviously money – vast sums of it – to be made from them and now there were promoters who would grasp the opportunity. Pyle was the trail-blazer.

By becoming professional, Lenglen stunned her fans, many of whom now turned against her. In any case, she was already a hate object in the United States, but this to Pyle made her the perfect proposition: 'People will pay to see anybody they hate.' He further enticed her by dangling the promise of fame as a film star in front of her. This never materialised, but he managed to sign up several other well-known, previously amateur, players and created a travelling circus of exhibition tennis matches.

At first, Lenglen seemed not to have understood how completely her turning professional would exclude her from the amateur world of tournaments and competitive play. Whether she was motivated by fear of losing her supreme position to Helen Wills, enraged by the humiliation she had suffered at Wimbledon, or lured by the promise of huge wealth and even a new career in movies, her decision to turn professional rather than leading to an exciting new stage in her life, resulted in disappointment and loss of direction. The bird of paradise no longer spread her wings. The goddess had been banished from Mount Olympus.

In 1933 she was appointed director of a tennis coaching school at Roland Garros. She also had a deal with Selfridges department store in London to make 120 appearances to give demonstration lessons and advice on racquets and dresses.[2] In 1938 she was made director of the French national tennis school, but in July of that year she died of pernicious anaemia at the age of thirty-nine.

By contrast, Helen Wills was on the threshold of a career as glorious and more enduring. In winning Wimbledon eight times between 1927 and 1935 she lost only two sets in finals matches. She became as famous as Lenglen had been and, just as the Frenchwoman had been seen as a symbol of all things French, so Helen Wills became a symbol of how Americans perceived their country and its values. She was 'Our Helen', a natural, simple girl of statuesque Grecian beauty, a young prodigy of a schoolgirl when she won her first titles, whose long brown plaits swung as she stormed all over the court. For her game was based on speed and power and she herself said:

'Nothing is more fun when playing than to hit the ball hard and see it go flying over the net. Speed, even with greater risk, has a certain fascination and charm that cannot be equalled by anything else in the game. If I had my chance I would much rather be the fastest player in the world than the most accurate, if to be the most accurate demanded slower play.'[3]

As the febrile gaiety of the twenties morphed into the anxieties of the depression thirties, she was the fastest woman player in the world.

As success followed success she changed from the sweet, shy all-American girl into a cold and queenly personality. In fact, she was never quite like other young girls. In describing how she was determined to get a Phi Beta Kappa at the University of California, she claims that she barely participated in the general student social life, which she seems to have despised. She simply attended the necessary lectures and did the necessary work in order to achieve her goal. In 1929 she married Freddie Moody, the young man who had consoled her after her loss to Lenglen, but in her autobiography ingenuously reveals that it took her several years of marriage to realise that he wasn't quite as interested in tennis as she was. It was as if she had a tunnel-vision determination to achieve and to do so in the most economical and devastating manner possible. The nickname 'Little Miss Poker Face' stuck to her because her expression never changed during a match, whatever the situation. She was a living marble statue, an ice queen. Over the years her inevitable triumphs over all other players began, perhaps, to bore the crowds. It became monotonous, and *she* was monotonous, 'powerful, repressed and imperturbable' as the sports correspondent of the *Herald Tribune* put it. 'Somehow she does not seem to be enjoying the game ... it strikes me that hers is a professional attitude,' he wrote (and that was not a compliment). She played without emotion, her features 'an absolute mask of serene austerity, with never the flicker of a smile to lighten them' and destroyed her opponents mercilessly, a transcendent exponent of the killer instinct.

Unlike the saturnine Lenglen, Helen Wills seemed ideal for the screen. James Phelan, a rich and influential San Francisco banker and lawyer (he had been mayor of the city and also a senator), was much older than Helen Wills, but their mutual affection went very deep and it may have been only the age difference that prevented their friendship from developing romantically.

Helen Wills Moody and King Gustav of Sweden

He encouraged Helen Wills to think beyond tennis, to become a writer and to star in films. He arranged a screen test, but, like Lenglen before her, Helen Wills was not right for the screen, although she was beautiful. She was told that she was too heavy; her statuesque, athletic figure did not fit with the vulnerable and infantile Hollywood heroine then in vogue. Later attempts also came to nothing, although she did appear in a propaganda movie supporting Herbert Hoover's bid for the presidency in 1928.

Yet if the movie industry failed to appreciate her beauty, sculptors and photographers certainly did. Most famously the Mexican muralist, Diego Rivera, wanted to celebrate her beauty by making her the symbolic figure of California as the centre of his mural for the San Francisco Stock Exchange. This was controversial. Many felt that the famous revolutionary communist should not be in the United States at all, let alone painting murals for a stronghold of capitalism. Objections to the portrait of Helen Wills were harder to understand; in the end Rivera altered her features, but still claimed her as the inspiration for the central figure.

The ice queen of tennis, not content to be a muse, was a successful journalist. Among her scoops was an interview with Amelia Earhart after the aviator's successful first solo flight across the Atlantic. In addition she was a painter, who exhibited on a regular basis. In contemplating the beauty of perfection in art, she seemed, she said, 'to be transported to another sphere ... Music, sculpture and to the greatest degree, painting ... Perfection and beauty fascinate me in any field, but most of all in art.'[4]

For years Helen Wills had no serious rival, but an obsession with rivalries has long dominated sports journalism, particularly those in which players compete as individuals. Her closest opponent was another Helen, Helen Jacobs. Jacobs was never able to escape from the shadow of the other Helen. The Jacobs family even (inadvertently) moved into the Berkeley house vacated by the Wills family and Helen Jacobs was allotted Helen Wills' old room.

At first Helen Jacobs was an ardent admirer of the player who was so like her, yet so different. Both came from the Bay Area of San Francisco, both were outstanding players. On the other hand, Helen Wills was not only the more successful; she was considered the beautiful one. Helen Jacobs might be friendlier and more outgoing, but by comparison with the queenly Wills, she was 'short and stocky' (although in a portrait photograph in the London National Portrait Gallery she appears quite glamorous). She could not *represent* tennis in the way Helen Wills could. Wills cultivated a feminine appearance, took pains over her clothing and always wore make-up. Jacobs by contrast 'wore a hair net on the court, used little make-up, wore no nail varnish and chain smoked'. In 1936 *Time* magazine reported that Jacobs had so far shown no interest in men.

She was a pioneer of shorts for women players. The short skirts of the twenties had been controversial, but in the 1930s the issue of bare legs was replaced by the idea that shorts for women were just as inappropriate. It would have been natural to assume that, with modesty assured, the divided skirt would be welcomed, but, on the contrary, an atavistic gender anxiety haunted the masculine half of the human race (at least in the West) lest in stealing their clothing women might steal men's power. In the 1930s the *Daily Sketch*, for example, expressed alarm at short hair for women and the 'loss of curves' that trousers and shorts were said to imply. The writer frankly admitted that trousers and shorts might be seen as 'a flaunting symbol of masculine superiority'.

Lili de Alvarez, one of the most beautiful stars on the 1920s circuit, whose femininity was never in question, appeared at Wimbledon in 1931 in a 'white trousered frock',[5] but trousers for female tennis players did not catch on. By contrast, most female players were wearing shorts by the mid 1930s, including the British stars Kay Stammers and Eileen Fearnley-Whittingstall. Originating as casual day wear in the United States, shorts were popularised by Hollywood stars.

Sexual modesty was apparently a primary concern at this period and there was 'an inherently British language of "correctness" that was used in attempts to maintain standards of appearance and decorum in England throughout the period'.[6] Shorts were not welcomed and the British Wightman Cup team chose skirts for the 1938 contest against the Americans. It was the continental and American players who were the pioneers in taking up

Ora Washington with her defeated opponent,
Lula Ballard, in 1939

practical and streamlined styles, but for all the players freedom of
movement was the overriding issue.

The two Helens met many times on the tennis court and
Jacobs eventually came to the conclusion that her rival's stony
demeanour on court was a form of psychological bullying. She
was described as one of those machine players whose concentration and willpower never flagged and whose ground strokes
were so powerful that they defied opponents to outwit her at the
net. Jacobs won four US championship titles and had many other
successes, but she was destined to go down in tennis history as
the loser to Wills and to remain in her shadow. This was partly

because she never beat Wills at Wimbledon – although the last time they played in a final she held a match point. And she did beat her in the 1933 final at Forest Hills. That was the occasion on which, in danger of losing the match, Wills unsportingly retired, thus depriving Jacobs of the lustre of a true victory.

The press played up the animosity between the two, something that each of the players themselves denied. A rivalry between women, to a profession obsessed with rivalries, was especially exciting, as it could be described as a 'cat fight' and surreptitiously used as a way of belittling both the women and their game.

Helen Wills Moody's only other potential rival could never meet her across a net. Ora Washington won seven straight singles titles in the tournaments organised by the American Tennis Association, the association for black players in the United States. From 1929 to 1935 she dominated, and won a further singles title in 1937.[7] Very little was written about her, other than that she was nearly 6 foot tall (1.83 m) and had an unusual grip, holding the racquet further up the handle than was usual. A fellow African-American player from the period, Bob Ryland said that: 'Ora was really angry about never getting a chance to play against the best white women … She'd hear about the white women winning at Wimbledon and the US Nationals and those other [grand slam] tournaments and she'd be saying, "I could beat them."' But while Helen Wills was moving in upper-class society on two continents, presented at Court in London and staying at country houses, Ora Washington had to work as a domestic and could never appear on the recognised international stage. It was not until after the Second World War that this situation would change.

8

The lonely American

THE PARADOX OF TENNIS WAS that while it was never the most popular sport, its stars were the most famous of all. Babe Ruth, the baseball star, might be a household name in the United States; Max Schmeling's boxing exploits might dominate the German news; but Suzanne Lenglen and Bill Tilden were international.

The American champion, William T. Tilden II, Big Bill Tilden, equalled Lenglen in every way. Like her, he condensed in his person – and even more dramatically – in all the conflicts resulting from the emergence of tennis as an inherently contradictory sport and spectacle.[1]

Once he had won Wimbledon in 1920 Bill Tilden rapidly became the most famous sportsman in the world. He took the game forward and indeed was, it has been said, the inventor of the modern game to which he devoted his life. Dan Maskell believed the American's strength was his enormous versatility: his 'great variety of stroke, his deadly use of spin, his keen sense of strategy and tactics'. He was not a natural volleyer, but he had so many other weapons – the heavily sliced drives, the vicious kicking top-spin serves or 'a raking forehand drive into an opponent's backhand corner' – that he could choose his moment to hit a volley with precision and win the point.[2]

He was also, like Lenglen, whom he heartily disliked, the star who sold the spectacle to the fans.

Born into the Philadelphia upper crust of Anglo-Saxon 'old money', he was reared almost entirely by his mother, who passed on to him her love of music and the life of culture. After the early death of her first two boys and a girl, she gave birth to two more sons, but she had longed for another daughter. She became especially fearful for William's health and he was educated at home until the age of fifteen.

Tilden's appreciation of all things artistic was fostered by the family's summer holidays in the Onteora Club, a fashionable resort in the Catskills. There Tilden mixed with the writers, actors and musicians who spent their vacations at the club, where they also played tennis. Tilden learned the game there and won his first tournament, the Onteora under-15 boys' championship, in 1901 at the age of eight.

After his mother died, when William was fifteen, he was sent to live with an aunt and older cousin, although his father was a wealthy man with a large house and a number of servants. They had never been close. Then in his final year at Pennsylvania University first his father and then his older brother died suddenly. His brother was only twenty-nine and Tilden had been deeply attached to him.

He abandoned his degree to become a journalist on a local paper, and now began to work seriously on his tennis. In spite of his precocious win at Onteora, he was a late developer as a player, unremarked at university and unable initially to get into national tournaments. He escaped active service during the First World War because he had flat feet and while serving in the medical corps had plenty of time to improve his game, winning his first national title, the Clay Court Championships in 1918. The following year he reached the final of what was then the National Championships (today the US Open) after defeating Richard Norris Williams in the semi-final.

He was already controversial and unpopular and the young sports correspondent, A. L. Laney watched Tilden with 'antagonism mixed with fascination'. By contrast his semi-final opponent Richard Norris Williams was the epitome of the gentleman player. He was distantly descended from Benjamin Franklin, his family came from the Eastern seaboard upper crust and he had survived the *Titanic* disaster in which his father had been drowned. Tilden's win upset tennis fans, on account of the Philadelphian's apparent arrogance and 'distasteful mannerisms'.[3]

In the final Tilden lost to the popular Bill Johnston, known as 'Little Bill'. Convinced that the loss was due to his poor backhand, he took a job with an insurance firm in Providence. His real 'work', however, was to coach the son of one of the executives, who possessed an indoor court. There Tilden spent the whole winter reconstructing his backhand and in 1920 he won Wimbledon for the first time at the age of twenty-seven.

The Americans adored 'Little Bill' (as we saw A. L. Laney was one of them) and never took Tilden to their hearts. But he was a popular sensation in London with his blue mohair teddy bear sweater, gangly figure and blistering tennis. For American audiences his Wimbledon win did not count, because 'Little Bill' hadn't played that year. Tilden's supremacy was only established when he beat Johnston at the National at Forest Hills. He was now firmly established as the top American tennis player – indeed the top in the world, set to become the winner of six straight US championships, more than any other player, and the only man ever to win his last Wimbledon ten years after his first, at the age of thirty-seven – and was propelled into sporting celebrity.

Tilden dominated world tennis from 1920 to 1926. He was largely responsible for keeping the Davis Cup in the States for seven years, until it was wrested away by the four Frenchmen who in their turn dominated the late twenties, the 'Four Musketeers'. They were significantly younger, but even as Tilden passed his peak, it took four players to beat him.

Great sporting events of the past – 'greatest' matches, memorable defeats, astonishing reversals – resemble dance and theatrical performances in that no film or video can truly

Bill Tilden wearing the mohair sweater that thrilled the
Wimbledon crowd on his first appearance

recapture them. Nureyev or Fonteyn on celluloid can never convey
the magic of what was actually there, physically experienced in
'the real'; the make-up is all too visible, the sets seem dated, the
costumes stiff. The same is true of recorded sporting events; and
even more so, since once the match is over, the outcome is no
longer uncertain. Old films of pre-Second World War tennis stars
in play capture but pale ghosts across grey turf.

The intensities surrounding the personalities of the players
can seem equally dimmed in retrospect. The preference of
American audiences for 'Little Bill' was due to his seemingly
better sportsmanship. Yet Tilden himself was almost obsessively
sportsmanlike, and would ostentatiously throw points if he felt
that a line call had been incorrect. He was also a performer and

a showman and it was this that alienated the American public. Typical was the way in which he would serve out a match by somehow holding five balls in one huge hand, then tossing four of them up, one after another, for four cannonball aces, finally throwing the fifth away in disdain.

Coco Gentien was convinced that Tilden enjoyed his lofty yet isolated status: 'Even more than the moral solitude of which his private life was the reflection, he loved opposition and he was never so happy as when he saw the eyes of the crowd trained upon him like revolvers.' Gentien perceived Tilden's pleasure in domination and aggression: 'You'd have said Mephistopheles had chosen a tennis court on which to reincarnate himself. He never played in the same way. There was something excessive in his manner when he came to the net to shake hands with a defeated adversary, his arm outstretched from the back of the court and a diabolical smile stretching his lips as if to say "you played better than I thought you would".'[4] And René Lacoste observed that he seemed to exercise a strange fascination over his opponents as well as his spectators. 'Tilden, even when beaten, always leaves an impression on the public mind that he was superior to the victor.'[5]

Urbane, with a clipped upper-class accent, he was cultured, loved classical music and literature, was a great bridge player and loved the theatre. He was also belligerent and opinionated, his personality overwhelming so that, as one fellow player put it, it was like a bolt of electricity when he came into a room. There was a sense of his greatness; he was tennis royalty, you couldn't argue with him and it was a relief when he left.

When in New York Tilden lived in a suite at the Algonquin Hotel, and stayed in the best hotel in whichever city he appeared. He mixed with the stars in Hollywood. He played on Cecil B. de Mille's tennis court with Douglas Fairbanks Jr and Charlie Chaplin. In Europe he socialised with actresses and aristocrats.

Tilden's supremacy began to slip in 1926, also the year Lenglen's reign came to a shocking end. It was the year when the four young Frenchmen, who had been plotting since 1922, with Lenglen's help, to find a collective way to beat the great American and win the Davis Cup, achieved their first important successes. They travelled to the United States, where Jean Borotra defeated Tilden in the indoor championships. Big Bill hadn't lost any important match for seven years, but suffered a second defeat when Henri Cochet beat him in five sets at Forest Hills and a third when René Lacoste beat him in the final match of the Davis Cup. Although America retained the cup, Tilden's defeat by Lacoste – who had also won the championship, defeating Cochet in the final – was another sign that Tilden's days of total dominance were over.

9

The Four Musketeers

THE SUCCESS AND REPUTATION of the four French players had been growing since the war. When Paul Champ (member of the French Tennis Federation, Vice President of the Racing Club of France and tennis correspondent of *Le Figaro*) hit upon a collective label for them, the Four Musketeers, the name cunningly evoked a French national myth.

The popular novelist Alexandre Dumas had published *The Three Musketeers* in 1844, since when this international bestseller had never been out of print. It told the story of three musketeers in the service of the King of France, Louis XIII, in his struggles with the sinister Cardinal Richelieu. These three heroic soldiers, Athos, Porthos and Aramis, were joined by a fourth, the youth d'Artagnan, who travelled from Gascony in the hope of joining the King's forces. After an initial encounter in which he challenged each of them to a duel, d'Artagnan became the fourth Musketeer and their leader, and the band embarked on a series of adventurous and dangerous exploits to defend the honour of their King.

Although set in the seventeenth century, the tale recaptured something of the medieval age of chivalry. These heroes were warlike, fearless and tenacious, yet brought to life-and-death combat a sense of honour. Their adventures celebrated a form of warfare that was morally justified and heroic, and, after the carnage of the Somme and the Western Front, the new Musketeers of tennis represented the return of honour in a simpler form of heroism, a heroism that had been crushed in the mud and gore of Passchendaele.

The Musketeers, both old and reborn, appeared to represent certain ineffably French characteristics of panache, daring and at the same time a lightness of spirit even in the face of danger and death. Theirs was also a collective patriotic effort and fitted well with the rampant nationalism that was part of the thrill and tension that electrified all sports. The collective label was therefore a clever one, for it captured the essence of the French tennis players' quest to regain the Davis Cup. This quest could be recast as something more than an extended tennis tournament. It reprised the aristocratic duel and the fearless adventurousness of the knights of old; it even became a new version of the Grail legend, or, as one French journalist put it, a new version of the Argonauts' quest for the Golden Fleece.

Dumas' Musketeers expressed the romance of warfare and personal dedication to something valued more highly than wealth and even than life itself: honour. The Musketeers' commanding officer, M. de Tréville, was the epitome of strength and fidelity. He had started life as a poor man, although of good birth, but 'with that fund of audacity, esprit and resolution, which makes the poorest Gascon gentleman often inherit more in imagination than the richest nobleman ... his daring and haughty courage – still more haughty in success – had raised him [to become] the confidential friend of the King.'[1] It might seem that the four Frenchmen who defended the honour of their country in the 1920s with racquet and ball were hardly in the same league as the swashbuckling cavaliers of the seventeenth century. Yet their exploits caught the imagination of their countrymen – and the world – partly because even though France had been on the winning side in the war, there was considerable resentment at the war debts France now owed the United States, and the unsatisfactory Treaty of Versailles had led to growing anti-Americanism.

(Ironically, many Americans loved France and especially Paris, not only because the strong dollar made it a cheap place to live, but also because they wished to escape Prohibition and the stuffy Puritanism of their native land.)

The Four Musketeers: Henri Cochet, Jean Borotra, René Lacoste and Jacques Brugnon on their world travels.

The Musketeers became sporting envoys, seen at the Quai d'Orsay (the French equivalent of the Foreign Office). After they won the Davis Cup a world tour was organised, with French embassies alerted wherever they went. In Sydney, the mayor and councillors welcomed them at the town hall; they played exhibition matches in many different cities and countries and the press always gave them massive coverage. They were, indeed, symbolic musketeers, restoring the prestige and glory of France through the symbolic form of warfare that was sport.[2]

The French tennis players' campaign was a collective endeavour on the part of four men who at the same time had very different personalities. Jacques 'Toto' Brugnon was the eldest, the son of a wealthy lawyer and three years older than Borotra. His tennis career had begun before the war and he had not intended to resume competitive tennis after 1918, but Lenglen chose him as her mixed-doubles partner and encouraged him to continue. He was the least flamboyant member of the quartet, but a superb doubles player.

Henri Cochet's father was a prosperous tradesman who was also director of the Lyon Tennis Club. Jean Borotra's father was a landowner turned man of letters who lived in a château near Bayonne, while the father of René Lacoste, the youngest, was a successful industrialist. All four players, therefore, came from that section of society that had become passionately involved in sport and perhaps particularly lawn tennis in the period immediately prior to the war. They represented the rising and successful French bourgeoisie, with its wealth and social aspirations. Tennis players were ideally suited to become representatives of this bourgeois class, because the game had the aristocratic associations its members aspired to in many aspects of their lives.

So as the Musketeers set off to storm America and defeat Cardinal Richelieu reincarnated as Big Bill Tilden, they personified the cultural identity of the class from which they came. Henri Cochet played a suave, almost perfect game. René Lacoste, as well as being the youngest of the four, was the least physically powerful and suffered from a weak chest. He had even had a bout of tuberculosis. His game, however, was successful because he approached it scientifically. He was an intellectual of the game, a player whose precision and stroke play could outlast any opponent. He practised relentlessly (even hitting balls against the wall of his hotel room while in the US) and he took detailed notes on the play of his opponents in order to learn from as well as to defeat them. He was nicknamed 'the crocodile'. One myth has it that this came from his having found a baby alligator and kept it in his hotel room in Boston; it may more plausibly have been because of his style of play – to wait patiently until his opponent could be caught unawares, when he would suddenly strike below the water line as it were.

Of the four, Jean Borotra was by far the most flamboyant.[3]

Known as the 'bounding Basque' he had grown up in south-west France playing the ancient game of pelota, which was related to early forms of tennis. This made his style controversial, yet it was very successful. His movement was peerless; he leapt about the court and could hit a smash or volley from any and every angle. He normally wore a Basque beret when playing, but what made him the darling of the crowds, particularly at Wimbledon, was his clowning on court. On one occasion, for example, during a doubles match with Brugnon as his partner, he leapt so far out of court in returning a volley that he landed in a female spectator's lap in the crowd. He apologised profusely, kissed her hand, doffed his beret, leapt back onto the court and won the point – Brugnon meanwhile having kept the rally going on his own. On the occasion at Wimbledon when Lenglen, partnered by him in a mixed-doubles match, was booed, he deflected the public mood by rushing to the service line, dispensing with the knock up and serving two double faults in quick succession, then generally clowning about until the crowd was distracted and forgot its anger.

This playing to the crowd frequently amounted to advanced forms of gamesmanship, a characteristic for which Tilden greatly disliked him. One tactic, for example, was to congratulate his opponent effusively at every change of ends. 'Oh Beel – you are playing so well – I shall never be able to defeat you.' Because this was so blatantly over the top, it became more and more irritating to Tilden, but when he tried to walk round the other side of the net, Borotra still followed him until in the end in desperation Tilden resorted to stepping over the middle of the net.

During one difficult match Borotra changed from his usual shoes into espadrilles. These were not strong enough to survive long games of tennis. As they began to disintegrate, Borotra first gestured his despair, then eventually would be given time to change them, causing a break in the concentration of the person on the other side of the net, but delighting the crowd as he gestured hopelessly at his toes sticking out of the shoe. Sometimes he would act as though he were fainting at the end of a testing game, clinging to the umpire's chair as though about to collapse before bounding about the court during the very next game. Laney also recalls the way in which he would frequently foot fault when serving and if challenged would apologise profusely, yet continue to serve in exactly the same way without making any attempt to correct his action.

Everything about Borotra was flamboyant. It was not just that he excelled at tennis. He had won the Croix de Guerre in the war. He was a graduate of the Polytechnique and rapidly became a dynamic businessman in the oil industry, working for the oil firm SATAM and modernising the design of the forecourt petrol pump.

This second role became part of his identity. At Wimbledon, for example, he arrived at the last minute, dashing breathlessly onto the court, but managing to bow to the royalty in their box and salute the crowd, acknowledging their ecstatic applause. He put it about that he had been delayed by extremely important business, and had flown from Paris, rushed by car from Croydon airport, changing into his on-court outfit in the limousine that drove him to the Centre Court, and had arrived in the nick of time. In this way he managed to combine the aristocratic values of the amateur sportsman with the business ideal of efficiency and progress.

He acted as spokesperson on the international trips made by the Musketeers, and on these occasions would speak of international relations in his role as ambassador. He was a genuine patriot, but also a monumental egoist who felt himself to be the incarnation of France, transforming his deep patriotism, as one critic put it, 'into an instrument in the service of his own renown'.

In the 1930s he was associated with the extreme right-wing organisation the Croix de Feu, possibly as a naive fellow traveller motivated by patriotism and his intense devotion to Général Pétain. Pétain was a hero of the First World War and had distinguished himself at Verdun, but during the Second World War he became head of state and led the Vichy government that collaborated with the Nazis under the Occupation. During the fighting that preceded the French capitulation, Borotra had been captured and escaped. However, he then accepted an appointment in the Vichy government as director general of sport. In this role he supported a national network of sports clubs open to all and attacked the monopoly of the universities in developing sports opportunities for the young. These attempts derived from the widely held view that the unfitness of the French had led to their defeat at the hands of the Germans in 1940, and the Nazis became increasingly suspicious of his sports initiatives, believing that sports such as skiing and fencing might be part of a plan to train an embryonic resistance. When Pierre Laval came to power he dismissed Borotra, who joined General Weygand in North Africa. In 1942 he was arrested and interned, first at Sachsenhausen and then in Fort Itter. He allegedly made several attempts to escape and claimed to have joined the Resistance. For these exploits he was awarded the Légion d'Honneur, a second Croix de Guerre and medals for his escape attempts and membership of the Resistance.

He seems to have managed to convince himself that he was not a collaborator and that Pétain had performed a double bluff and had been genuinely committed to opposing the Nazis. There were those, nonetheless, who took a more sceptical attitude to his wartime activities. Certainly his devotion to Pétain never wavered. He became for many years president of the Association for the Defence of the Memory of Général Pétain, an organisation many of whose members were of the extreme right.[4]

In 1946 his application for entry to the Wimbledon championships singles and doubles was refused on the grounds of his wartime association with Vichy. (Another Frenchman, Yvon Petra, won the tournament.) He continued as an active player, one of his last heroic efforts being to play Davis Cup against Sweden in 1955 at the age of fifty-seven, when with his partner he won a doubles match against the much younger Swedish pairing of

Nielsen and Larsen. He continued to promote his ideas about the role of sport in a complete education of mind and body and his last appearance on an international tennis court was in the mixed doubles at Wimbledon in 1973. He was still wearing his beret.

The Musketeers, and Borotra in particular, personified a French cultural identity that combined flair, heroism and personal magnetism. The international appeal of this collective / individual identity was typical of the 1920s. Sensational occurrences seemed to take place all the time in sport and sport-related activities. The French yachtsman Alain Gerbault sailed the Atlantic alone and later attempted the return crossing and disappeared, never to be seen again. Charles Lindbergh flew the Atlantic in the opposite direction. There was the Lenglen-Wills match. Land, air and sea speed records were broken. In men's and women's fashions the streamlined, sporting ideal was dominant. This new age of sports meshed perfectly with the heady hysteria of speakeasies, dance bands and silent movies.

Even in the Golden Twenties, however, there was another tennis story.

10

Working-class heroes

THE SURFACE GLITZ OF THE 1920s created an impression of modernity, a world in which emancipated women and dashing men were determined to flout and overturn the stuffy conventions of the Victorian age. Yet beneath the mask the old order persisted. Even after the Wall Street Crash of 1929, the resulting Depression fell very unevenly within and across regions and nations. Industrial areas were the worst affected. In the south of England, in California and parts of the Eastern seaboard of the United States, and around Paris, the suburban and exclusive tennis clubs that were now well established continued to facilitate a relaxed and informal way of recreational life, provided you came from the 'right' social class. This life rested on the belief that sport was to be enjoyed and the gentleman amateur continued to be the unquestioned ideal.

Paul Gallico criticised the hypocrisy involved. Already in the 1920s there were no longer true amateurs in any sport, he said. Any serious athlete had to devote himself to his sport full time. Yet the fiction of the gallant amateur, unsoiled by anything as unpleasant as money was maintained and anyone caught flouting the rules would be expelled forthwith.

All the amateur rules actually ensured was the exclusion of any talented individual who lacked the means, or whose family lacked the means, to support full-time tennis for no pay. Even if (as was indeed the case with Tilden and Lenglen) all sorts of ways were found for under-the-counter 'gifts', 'expenses' and so on to an established star, a player had to begin from a position in which he could already afford to forego earning a living. In any case, a working-class child was unlikely to have any contact with a game played only at private schools and clubs.

Dan Maskell, who by the end of his long life was famous, to the British, as the voice of Wimbledon, since he was a commentator on the BBC from 1949 until his retirement in the 1980s, provides a classic example of how exclusion worked in practice – even if he was the exception in overcoming the obstacles it presented in establishing himself at the centre of the British tennis world. His father was an engineering worker, who later managed a pub. The family lived in the inner London, then largely working-class district of Fulham, and it was by chance that Maskell encountered tennis at all. The exclusive tennis venue, Queen's Club, happened to be situated in Barons Court nearby. As a young boy Maskell would pass its grounds while running errands for his mother and would gaze through the wrought-iron gates in fascination at this other world, in which gentlemen and ladies attired in spotless white arrived in limousines to play the elegant game.

Dan Maskell was a bright child. He passed the scholarship examination to Latymer School, one of the best selective secondary schools and situated in nearby Hammersmith, but his father could not allow him to take up the offer as it would have committed the boy to staying on at school until he was seventeen. In a poor working-class family with seven children this was just not possible, so he had to complete his education at the elementary school. However in the holidays he became a part-time ball boy at Queen's. Naturally, the work consisted mostly of retrieving balls, but a ball boy might also sometimes hit balls across to the club member who was having a lesson if, for example, the coach wished to stand next to the learner to demonstrate his advice. Maskell's talent was noted and on leaving school in 1923 he became a permanent ball boy at the club at the age of fifteen.[1]

The ball boys were lowest in the pecking order of the club's employees. At the top were the professional players, the coaches who taught and played sets with the club members, but they were essentially upper servants. (The development of the coach as a specific role seems to have emerged gradually, sometimes as groundsmen and other peripheral figures developed their observation of the game into a teaching skill.) Club members enjoyed a wide choice of courts, changing rooms, bar and dining room. The professionals had just one sitting room and bathroom.

'In love' with the game as soon as he came into contact with it, Dan flourished in this socially segregated world and viewed his employment by the club as a tremendous opportunity. 'I learned that the world was composed of the haves and the have-nots; the boys who went to public school and those who, like me, went to the elementary school. Not that I have ever resented the early lack of opportunity.' On the contrary he felt 'completely at home at Queen's Club'. Within a year he had been promoted to top ball boy, responsible for assigning the boys to the various courts.

The ball boys were sometimes allowed to play tennis on the hard courts – never the grass – at the end of the day, but more often on a makeshift court on an unused stretch of concrete that had been a skating rink (perhaps left over from the days of roller 'rinking'). At first they fashioned their own racquets from bits of wood and used old balls they found lost at court edges or even in the system of pipes below one of the indoor courts. Eventually Maskell begged an old real tennis racquet from the head professional, who later sold him a proper second-hand lawn tennis racquet. Even with these unpromising implements Maskell managed to demonstrate his natural talent for the game and soon became a junior professional.

The job of coach was not necessarily the best way to improve his own game, since a coaching session was designed entirely to suit the play of the member. Members often had a favourite coach – even favourite ball boys – and therefore the success of the coach was dependent on his ability to relate to (and perhaps flatter) the member. Yet, however well a coach got on with a club member, and however much that member might want to offer him a drink at the end of their game, this was not possible, for the professionals were never permitted to sully the bar by their presence and therefore the drink had to be consumed while the pair of them stood awkwardly on the steps outside.

Maskell's success as a coach soon led to invitations to weekends at members' country houses. There he would coach their children, play sets with other weekend guests, and also participate in the general fun during the day. Of course in the evenings he ate with the butler and the other domestics in the servants' hall.

Professional tournaments were now beginning to be organised and in 1928 Maskell became the British Professional Champion (not that any notice was taken of this by the sports press). Then, in 1928 he was appointed the first tennis coach at the All England Club at Wimbledon, aged only twenty. On this occasion protocol was abrogated, and he was offered a locker in the members' dressing room, an unheard-of concession. The consternation of Ellis, the dressing-room attendant, was plain. Dressed in 'the striped trousers and waistcoat of his days in service as a gentleman's gentleman ... he blanched visibly', Maskell recalled.[2]

Two years later Maskell was invited to the United States to play in the professional championship there. Startled by Prohibition New York, he was nearly shot down by a hail of bullets unleashed by rival mafia gangs in a Manhattan street; and the Chinese laundry where he had left his clothes to be cleaned was blown up, also by the mafia. Apart from these incidents, his visit was enjoyable and successful. A whole parallel world of professional tournaments was organised in America and was just beginning to interact with the much more high-profile operation run by C. C. Pyle, who had recruited Lenglen. The professional circuit as such, however, was ignored by the sporting press and the exploits of its players were unknown and unsung.

Maskell never seemed to have a chip on his shoulder, although he was acutely aware of the *Upstairs, Downstairs* attitudes of the period. He always reacted positively and was rewarded by achieving his own kind of fame and a place at the centre of British tennis. Yet in 1933 when he travelled with the Davis Cup team as their coach to Paris, he was booked into a modest hotel, while the players stayed at the Crillon. To their credit the players protested, the LTA relented and Maskell was transferred to join the team. Attitudes *were* – slowly – changing.

While Maskell accepted the situation gracefully, Fred Perry, the most successful and best-known member of that Davis Cup team, was chippy and combative. His autobiography opens with a double missile launched at the tennis establishment. 'I never thought I'd live to see the day when a statue was put up to the son of a Labour MP inside the manicured grounds of Wimbledon … a few former members [will] be revolving in their graves at the thought of such a tribute paid to the man they regarded as a rebel from the wrong side of the tennis tramlines.'[3] Then, while acknowledging how things had changed by 1984, when the book was published, Perry nevertheless adds a second sally, recalling the day he won Wimbledon for the first time in 1934. In those days, he says, there was no formal trophy presentation. After his triumph he was enjoying a hot bath in the bathroom adjacent to the dressing rooms when he heard Brame Hillyard, chosen to represent the Club committee, talking to the losing finalist, the Australian Jack Crawford, on the other side of the bathroom door: 'Congratulations. This was one day when the best man didn't win.' (In 1930, when he was only just emerging as a significant player, Perry had beaten Hillyard in an early round of Wimbledon, which may have given an additional edge to the committee man's snobbery.)

Perry emerged to find Crawford holding a bottle of champagne. Every winner was automatically made a member of the All England Club and Perry's tie had been left draped over the back of his chair. But no one congratulated him or shook his hand. As far as he was concerned, the message was clear. He wasn't wanted. Two years later, after his third Wimbledon victory, he turned professional.

Perry and Maskell became good friends, their shared background a bond. Both describe their fathers as being 'old school' disciplinarians, lord and master at home, where their word was law. They insisted on high standards of behaviour, but were kindly. Neither Maskell nor Perry makes any mention of beatings or harsh treatment. Perry's childhood, however, was a lot less impoverished than Maskell's. His father, Sam Perry, originally a cotton spinner in Stockport, had been in a position similar to Maskell himself; that is, he gained a place at grammar school, but had to leave because his father died and the weekly shilling (5p) he could earn at the mill was a significant addition to the family budget. However, he became an active trade unionist and this led him to make a political career for himself in the Cooperative Party, soon becoming a paid official. He later stood for Parliament on the Cooperative ticket and eventually became a Labour MP when the parties merged.

His progress in the Cooperative movement led to a post in London, and the family moved to the garden suburb of Brentham, near Drayton Park and Ealing. This was a piece of luck for Fred, for the Brentham Institute and its cricket field, football pitch, tennis courts, bowling greens and table tennis facilities were open to all local residents. The opportunity to play tennis was unusual and one that few boys of his social milieu would have had, although Sam Perry was sufficiently well off (and had only one other child, a daughter) to be able to afford to allow his son to take up a place at the selective Ealing County School.

Fred Perry's first sporting love was table tennis and throughout his teens he played both table and lawn tennis obsessively. In the world of table tennis he was befriended by the aristocratic communist, Ivor Montagu. Montagu, the youngest son of the second Lord Swaythling, had two great passions; cinema and table tennis, the latter because it was a sport suited to the lower paid – all it required was a room and a table, in contrast to so many sports necessitating outdoor space and elaborate equipment. The two class rebels from opposite ends of the social spectrum found much in common.

However, once Perry had won the world table tennis championship at the age of twenty, he transferred his affections to lawn tennis. He may have been swayed partly by his father's observation that table tennis was a thoroughly unhealthy activity, played at night under lights in a smoke-filled atmosphere. Lawn tennis also had considerably more glamour than ping pong and, as with Dan Maskell, it was the glamour of tennis that first drew Perry and began the 'love affair' he conducted with the game. On holiday at Eastbourne he wandered into Devonshire Park where the prestigious pre-Wimbledon tournament was being played and was dazzled by the sight of the players in white against the rich green of the grass and by the Daimlers, MGs and Hispano-Suizas parked outside. 'I asked my father if all those big cars belonged to the players, and he said they did. "Then that's for me," I said.'

He left school at sixteen and after a false start with a tea merchant he worked for several years for Spaldings, the sporting goods company, while continuing to play both table tennis and lawn tennis. By the age of twenty-one he was making spectacular progress in tennis and won through two rounds at Wimbledon in 1930. One of the players he defeated was Baron de Morpurgo. So annoyed was the Baron that a working-class upstart had beaten him that instead of shaking Perry's hand at the net, he slapped him in the face. Gentlemanly sportsmanship evidently had its limits.

That year Perry came close to beating the top British player, Bunny Austin, at Bournemouth. At this point his father, who by this time had twice been a Labour MP, stepped in and offered to support him financially for a year. Here too Perry was luckier than Maskell, whose father could never have made a similar offer.

There was criticism from some quarters that this support flouted the spirit of amateurism, but Perry senior defended his decision by citing his own impoverished childhood. He had had to 'beg pennies from door to door in order to pay the rent of a football field' and he felt that no one had any right to criticise his wish to give his own son a better chance.[4] It is certainly hard to see how the help Sam Perry gave his son differed from the family support taken for granted by players whose parents saw them through private school, university and life on the amateur circuit. Presumably their families, too, paid the entrance fees to tournaments and travel expenses, all of which cost about £10 a week, then a large sum, so the criticism was unmerited and hypocritical. The controversy over Sam Perry's support for his son was soon pre-empted, for by the end of the year it was no longer needed as Fred Perry was doing so well.

Teddy Tinling described Perry as 'brash and cocky' and with 'handsome hero looks, enhanced ... by a flashing smile'. He was sharp-tongued and witty – which didn't always please everyone. And he didn't speak with a 'cut-glass' or 'Oxford' accent. Tinling took him with a team to play the Cambridge University team, but after a couple of visits the Cambridge tennis establishment suggested that Perry should be excluded from any future contests. Tinling believed it was not just owing to his accent, but because he was 'unsporting' enough to reveal his 'consuming desire to win at all costs'. It was just not done to *appear* that competitive. It was against the amateur spirit.

Perry was frank in his autobiography about the role dress and self-presentation played in the men's as well as the women's game. He was very conscious of his appearance, not only because he was a star, but because of the effect it could have on his opponents. He described how: 'if I was involved in matches with a ten minute break at the end of the third set, I'd start by wearing off-white gabardine trousers and an off-white shirt. Then, after the rest period, I'd re-emerge in dazzling white duck trousers and a fresh white cotton shirt, my hair neatly parted. The crowd always thought I looked twice as fresh as the other man, but of course it was just window dressing.' This was one of his 'little tricks' – the gamesmanship so many of the top stars indulged in. For more practical reasons he was also concerned to have the ideal shoes on court: 'specially made plimsolls, of buckskin laced to the toe (this gave greater comfort and room for movement) and with a very thin leather sole, under which was stitched a slightly thicker crepe sole – extremely light and durable and fitted like a glove.'[5]

Fred Perry and the majority of male players continued to favour long trousers, but shorts were beginning to seem more practical. The first man to wear shorts during the Wimbledon tournament was in fact Brame Hillyard. (Hillyard was the older brother of George Hillyard, an influential figure on the British tennis scene; George was married to Blanche Bingley, women's champion in 1886, 1889 and 1894 and four times runner up to Lottie Dod. Miss Bingley's on-court outfit invariably included gloves, but this was said to be for practical reasons: to absorb sweat and obtain a better grip.) The British player Bunny Austin introduced shorts to the Centre Court in 1932.

Perry was included in the Davis Cup team and travelled with the team to the United States at the expense of the LTA. Hollywood was now in competition with the Riviera as a star-studded playground uniting tennis and glamour; and 'when the Pacific Southwest tournament was on and the tennis players were in town, everybody was tennis nuts. All the stars had private boxes at the championships – Harold Lloyd, Ben Lyon and Bebe Daniels, Marlene Dietrich, Clark Gable, Charlie Chaplin and the Marx Brothers. Everybody wanted to throw a party,' recalled Perry.

Charlie Chaplin hosted tennis parties and he and Errol Flynn were the film colony's best players. After 1933, when the Nazis came to power in Germany, the Los Angeles area became home to many German, often Jewish, exiles from the lost Weimar Republic and to other Europeans. Some of these had enjoyed tennis in Germany, where, as everywhere else, the game had become fashionable after the end of the war. One of the most fanatical of these players was the avant-garde Austrian composer, Arnold Schoenberg. Schoenberg felt at home in Hollywood and

stayed on after 1945, but many of the refugees missed the sophistication of the central European urban life they had left behind
and could not feel at ease in a huge suburban agglomeration
where there were no pavements – and no cafés.

Fred Perry on the other hand took to the place like a duck to
water. 'My first trip to California in 1931 marked the start of a
new era and changed my life forever. I became an annual visitor
to the Pacific Southwest tournament and very much a man-
about-Hollywood, where the lively life style suited me down to
the ground. I played the Pacific tournament for five years, losing
the 1931 final, winning it the next three times and again getting
to the final in the following year.'[6]

On his first arrival in 1931 with his doubles partner, Pat
Hughes, each was whisked off separately to be shown the town
by a real-life film star – in Perry's case Jean Harlow. However it
wasn't just the film stars. He loved everything about the place and
was especially intrigued by the rather fake interiors of some of
the stars' homes, where rows of leather-bound books would turn
out to be mock-ups and resembled the film sets where doors had
nothing behind them.[7] It may be that the illusory nature of this
world appealed to him as he too was, if not an intruder, at least an
interloper into the world of privilege, an actor in a masquerade.

Perry was equally successful when it came to his relationships
with Hollywood women. Nothing serious seems to have come of
his initial date with Jean Harlow, but the good-looking Perry later
had his name linked with several stars, including Loretta Young
and Marlene Dietrich; in 1938 he became engaged to a less well-
known actress, Mary Lawson and was later married unsuccessfully three times to the actress Helen Vinson; to Sandra Breaux, a
model; and to Lorraine Walsh who had been married to the film
director Raoul Walsh. However his fourth marriage, to Barbara
Riese, another Hollywood habituée, lasted for forty years.

Perry was seduced by the idea of acting in movies. 'I intend to
fool around in Hollywood for a while,' he said in an interview in
Time magazine in 1934. He felt that sport and show business went

Fred Perry, 'man about Hollywood' with Marlene Dietrich

together. 'Sporting people tend to gravitate to show business people, and vice versa; basically we're all in the same game,' he wrote.[8] After he won the United States title for the second time, there were offers from Hollywood, but when he requested permission from the LTA in London it was refused. B. P. Schulberg, on behalf of Paramount, offered him a two-year contract to appear in pictures and on the radio. He was, he wrote, sorely tempted, but it would have violated his amateur status and he was not quite ready – yet – to turn professional.

The following year there was an even more tempting offer. RKO offered him a contract for two pictures a year at $50,000 a picture. The contract was to run for two years and he would not be required to play tennis in any of the sequences. He got as far as taking a screen test for RKO 'immaculate in white tie and tails' and he was to have had a part alongside Fred Astaire and Ginger Rogers in *Top Hat*, but nothing came of any of these plans. The amateur issue was still an obstacle. It may also have been that the good looks and dazzling movement of the tennis player didn't translate well to the screen.

Above all, though, America appealed to Perry because it was

all 'a breath of fresh air' after English class consciousness. He liked the fast life 'because I'm a fast acting character myself. I played tennis in the same way.'[9]

He eventually spent most of his time in the States. Like Dan Maskell, in a different way he had escaped the snobbery so irksome in his home country. In later life he became a successful sportswear manufacturer, and the iconic Fred Perry shirt was evidence of the continual crossover between fashion and sportswear, worn successively by the Mods of the 1960s, by two toners, soul boys and Britpop bands and even by singer Amy Winehouse.

11

Tennis in Weimar – and after

DURING HIS GLORY YEARS BILL TILDEN lived the celebrity life. He hung out in London with actresses Tallulah Bankhead and Bea Lillie and basked in the limelight when seen escorting the silent-screen femme fatale, Pola Negri. But the city in which he felt most at ease was Berlin. He loved the unbuttoned lifestyle and atmosphere in Weimar Germany.

Baron Gottfried von Cramm described late-night partying with Tilden in Berlin. Tilden always stayed at the Hotel Eden where his entourage gathered in the rooftop bar. The evening would develop with everyone except Big Bill downing cocktails. Tilden never touched alcohol and was so famous for drinking iced water that a glass of water came to be known as a 'Tilden' or a 'Tilden cocktail'. On the other hand, he would demolish several beef steaks in the course of an evening and also chain-smoked and sustained himself on strong coffee. The party would proceed from one bistro or nightclub to the next and at the end of the evening – or night – Tilden would entertain the survivors back at the Eden once more. He appeared to need almost no sleep, for following these activities he would be out practising on the tennis court early the next day.[1]

The nocturnal excursions were always at Tilden's expense. He not only beat allcomers on the tennis court; he beat everyone to the draw when it came to paying the bill for these hedonistic explorations of the most modern city on earth.

The liberal Jewish politician Walter Rathenau joked that while Berlin had been an elegant 'Athens on the Spree' in the nineteenth century, by 1920 it was more like 'Chicago on the Spree'; all too true in his case as in 1922 he was assassinated when extreme right- wingers gunned him down. The city was the epicentre of a fervid culture clash. It was the headquarters of sexual freedom, of emancipated women, of cabaret, nightclubs and revolution. There were more gay and lesbian clubs in 1920s Berlin than in New York in 1980. Every kind of artistic avant garde flourished: decadent dance-theatre, expressionist film, the plays of Bertolt Brecht, movements for sexual liberation and political satire.

Yet the mask of modernity was deceptive. For a few years, the illusion could be maintained that the new, the radical, the shocking and the *modern* had won, but the political and social differences within and between classes and interest groups were irreconcilable. Long before the Wall Street Crash of 1929, the 'great inflation' of 1923 had destroyed the German middle class. Nazis and communists fought on the streets; the various fragmentary political parties spoke only for narrow constituencies. The divisions between the urban workers and rural peasants, between a radical intelligentsia and the conservative *petite bourgeoisie* became ever more bitter. National unity was impossible, until gradually the sinister, compelling figure of Adolf Hitler rose above the turmoil and announced himself as the man beyond politics, the saviour of the German race.

The new fashion for tennis epitomised German modernity. The Germans had originally preferred drill and gymnastics to organised sports, but gradually the sporting mentality gained ground. Before 1914 tennis had been played seriously only at spas such as Bad Homburg, but in the 1920s it became an irresistible and glamorous addition to Weimar culture. Clubs sprang up everywhere and the fashionable Rot Weiss club in Berlin was the headquarters of the sport in Germany. Tennis and its fashionable profile could be seen as one expression of the freedom of movement and the liberation of the body that the times demanded.

The game, as elsewhere, trailed clouds of social cachet. It also brought Weimar androgyny to the court. The male player was an internationalist and cosmopolitan, a glamorous figure, elegant rather than manly, the men's game one of artistry rather than pugilism. But women players such as Cilly Aussem, who won both the French national tournament at Roland Garros and Wimbledon in 1931, belonged to a race of Amazons, and played in an aggressively modern style. They expressed the new, sexually liberated Germany found above all in Berlin – but the whole ethos of tennis was utterly contrary to the German tradition, which associated masculine athletic activity with 'strict self denial and abstinence from food, alcohol, sex and pleasure'. Tennis shockingly celebrated an androgynous model of masculine sexuality and heterosexual flirtation.[2]

Elsewhere, far from the capital, landowners and peasants lived as if the nineteenth century had yet to begin. Baron Gottfried von Cramm came from just such a milieu.[3]

Born in 1909, Baron Gottfried Alexander Maximilian Walter Kurt Freiherr von Cramm was the third of the seven sons of Baron Burchard von Cramm. The family had owned land in Lower Saxony since the thirteenth century and Gottfried's mother, Jutta von Steinberg, was sole heiress to the fortune of another ancient landed family. Gottfried was born at the family estate in Nettlingen and brought up in the castle at Brüggen inherited by his mother. Every summer the family transferred to a third castle, at Oelber.

As a student at Oxford, Gottfried's father had noticed how important sport was to the English and continued to interest himself in sport on his return, encouraging his sons to play games and keep fit. He had a tennis clay court laid out at Oelber and invited the top German Davis Cup doubles pair, Robert and Heinrich Kleinschroth, to stay and to play tennis with the whole family and their guests.

Burchard von Cramm had served in the cavalry reserve, but the lives of these aristocratic landowners were relatively untouched by the war. Nor did the Junkers, the land-owning class, suffer from the Great Inflation as did the middle classes; land actually became even more valuable.

The cultured Cramm family seems not to have followed the stereotype of the militaristic, ultra-bellicose and right-wing German ruling class. Burchard von Cramm was involved in a number of peace initiatives after the end of the war. Instead of being sent to one of the fearsome authoritarian German boarding schools, Gottfried was educated at home, for a time by the governess who had taught the prince who was to become Edward VIII.

Gottfried became fascinated by tennis from an early age and when the Kleinschroth brothers brought Bill Tilden with them to Oelber in 1927, the American quickly saw how promising this cadet of the family was. Keen, though, as the boy's father was on sport, the family did not regard tennis as an appropriate full-time career, even as an amateur. Indeed, dedicated but well-connected players often used a pseudonym when they entered a tournament. (King Gustav of Sweden, for example, played as 'Mr G'.) Gottfried was destined for the diplomatic service.

He arrived in Berlin in 1928, aged nineteen, ostensibly to study law, but once there spent most of his time at the Rot Weiss club and rapidly emerged as the most promising German star, which was soon noted when he played on the Riviera circuit. He formed friendships both with the seventy-year-old tennis fanatic, King Gustav, and with Daniel Prenn, the number two German player, soon to be his doubles partner. By 1930 it was becoming clear that Gottfried's future lay with tennis rather than diplomacy. As he wrote to his mother, 'Prenn is trying to commandeer me for tennis' – and Gottfried was only too happy to be commandeered.

American sports writer Allison Danzig described Cramm's style as elegant and a bit stately. His drives were wide and clean and his 'offensive' service was mechanically perfect. What he lacked was 'a certain subtlety, an ability to break up the other fellow's game'. He struck the ball very quickly, but 'must have his feet planted and must address the ball, whereas a player such as [Don] Budge or Perry can perform miracles on the run'. But he could hit startling winners and could 'blind' the gallery with his flat backhand.[4]

Perry described the German's style more sardonically in recalling a match between him and Bunny Austin: 'Austin believed in the purity of stroke play ... it should be straight out of the instruction manual, line for line, word for word. To see him and Cramm play a match, as I did at Wimbledon once, was like reading a book on tennis. Nothing much happened, but it was lovely to watch.'

In September 1930 Gottfried was married to Lisa von Dobeneck, the daughter of a neighbouring landed family. Like her new husband, Lisa, at eighteen, was sports mad, a tennis and hockey player who also skated, swam and danced. She absolutely typified the New Woman of Weimar Germany. Installed in Berlin, she and Gottfried became Germany's most glamorous couple. She was as dark as Gottfried was fair; indeed with his wheat-coloured hair, cold blue eyes and tall, elegant figure, he was 'a new star fallen from heaven', and was soon to outdo the German boxing champion, Max Schmeling, as Germany's most popular sporting idol.

When Cramm became fully aware that his erotic desires inclined him towards men is not recorded. Not that it mattered very much, for same-sex love was as fashionable as tennis and the young couple were perfectly in tune with the polymorphous sexual culture of Berlin, frequenting dives that catered to every sexual taste. Sooner or later, though, Gottfried did discover his true nature and seems to have embarked on an affair with an actor, Manasse Herbst.

The cocktail-circuit life was not allowed to interfere with his tennis, which went from strength to strength. Germany had been

Gottfried von Cramm and wife Lisa, the fashionable
Berlin couple

readmitted to the International Tennis Federation in 1927 and
with Cramm the rising star these were great years for German
tennis. In 1931 he won his first international title in Athens, where
he also played mixed doubles with Lisa and in 1932 he joined the
German Davis Cup team. Cramm and Prenn won through five
rounds and then, astonishingly, defeated Britain in the interzone
final. Gottfried was easily defeated by Fred Perry, but won his
match against Bunny Austin. Finally Prenn pulled off the miracle
of defeating Perry, who was shortly to become 'world champion'
and although the Germans didn't win the Davis Cup, their heroic
triumph over the British meant that Gottfried von Cramm became
a household name.

Cramm was the perfect gentleman, but his background
differed from Tilden's. Tilden came from an upper-middle class

or bourgeoisie made up of professional men, such as lawyers and successful industrialists and businessmen. Some acquired land, but they did not conform to the European notion of a landed gentry or aristocracy. Cramm, by contrast, was the aristocrat of aristocrats and his point of view essentially that of the paternalist landowner who owes a duty to his peasantry in a reciprocal relationship with rights and responsibilities on both sides.

Cramm explained this view to the American player, Don Budge, the first time they met, which was during the Wimbledon fortnight, when they were to play each other the next day. Cramm took the young American to task, in the nicest possible way, for his lack of sportsmanship. Budge was astounded because he had done what Tilden always did and what he had believed was the essence of good sportsmanship. During a big Wimbledon match against Bunny Austin, Budge was convinced that the linesman had made a wrong call that had gone in his, Budge's, favour and he therefore deliberately and ostentatiously threw the next point, eliciting approving applause from the crowd. Budge assumed he'd done the right sporting thing, but Cramm disabused him: 'Absolutely not. You made a great show of giving away a point because you felt the call had wronged Bunny. But is that your right? You made yourself an official, which you are not, and in improperly assuming this duty so that you could correct things your way, you managed to embarrass that poor linesman in front of eighteen thousand people.'[5]

In January 1933 Hitler became Chancellor of Germany. The perfect aristocratic Baron from Hanover presented the Nazis with a dilemma. Some, Heinrich Himmler in particular, loathed the land-owning upper class, the Junkers, and their steely grip on the army. Others, Hitler included, were more ambivalent. They were so Germanic! The very essence of *das Volk*, the true Germans, descended from the Vikings. Cramm, furthermore, so very much looked the part. He was the epitome of the Aryan ideal.

Gottfried, the Prince Charming of tennis, was, however, no Prince Charming of fascism. The family of brothers, wrote Tatiana

Metternich, who knew them well, were patriotic Hanoverian monarchists, who hated the Prussians.[6] Some politically active German aristocrats did hope to see the return of the Kaiser, but Gottfried's views are not known; he had never seemed interested in politics. However, although many of Gottfried's class held very right-wing views, that did not mean they liked the Nazis, who, after all, were vulgar, low-bred, vicious upstarts, many of them downright criminal. Besides, the grandfather of Cramm's wife was Jewish.

One of Hitler's first orders on coming to power was to ban all non-Aryans from every form of sporting club and institution. Cramm's doubles partner, Daniel Prenn was a Lithuanian Jew from Vilnius, who with his family had escaped the continual persecution of the Jews both before and after the 1917 Russian Revolution and arrived in Berlin in 1920. Then, Berlin had appeared as a haven of tolerance. Now he disappeared from the Rot Weiss tennis club and was barred from every German tournament.

Bunny Austin and Fred Perry protested in a letter published in *The Times*, but international protest was otherwise shamefully non-existent. Luckily for Prenn, Simon Marks, head of Marks and Spencer, was a tennis fan, as well as being Jewish. He sponsored Prenn and his wife Charlotte, enabling them to leave Germany for Britain and avoid the fate of so many of their fellow Jews. The up-and-coming Henner Henkel replaced Prenn as Gottfried's doubles partner. Gottfried himself was now Germany's number one player.

He achieved outstanding successes between 1933 and 1937. In 1933 he won the Wimbledon mixed doubles with Hilda Krawinkel, who also reached the women's final, losing to her countrywoman Cilly Aussem. He twice won at Roland Garros, beating Fred Perry in 1936. But Perry twice beat him in Wimbledon finals – although in 1936 this was partly due to Gottfried having strained a leg muscle in the first game of the match and being virtually unable to compete thereafter.

In 1935 Germany came close to triumphing over the United

States in the Davis Cup in the interzone final. In the last set of the final (and decisive) doubles match with the Germans they actually reached match point. Then, however, came the most famous example of Gottfried's legendary sportsmanship and fair play. He was serving. It was a near ace, but the American on the other side of the net just managed to get it back. Gottfried's doubles partner, Kai Lund, appeared to hit an unreturnable stroke off the weak return. But Gottfried spoke quietly to the umpire to point out that his own racquet had touched the ball before Lund hit it. Therefore the point was the Americans'. No one but von Cramm had noticed this. The Germans lost the match and their hopes of meeting Britain in the Challenge Round.

Two years later, in 1937, Gottfried was again at Wimbledon. He had again lost in the singles final, this time to Budge. Now the two were to meet again in another Davis Cup interzone final to see which team would face the British holders in the challenge round. It was almost taken for granted that the British, weakened by Perry's departure to the professional ranks, would lose to whichever team won the tie, so this was effectively the contest for the cup.

One thing had changed. The swastika flew over the All England Club. However reluctantly, Gottfried was representing the Nazi regime. Don Budge reports in his memoirs that before the match Gottfried received a telephone call from the Führer himself and that Cramm held the handset, repeating 'Ja, mein Führer' several times, afterwards saying that Hitler had wanted to wish him luck. The Baron's biographer, Egon Steinkampf, disputes this. Gottfried's friend, Wolfgang Hofer cast doubt on the story, and said that Cramm himself had called the story a 'fairy tale', so it may well be one of the many myths that attach themselves to famous matches. (Marshall Jon Fisher, whose book, *A Terrible Splendor* is built round the match, researched the anecdote exhaustively and shares Steinkampf's scepticism.)[7] This match was for many years held to have been the greatest ever played, played at the highest level between two friends until the very last point that clinched the final set 8–6 in Budge's favour.

There was a third defeat for Cramm at the hands of Budge, when the American again beat him at Forest Hills for the US Open title. Budge was now on his way to winning his 'calendar' grand slam. Cramm was on the first swing of a world tour with Henner Henkel, Heinrich Kleinschroth and the new German woman number one, Marlies Horn. After New York they travelled by train to California, Hollywood and the Pacific Southwest Tennis Tournament at the Los Angeles Tennis Club.

The tennis-loving Hollywood stars had planned to walk out of Cramm's first match in order to demonstrate their outrage at what the Nazis were doing to the Jews. Yet when Gottfried appeared, smiling and golden, not a soul stirred. Groucho Marx told Budge later that he had only to see Cramm to feel ashamed of what had been planned. What convinced them that the dashing blond German was not a Nazi the moment they set eyes on him we cannot know, especially given his stereotypically 'Aryan' looks. Their instincts were correct, however, and later in the tour, after the Germans had visited Japan and arrived in Australia, Cramm took the risk of criticising the German government to the extent of saying that the three years' military service all German youth had to serve was a bad idea that delayed their improvement in tennis. He also attended a screening of *The Road Back* directed by the gay British director, James Whale. This, an adaptation of Erich Maria Remarque's sequel to his more famous anti-war novel, *All Quiet on the Western Front*, was banned in Germany.

On his return, he was arrested and questioned by the Gestapo and then charged with having an illegal sexual relationship with Manasse Herbst. That he avoided the concentration camps may have been due to Göring's intervention. It was Heinrich Himmler who was the chief scourge of homosexuals. Göring was not only more easygoing morally, he was also a tennis fan and member of the Rot Weiss club. He had tried to enlist Gottfried as his protégé and to persuade him to join the Nazi party. Gottfried always refused and it was known that his family was unsympathetic to the Nazis. If Germany had won the Davis Cup and if Gottfried had won Wimbledon it would have been impossible to arrest him, given his popularity at home. Even as it was, his execution or disappearance would have been an international scandal, but he was lucky to get off with a year's imprisonment in a Berlin prison for moral turpitude and to be found not guilty of a second and even more serious charge of illegal foreign-exchange dealings.

Cramm's biographer points out that there is no evidence of a homosexual relationship with Herbst, other than the Gestapo records of the interrogation – during which Cramm confessed to the relationship – or of relationships with other men. It seems certain that the tennis player was instrumental in securing Herbst's escape from Germany and this was followed with sums of money that he managed to spirit out of the country (hence the accusation of illegal money dealings). After the war Herbst, now married, returned to Germany in order personally to thank Cramm for having saved his life.

In fact it was widely known that Cramm was a lover of men. He discussed his sexuality with Don Budge and was quite open about it; and while in London he had an affair with Geoffrey Nares, a young British actor, described by Cecil Beaton as 'elf like' and a 'sad, striving, rudderless young man'. (Geoffrey was the son of the famous matinée idol, Owen Nares, who was so enraged by his son's sexual preference that he had Geoffrey's name obliterated from his own entry in Who's Who.)

Released from prison, Gottfried returned to tennis in the months before the outbreak of war. By this time Budge had turned professional and the top American amateur was now Bobby Riggs. Cramm beat Riggs easily in the final at the Queen's Club tournament. But he was disbarred from Wimbledon on account of his conviction; Riggs won the Championship.

In spite of being one of the greatest tennis players never to have won Wimbledon, Cramm was in a sense a lucky man. With war under way he was deemed unfit to be an officer in the Wehrmacht and as a private was in 1941 sent to the Russian front, but, suffering from frostbite, he was invalided home. He had been awarded the Iron Cross for bravery, but was given a dishonourable discharge. That mattered little, given that he was now reunited with what was left of his family (his father had died and two of his brothers were killed) and he remained in Germany until the end of the war, spending most of his time in Berlin or in Brüggen with his mother.

He also paid at least three visits to Sweden, an unusual freedom for a man distrusted by the government. True, he played tennis there and visited his friend King Gustav; and the Nazis may have viewed the handsome aristocrat as a suitable ambassador to speak up for the German government as it sank further and further into the frozen mud outside Stalingrad. Tatiana Metternich, however, was confident that Cramm was acting as courier for the small German resistance movement led by fellow aristocrats, most famously Claus Schenk Graf von Stauffenberg. 'He was often away on trips as messenger for the opposition,' she wrote. Her sister, Marie Wassiltschikow, became a close friend of Cramm during the time when both were staying in Berlin with Heinz and Maria von Gersdorff. She wrote in her war diary of the intensity of their friendship in the anxious days after the Stauffenberg assassination attempt had failed. The Gersdorff home acted as a social centre for opponents of the Nazis, among them Adam von Trott, who had contacts with the Swedish Wallenberg brothers who were active in helping Jews to escape from Germany.

Seen purely in tennis terms, Gottfried von Cramm might appear as an unlucky player. Although brilliantly gifted, he was unfortunate to play in the same years as Fred Perry and the even more gifted Don Budge. It was also unlucky – and rather shameful – that the Wimbledon authorities refused him leave to play in the singles in 1939, which many felt was his best chance finally to win the title.

On the other hand he was a homosexual anti-Nazi who survived the war. Thereafter he led an active and successful life both as a tennis player and as a businessman, developing a successful cotton import–export firm based on his contacts in Egypt, where he was held in enormous esteem.

He almost single-handedly revived German tennis, finally returning to Wimbledon to great acclaim in 1951 and playing once more on the Centre Court, still wearing long trousers. (While in London he also had a reunion with Daniel Prenn.) Later, he did all he could to ease relationships, at least so far as tennis was concerned, between East and West Germany and more generally tried to improve sporting relations between the West and Eastern Europe and the USSR.

He was even briefly remarried, to the Woolworth heiress, Barbara Hutton. (He and Lisa had divorced before the war, but remained lifelong friends.) Barbara Hutton was the archetypal 'poor little rich girl' of the period, regularly in the news on account of her marriages to various displaced European princelings and also to Cary Grant. She conceived a hopeless passion for Cramm, which seems to have haunted her for most of her life, but inevitably their marriage was doomed.

The marriage baffled his friends as he was apparently neither in serious need of money nor of a wife to conceal his sexuality. Perhaps he acted out of misplaced kindness, for no one spoke ill of him – and he was often kind. He helped some of his maimed fellow soldiers and his former doubles partner, Kai Lund, who returned from battle minus a limb, purchasing for the latter a hotel in Baden Baden. Perhaps it was just as Barbara Hutton wrote: 'We were such good friends for so long, but friendship and marriage don't particularly go together.'

Gottfried was killed in a car crash on the road between Alexandria and Cairo, in 1976 at the age of sixty-seven. He had always said he would prefer to die an unnatural death rather than suffer from protracted illness, so in this respect too, it would seem that his luck never ran out.

12

As a man grows older

AT A CRUCIAL MOMENT IN the 1937 Cramm–Budge Davis Cup match at Wimbledon, who should rise from the stands to applaud the German, but Big Bill Tilden: the greatest American player rooting for the enemy! The Americans were beside themselves with fury.

It was true. Tilden had been coach to the German team for over a year. He had no truck with the regime, but Germany had become a refuge from his escalating problems.

Since his heyday in the 1920s Big Bill had indulged an expensive obsession: acting and the theatre. His first forays were in film: his own production, *Hands of Hope*, was followed by a contract to star in films written by the poet Ella Wheeler Wilcox, but these came to nothing, nor did rumours that King Vidor had signed him for a leading role ever result in his appearance on celluloid. In 1935 he was again signed, this time by Universal, to appear in another film that never materialised.

In the 1920s he spent large sums on mounting plays in which he himself starred, even including one about Dracula (a part for which many considered him well suited), but his stage performances embarrassed both friends and the public, bringing out the least attractive aspects of his personality. He did have his debut on Broadway, but in a melodrama that was universally panned.

As he became involved with film and theatre in the mid-1920s his supreme winning tennis record began to slip. In 1926 he lost to Jean Borotra in the quarter-finals of the US indoor championship, to Lacoste soon afterwards, to several lesser players in the spring of 1927 and finally to both Lacoste and Cochet in the Davis Cup at Forest Hills.

The US had held the Davis Cup for six years, but lost to the French in 1927 and, despite Tilden's participation, were unable to regain it in 1928. Tilden was past his best by now, whereas the French four were at their peak.

Tilden had always vociferously supported the amateur ethic. As a young man he seems to have shared the snobbish attitude that relegated professional players to the status of servants. It was one expression of the view that no gentleman would play a sport for money. This suited Tilden when in the 1920s he was a rich man, for he had continued his career as a journalist after becoming the world's greatest and most famous sportsman. He argued that just as a banker or lawyer was, or would be, permitted to continue to earn his living in his chosen profession while playing the amateur tennis circuit, so should he be permitted to work as a journalist. Since, however, he wrote about tennis, including tournaments in which he himself played, this flouted the rules of amateurism. As a result he was judged by the United States Lawn Tennis Association (USLTA) – with whom he had often crossed swords – to be profiting from the game and by 1928 its officials, notably the powerful Julian Myrick, were determined to expel him from the Association.

Unwisely, they struck when Tilden was in Europe as captain of the Davis Cup team, about to face the French in Paris in the challenge round. The ban rapidly degenerated into the realms of farce and international diplomacy. The French – players, officials and public alike – were appalled at the thought that this hugely anticipated five-match contest was to be deprived of its major attraction. When ticket refund demands started to pour in, the French officials contacted their government and the American ambassador in Paris, Myron Herrick, had to ring the State

Department in Washington to get them to persuade the USLTA to relent. It has even been suggested that the crisis may have reached President Coolidge himself. Laney, however, believed this was one of those typical tennis legends, whereby what actually happened was amplified and exaggerated and that in reality Herrick simply called the President of the USLTA, who was in Paris at the time, and asked him to reinstate Tilden.

Tilden was irksome to the managerial officials of American lawn tennis on many counts, not just because of his journalism. He held strong and often controversial opinions and was not afraid to air them. For example, he thought that the Davis Cup was too protracted (an argument still being made by players in the twenty-first century) and argued for the abolition of the challenge round, which was abolished at the Wimbledon championships in 1922, but lasted for the Davis Cup until the early 1970s.

One of his last triumphs was his win at Wimbledon in 1930 at the age of thirty-seven, beating Borotra en route to the title, but by the early 1930s his best days were past. Moreover he had squandered a fortune on all those unsuccessful theatrical adventures. So it was that, with the money running out, despite having stated violently that he would never turn pro, in 1931 he finally did.

At first the pro tour seemed to re-ignite the flame of his stardom. To begin with it did not matter that Tilden was the only star, and that no established professional tennis circuit yet existed. Tilden was the attraction and a crowd of 13,000 flocked to see him in Madison Square Garden when in 1931 he beat the then professional champion, Karol Kozeluh. The exhibition made $36,000. A trickle of star players joined him; Cochet in 1933; Ellsworth Vines, another top American player, in 1934; and Fred Perry in 1937. Finally, the last great player to turn professional before the Second World War was Don Budge, the first player to win the 'calendar slam' – all four 'majors' in the same year.

The tours were punishing affairs. The convoy drove through the night between one-night stands throughout the United States.

Often the fixtures were hundreds of miles apart. The court itself, a heavy affair made of sailcloth, travelled with them on a truck. It came in two halves, each of which weighed 900 pounds with block and tackle. Three hours were needed to lay it down. The troupe therefore consisted of not only the players and the tour manager, but also the truckers. In addition there was a ball boy.

The presence of a succession of teenage ball boys indicated the 'cruel wound', as sociologist Digby Baltzell put it, of Tilden's homosexuality. His journalism had been a sore point because it highlighted the ambiguity at the heart of amateurism itself, but far worse was his sexual ambiguity. That, more than all the arguments about Tilden's journalism, had been the thorn in the side of the USLTA, terrified lest the scandal become common knowledge and contribute further to the effete image of the game.

The masculine paranoia crystallising around homosexuality is central to the history of twentieth-century sport, spreading far beyond tennis. The enduring nineteenth-century sporting ideal incorporated an intense emotional bond between men. It was terrifying to think that this might become overtly sexual. In Britain and Europe tennis was more critically associated with class than with sexual orientation and in general people were less phobic about what were perceived as 'sissy' manners, but to the American jock the polite protocols of its elite origins were an alien and sinister challenge to red-blooded manliness.

Paul Gallico gave full vent to this terror. His sports-writing career began with an account of being knocked out by the famous boxer Jack Dempsey – one way of proving you were a real man. Boxing was an unquestionably masculine sport, but when it came to tennis Gallico seemed hard put to contain his loathing. Something more than mere dislike poisons his tennis-bashing polemic, 'Funny Game'. Tennis, he dared to admit with bated breath, was 'sissy'. He conceded that most male tennis players were 'stout, masculine fellows, able wenchers and good two-fisted drinkers', who lived 'normal lives', kept their hands 'off

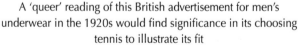

A 'queer' reading of this British advertisement for men's underwear in the 1920s would find significance in its choosing tennis to illustrate its fit

their hips' and got married. But even they, once they got out on the tennis court, 'began to swish a little'. They dropped into 'silly gestures, little shrieks of annoyance, fluttering and remorseful, petulant cries over a missed shot' or cooings over a great one. So far as Gallico was concerned, merely to cry out 'lovely shot' was to consign the tennis player to the hell of being a 'fruit'.[1] He was sufficiently generous to excuse Tilden's effeminate gestures and behaviour on the grounds that he was an artistic genius, yet was clearly repelled by any hint of camp. He judged baseball a far superior game to tennis, not just in terms of its more macho image, but because of the much greater skill he believed it required. As well as being a sports writer, Galllico was the author of a number of sentimental fictions, expressing a more 'feminine' sensibility; and one might speculate that the writer's phobic dislike of tennis expressed some fear of femininity or weakness in himself.

Journalist Steve Tignor credits Tilden's biographer, Frank Deford, with having done much in the 1970s as a leading sports journalist to bring tennis to a wider popular audience.[2] Deford felt that by then it had got rid of the 'fairy' image, possibly due to his own reportage, although he does not say as much. He clearly admired Tilden the tennis player, but his otherwise excellent biography is marred by the double stereotype he deploys: the genius and the homosexual.

The Romantics invented the modern idea of genius. For Byron and Shelley the individual genius possessed more than simply outstanding skill. He possessed creative originality. The genius made things new. By force of will, conviction and artistry he imposed an original vision on his audience. By contrast with debunkers who insisted that genius was simply 'ninety-nine per cent perspiration' or 'the art of taking infinite pains', the Romantics held the genius to be a hero.

The painter, Amedeo Modigliani, expressed this when he wrote that the artist 'is created for intense life and joy'. The artist, he said, had 'rights that others have not, because we have different needs that place us above ... their moral code ... You must hold sacred ... all that which may exalt and excite your intelligence. Seek to provoke and multiply all such stimulating forces which alone can drive the intelligence to its utmost creative power.'[3] The genius was more than a hero; he was even a kind of god.

Tilden was hailed a 'genius' of the tennis court because he displayed originality in his development of the game, being widely acknowledged as the single player above all others who brought the game forward. He played all-court tennis, although he preferred baseline play, he transformed the drop shot into a killer move; and he could discourse for hours on different kinds of spin. Tilden's performances on court – glaring at linesmen, throwing points or even sets, provoking the crowd – were theatrical and melodramatic and expressed the other side of genius: capricious behaviour.

Tilden certainly resembled the stereotype of the genius-artist in that he was 'refractory'. The nineteenth-century revolutionary French communard, Jules Vallès, wrote of the 'refractory ones' as those who felt compelled always to go against the grain. 'Instead of accepting the place in life to which they were destined, [they] wanted to make a place for themselves by dint of their own efforts alone, whether by audacity or talent.'

Tilden was just such a square peg in a round hole. He, too, 'cut across the fields instead of sticking to the main road' and was one of those who had 'a mission to complete, a sacred trust to carry out, a flag to defend … all those who have no roots in life, no profession, no standing … whose only baggage … is the obsession they make of art, literature … or who dream of founding a school … or a religion.'

The genius was for Deford a positive, if controversial stereotype; that of the homosexual was wholly negative. He interprets Tilden's life as completely blighted by being gay. He assumes that Tilden himself believed his life was a 'wrong call', in other words that he should not have existed. To be homosexual, thought Deford, meant that 'he lived one great lie in shame for a lifetime'. It was a 'massive ongoing deceit of himself, of his every day'.[4] In other words, Deford's explanation for Tilden's extreme sportsmanship and his demands of himself is that it and his whole life can be explained by this single feature. The tone of horrified pity tells the reader more about Deford than Tilden. It also reveals the depths of the rejection of the gay man and how impossible it was for a sportsman to be a lover of men, still less adolescent boys.

The worm in the rose, the 'one great lie' was not Tilden's,

but the lie at the heart of all sport. Tilden himself was, it is true, not at ease with his own problematic inclinations, but felt more relaxed about it in Europe than in the US. (Coco Gentien, gay himself, advised Tilden to make Europe his permanent home for that reason.) In any case his friends and contemporaries believed him inhibited and more or less 'sexless' during the years when success and fame and the endless playing of tennis gave his life fulfilment.

By the late 1930s his reasons for staying in Europe were financial. It was estimated that Tilden had made half a million dollars as a professional in the years from 1931 to 1937, but by 1938 the money had simply run out. The Algonquin, where he had so often had a suite in New York, was demanding thousands of dollars in unpaid rent and Tilden, then on his last ever visit to Europe, was forced to delay his return to the States until Ellsworth Vines, who, commendably, was one of the few to stand by Tilden until the end, had sorted out his affairs – insofar as they could be sorted out.

By 1939 the aunt with whom Tilden had lived as a teenager had died and his cousin had settled in Yorkshire. Their house in Philadelphia, which had provided a base during his nomadic life, was sold and Tilden moved to California. Now he was dependent on work as a coach, but the growing rumours concerning his sexuality had spread, and many clubs refused to employ him. Chaplin and Joseph Cotten continued to befriend him; Clifton Webb, who was gay, employed him to teach tennis to Katharine Hepburn, Garbo and the designer, Valentino, and he was still welcome at San Simeon, where he played Errol Flynn.

When war came he organised a travelling tennis troupe to entertain the armed forces in the States. The group included Gussie Moran, later famous for her frilly knickers, and Gloria Butler, whom he'd known as a child in Monaco, where her father, the tobacco baron George Pierce Butler, had sponsored the tournament. They visited wounded soldiers and from Moran's testimony seem to have had good times.

After the war, though, the decline continued. By this time Tilden's appearance and personal hygiene had deteriorated. His clothes were dirty, his body odour bad. One evening he was picked up by patrol police, on account of the erratic driving of the fourteen-year-old boy who was at the wheel of Tilden's Packard. Worse, the boy's flies were open and Tilden had his arm round him.

The boy had appeared willing and already had an immorality conviction. Because of this Tilden was advised by his lawyer to plead not guilty and if he had done so, he would probably have got off. His sense of sportsmanship refused this. Even the guilty plea might normally have been punished with probation, but the judge was so horrified that a sportsman of all people, a man who was a hero and idol to the young, should have committed such a heinous crime, that Tilden was sent to a prison farm where he served seven months.

Soon after his release he propositioned a hitch-hiker he'd picked up. This time the young man was not willing, and reported him to the police. Tilden returned to prison, Dunlop removed his name from all their products, his records at the University of Pennsylvania were suppressed and his portrait at the Germanstown Cricket Club in Philadelphia was removed.[5] When he appeared at Forest Hills one year, erstwhile friends cut him dead. Chaplin and Cotten still stood by him, but by this time the anti-Red witch hunt had begun and Chaplin had to leave the United States shortly afterwards.

Tilden still had a few friends. Throughout his career he had coached many boys in the hope each time that the youth would be his tennis heir. There was no suggestion that he ever attempted to molest any of these protégés. The last of them was Arthur Anderson. He and his mother, Miriam, became faithful friends and, interviewed in later life, Anderson had nothing but praise for his mentor.

Tilden had lost touch with Gloria Butler, but then by chance she caught sight of him playing on a shabby public court in

Hollywood. It belonged to the owners of Grauman's Chinese Restaurant, who, it seems, felt that even now Tilden's name was some kind of draw. At first he seemed afraid that his former friend, like so many others, would refuse to speak to him, but after a moment of hesitation they fell into each other's arms. He seemed not to mind his lowly occupation. 'I'll play tennis with anyone who wants to play.'

In 1953 he was due to depart for the professional championships, held in Cleveland. The previous evening Miriam and Arthur Anderson had invited him to dinner. He didn't turn up, so Arthur drove over to Tilden's shabby one-room, walk-up apartment to find that Big Bill, dressed in his overcoat with his bags packed, lay dead.

Ellsworth Vines, Gussie Moran and a few others attended the funeral, but Tilden seemed to be forgotten and disgraced. He was nevertheless posthumously inducted into the Tennis Hall of Fame in 1959.

13

Three women

BILL TILDEN AND ELEANOR TENNANT may or may not have met, but she, like him, was familiar with the Hollywood courts and stars. Her background was different, for her family had fallen on hard times. Her father had found wealth in the gold rush and had become a hotel owner, but then got involved in local San Francisco politics and lost his money. Eleanor's parents were estranged. They lived in the same house but never spoke to each other, as Mrs Tennant tried to make ends meet.[1]

Tennis was Eleanor's escape from the unhappy household, and like the pre-First World War champion Maurice McCloughlin, she learned to play on the public courts in the Golden Gate Park in San Francisco. There was a girls' tennis club there, run by a Mrs Fletcher, who noticed Eleanor's talent and invited her to join.

Like so many others, Eleanor was madly in love with tennis. She soon stopped attending school and spent all her time improving her game. By the time her mother found out that she'd simply abandoned her education, it was too late to send her back, but she was made to train as a secretary.

She was an exceptionally independent and resourceful young woman. Secretarial work did not suit her and in 1917 she became the only woman commercial traveller for Standard Oil. With the money she saved she took a two-week holiday to Los Angeles. On her arrival she again showed initiative – not to say cheek – in introducing herself to Maurice McCloughlin and asking him where she could get a game of tennis. She must have been persuasive and attractive, because McCloughlin (who was America's top player at the time) at once asked her to join him in a foursome that afternoon. The other players were Willy de Mille, brother of Cecil B. de Mille, and Admiral Winslow.

Admiral Winslow and his family had rented the whole top floor of the Beverly Hills Hotel – the 'blue bloods' from Newport, Rhode Island staying at the best hotel in southern California. So everyone noticed when they took up Eleanor Tennant. The hotel manager noticed too and employed her as the hotel tennis coach. Her tremendous initiative soon had the guests playing all the sports available, including pony trekking up into the hills. She even organised the older residents into bridge tournaments.

As California was a more relaxed society than post-Edwardian London, Eleanor did not experience the rigid class distinctions that kept Dan Maskell in his place, but she was still a hard-up young woman trying to make her way in the world. She was also learning as she coached, observing her own game in order to understand how to teach others – including the film stars who began to hear of her and come to her for lessons. Before long she was known all over southern California as 'Miss Beverly Hills Hotel' and had effectively become the hotel's unpaid PR person at the age of only twenty-two.

She got along really well with show business people. Like Fred Perry, she believed there was a great deal in common between tennis and show business. 'Tennis has all the high lights and all the coloured things ... and their footlights were our tournaments.'

A pattern of highs and lows was to develop in her life. Each employer liked and valued her to begin with, but eventually there was usually a falling-out. After a period of being feted by wealthy families in Cleveland and the East Coast, when she was able to play tennis as an amateur, she tried a career in the catering business and then was briefly married, but neither experiment was a success. She went back west and became a tennis pro in

La Jolla. There she coached at a girls' school and invented the idea of the 'tennis clinic' at which she taught up to 100 pupils at a time – in some ways prefiguring the tennis academies that were to develop after 1970. She also earned money through her association with Wilson sporting goods.

She took up with the Hollywood crowd again. Elizabeth Ryan invited her out to Randolph Hearst's fantasy castle at San Simeon, and she became a close friend of his mistress, Marion Davies. Like Tilden, she played tennis with Clifton Webb, Charlie Chaplin, Marlene Dietrich – and Carole Lombard, another top Hollywood film star and Clark Gable's lover and future wife. Lombard became a close friend and gave her a nickname: 'Teach'. Henceforth she was known everywhere as 'Teach Tennant'.

This was a pleasant life, but not quite enough for a woman as ambitious, energetic and determined as Eleanor Tennant. There may have been an inner dissatisfaction that her own tennis talent was subordinated to the lesser talent of the rich, for she herself had to work hard to earn her living. She sent money to her mother. Her sister was sick – and eventually came to live with her as a chronic invalid. So when a young woman player began to make a name for herself, Teach noticed and grabbed her opportunity.

Alice Marble wanted to be a baseball player.[2] She was mascot to the San Francisco Seals and attended their practice sessions, acting as ball girl. But baseball was a man's game; and when she was fifteen Alice's brother Dan spoke to her about it. He bought her a tennis racquet and told her she had to stop being a tomboy. She was to play the more ladylike tennis, which she could enjoy for the rest of her life.

Alice was furiously resentful, heartbroken and humiliated. Because she was well known locally as the 'queen of swat', the girl who practised with the Seals, the boys at school jeered at her demotion to the sissy game. But she gritted her teeth, learned to play and worked her way up the juniors until she was beaten by one of Teach's pupils. Noting the superiority of the girl's ground strokes to her own, Alice wrote to Teach to ask her if she might become her pupil too.

Thus began one of those Svengali relationships that tennis seemed particularly to favour. The close bond between coach and player can reach the intensity of a parent–child relationship (and often is, literally) or become something more than a love affair. Such affinities are not exclusive to tennis. In the 1960s the dancers Rudolph Nureyev and Margot Fonteyn created just such a relationship. In the modern age erotic fulfilment tends to be presented as the touchstone of intensity and ecstasy. Sports stars and other physical performers, in trying to express the experience of some pinnacle of performance, sometimes described their triumph as 'better than sex'; as if it went to some ecstasy beyond the erotic. Fonteyn's biographer suggests that the dancers may once have spent the night together, but that, even if true, is irrelevant to their art, which transfigured and transcended sexual attraction. In like manner the skating partnership of Torvill and Dean in the 1980s was an all-consuming bond, lifting sublimated eroticism to an almost abstract sphere.

These, though, were equal partnerships. The contract between coach and player is different, and doubly unequal in that the coach may always be tempted to live vicariously through the triumphs of the player, while at the same time dominating through his or her status as the teacher; and there is the further ambiguity that the coach is employed by the player.

Teach Tennant's relationship with Alice Marble was different in that the coach supported the pupil economically. Alice moved in with Teach and in return for coaching she helped Teach with her school pupils and did secretarial work for her. Her tennis blossomed.

In July 1933 Alice won the California women's singles title, rising to third in the women's national rankings, and travelled east alone to play in a series of four tournaments, the results of which would decide whether or not she was chosen for the Wightman Cup team. She did well in the first three tournaments, winning two of them. She lost in the final at the third, but with her partner won the doubles, defeating the national doubles champions. When she arrived at the fourth and last, at East Hampton, she was greeted with the news that she was to play in the doubles with no less a partner than Helen Wills Moody.

The smart East Hampton tournament was run by a committee chaired by Julian Myrick, he who had persecuted Bill Tilden a decade earlier. Myrick was a member of the well-connected amateur establishment that controlled the tennis circuit. He was also chairman of the Wightman Cup. He decreed that Alice was not even to be considered for inclusion in the Cup team unless she played in all the East Hampton events. As a result Alice played 108 games over nine hours in 104° F heat and collapsed with sunstroke and anaemia. This unfair and arbitrary treatment exemplified the autocratic and arbitrary power of the establishment network.

There followed a series of setbacks due to ill health. Nominated for the Wightman Cup and sponsored by the USLTA to travel to Europe, she collapsed at Roland Garros and returned to America diagnosed with tuberculosis. Julian Myrick and the USLTA washed their hands of her. That would have been the end of Alice Marble's career as a tennis player had it not been for Teach. Teach guided her gradually back to health and by 1937 they were ready to set out again to conquer the world. At first the USLTA refused even to invite Alice to play in any tournaments, but eventually she was admitted. Triumph followed, for she beat Helen Jacobs in the final of the US National, 4–6, 6–3, 6–2.

She also won the mixed doubles at Wimbledon with Don Budge. In 1938 they successfully defended their title and Alice also won the women's doubles. In 1939 she won all three trophies at the last Wimbledon before the war and won all three titles at Forest Hills as well.

Don Budge claimed that Alice was the first woman to play 'like a man', using serve, volley and smash instead of playing a predominantly baseline game. That made Alice special, he claimed. Budge may well have been correct to say that Alice

Marble took the game forward by serving and volleying like a man. Yet it is also true that the outstanding women players from Lottie Dod to Helen Wills had always practised with men and aimed to play a man's game in the sense of power and speed of stroke. Lottie Dod was also known for her volleying. Until the 1950s, however, it was probably only the outstanding women players whose game rose above the ground-stroke play with which most women were content.

Eleanor Teach Tennant had relieved Alice of all financial worries, and nursed her through serious illness. She made Alice into an international tennis champion. She introduced Alice to the celebrity world and to the exclusive social life that could open to the big tennis stars. But there was a cost. They were not lovers, although Teach was a lesbian; but the powerful coach demanded control over every aspect of her pupil's life. Under Teach's iron discipline Alice reworked her strokes and developed the orderliness and discipline that had been lacking. Teach described Alice as a Pygmalion – completely remoulded by her teacher. She stuck to a rigid regime of early bedtime, continual practice and no boy friends.

Carole Lombard and Alice became close friends and in 1938 the actress urged Alice to develop her singing voice. She became the vocalist for Emil Coleman's band for a short season at the Waldorf Astoria in New York. Some of her fans, however, didn't approve, as a life of night clubs and decadence didn't sit well with the wholesome image of a sportswoman. It also interfered with her tennis. Most important of all, Teach didn't like it.

Alice complied, but eventually the relationship became too combustible. The pair quarrelled and separated. Alice married and had a miscarriage; her husband died on active service. Carole Lombard was killed in an air crash. Meanwhile Alice turned professional and had a small part in *Pat and Mike*. She never remarried.

Teach moved to Palm Springs and became coach at the Racquet Club which was managed by two former pupils who were also film actors. Once more she was coaching the stars. She had also coached Bobby Riggs and she was now looking for a new budding champion. She found one in Pauline Betz, who won Wimbledon in 1946, and then in Maureen 'Little Mo' Connolly.

Little Mo's confidence was in no way dented by her short stature and lack of conventional good looks and she was no Pygmalion. She came up to Teach at the age of twelve and asked – or rather demanded – that she become her coach. At the age of seventeen she won Wimbledon. En route to that triumph she confronted Teddy Tinling and told him that he must make her court outfits. 'She has always known where she was going,' said Teach. It was an understatement.

The budding champion came from the municipal courts, like Marble and Betz before her, but she was so promising that she was soon being sponsored by the Southern California Tennis Association. Born left-handed, she had switched to the right hand to play tennis, for at the time it was believed that no lefthander could become a top-flight star (and there was still a general stigma attached to left-handedness). The change of hands had hampered her serve. For this reason and because Maureen was not yet fully grown, Teach concentrated on training her to be a baseline player. This was controversial in the age of the serve-and-volley game as played by Alice Marble, but was a winning strategy because most of the serve-volley players had weaknesses in their ground strokes. Teach maintained that although Maureen did not have a cannon-ball type of serve, hers was accurate and her placement exceptional, but the player was always to be seen as having a weak serve. Even without an obviously killer serve, the precocious star was able to defeat her opponents by the power and speed of her strokes and above all because she had the ability to breathe correctly, something that Eleanor believed was very rare.

Like Alice Marble before her, Little Mo rebelled against her mentor after she won Wimbledon for the first time. There was an acrimonious split in London, much reported by the British tabloid press. Two women, each with such willpower, were sure to clash eventually.

Coach and pupil: 'Teach' Tennant and Little Mo in 1952

Little Mo won Wimbledon three years running and in 1953 became the first woman ever to hold all four major titles at the same time. During her brief career she absolutely dominated the women's game and was considered one of the most devastating players in the history of tennis. But her triumphs were cut short at the age of twenty. Riding was her second passion and in 1954 a serious riding accident ended her tennis career. She married and had two children, but died of ovarian cancer at the age of thirty-four.

Teach Tennant's career bridged the glamorous Hollywood years and the slow transition to professionalism after the Second

World War. But essentially she was a figure of the future. She carried a flag for the prospects of independent women in the sport. She was also a prototype of the key role of the coach in future years.

PART TWO

THIS SPORTING LIFE

14

Home from the war

S UZANNE LENGLEN HAD PERSONIFIED the frenetic gaiety of
the 1920s and the spirit of rebellion that swept away the stuffy
social restrictions of an earlier age along with the horrors of the
First World War. After the Second World War the mood was very
different. It felt as if shattered societies could only be mended by
a return to established relationships and familiar customs. Europe
was devastated with hundreds of thousands of 'displaced persons'
– refugees – in desperate flight across the continent. There was
civil war in China. India became independent. Pakistan was born.
The old European colonial systems were breaking up. Hiroshima
and Nagasaki had been flattened by atomic bombs and Japan
was being reinvented by the occupying forces under General
MacArthur. In Britain the victory celebrations soon gave way to
shortages and austerity. The United States was neither invaded
nor bombed, but a gloomy mood prevailed and the gloom became
international as it settled into Cold War paranoia.

This was a world of mass production and mass entertainment.
Writing of his childhood in the 1940s, historian Raphael Samuel
remembered how 'the principle of collectivity' dominated every
department of national life. His point of reference is Britain,
but his description applies to much of Western Europe and the
United States – and even more to the Soviet Union and its allies.
'Standardisation and uniformity were the keynotes of planning'

and this applied as much to leisure as to work and reconstruction. There was 'dancing in step' in the ballroom, there was regimented mass 'fun' in the holiday camps, indeed mass leisure of every kind from the queues of men at the football grounds every Saturday to the queues of courting couples outside the huge cinemas. Samuel felt that the 1940s 'constituted … a kind of zenith of mass society', in which rigid codes of dress clearly marked social position as did styles of interior decoration and – as soon as rationing was over – tastes in food.[1]

Yet this mass-production world was curiously at odds with the growing emphasis on individualism that set the West against the collectivist regime of the USSR. The West called itself the 'free world', posing as the citadel of individual freedom and priding itself on its democratic credentials; there was a dread of 'mass man' and the crushing of the individual by big business and the overweening state. And there were other contradictions. Existential angst combined uneasily with the push for economic growth and material betterment. Governments and experts preached a return to conservative forms of family life, but this was thwarted by mass culture and its often boisterous promotion of erotic themes and romantic music.

How the traditions of tennis were to fit into the post-war world was not altogether clear. In wartime Europe the game had come to a halt. Dan Maskell spent the war in the auxiliary medical services. Cramm's ex-boyfriend Geoffrey Nares met his death in the Egyptian desert. In the United States the new young American star Margaret Osborne worked in a munitions factory in Sausalito. Alice Marble entertained wounded soldiers and others about to replace them in far-flung theatres of war, as did Tilden and his touring troupe. Many players joined the armed forces. Allison Danzig reeled off a list of names of those who had exchanged a racquet for a blue or khaki uniform. There was Wilmer Allison who had been 'practically living in Army bombers, flying the oceans to set up radio installations … Lieutenant Ernest Sutter, former intercollegiate champion [was] in the landing force that invaded French North Africa and has a shattered right arm that may never wield a racket again … '

Tennis continued in the US, with the result that by 1947 American players were better prepared than any Europeans to dominate the game. The new tennis stars were no longer like the old 'amateur gentlemen' who had played the game for love and then moved into 'adult' careers. Bobby Riggs (who'd won all three titles at Wimbledon in 1939), Frank Parker and Jack Kramer came from modest backgrounds and Pancho Gonzales from a poor Mexican–American one. For them the game was a route to a better life. It was a career and they spent their whole lives in the sport. Each won the American national title twice and that was the signal to turn professional.[2]

That they were able to turn sport into a career was in part due to the changing role of sport itself in public life. It was becoming an entertainment spectacle. Businessmen, promoters and entre- preneurs were investing increasing amounts of time and money in the commercialisation of entertainment in general and sport in particular. Even tennis, a minority, exclusive sport could become big business.

The problem with this was that tennis, to a greater extent than other sports, was fettered by its strict adherence to amateur status. This was further complicated by the situation of the player as a lone individual, unsupported by a team, a manager, and roots in a local culture of support. The same problem – of how to square the circle between amateur status and earning a living – that had bedevilled the 1930s became ever more acute with the emergence of players who could not rely on wealthy parents or afford membership of a club. It was hardly surprising that 'shamateurism' already a problem before the war, became even more flagrant and more damaging to the game.

As an amateur Bobby Riggs had no trouble once he reached the top ten in supporting himself and for a time a wife and child on 'expenses'. He was effectively bank-rolled by Edmund C. Lynch, of Merrill, Lynch, Pierce, Fenner and Beane, 'paid' in one way or another to play tennis with the banker and his friends on estates in Southampton on Long Island, Indian Creek in Miami and Nassau. Riggs travelled everywhere on Lynch's private yacht and often stayed on it too. Apart from this, he was supported in different ways by the tournaments at which he played, with courtesy hotel rooms and free equipment.[3]

'Shamateurism', however, was not necessarily beneficial to the players in the long term. It could damage a promising career – that of Pancho Gonzales, for example. His talent took him precociously to the top. He won at Forest Hills in 1949 and 1950 and then turned professional at the age of twenty-two. Jack Kramer, Wimbledon champion in 1947, also turned pro and became one of the most influential post-war figures in tennis, more or less in charge of the tour. He believed that Gonzales, by joining the professional tour before he and his game were mature, irreparably damaged his development. He was an exciting and hugely talented player, but his game was stalled by the demands of the pro tour and the absence of proper tournament play against a whole variety of different players in different competitive circumstances. He made $100,000 dollars in his first year on the pro tour, but then for several years Kramer refused to let him play because he wasn't winning enough matches.

Kramer hated the whole system. In 1979 he wrote: 'things are not pure in tennis today. But at least the players do have a voice and a piece of the action. In the shamateur days we were only athletic gigolos – which is what Tilden called us.'[4] Shamateurism was a dirty secret, tolerated even as it was attacked. The press was certainly never silent on the subject. In 1953 an *Evening Standard* correspondent, John Mallalieu complained of the joyless demeanour of the players, who seemed to endure rather than enjoy playing tennis. 'There's no livelihood at stake – or is there?' wondered Mallalieu and felt it would be better if Wimbledon became an open tournament – or rather, tennis became an open game, like cricket and golf. Then it would no longer be 'half a sham'.

Kramer felt that the amateur hierarchy that ran the sport also exploited the players. The officials usually owed their positions of power to social status in the clubs and were as much preoccupied with preserving the status quo as with fostering the abilities of the players. Indeed, many players resented the snobbish disdain with which the amateur establishment often treated the players.

Other players wholeheartedly supported the amateur system. Bill Talbert, one of the top post-war American players (he partnered Margaret Osborn in some of her many mixed-doubles triumphs among other things), loved the whole atmosphere of the exclusive clubs. He saw it as 'a fantastic kind of melting pot'. His father had lost his job in the Depression. As a result Talbert had to go to work from the age of fourteen, but he managed to work his way through college and continue to play his tennis. He took to the club atmosphere immediately. For him, the Merion Cricket Club in Philadelphia was the gateway to a wholly different life and he loved everything about the air of easy privilege and sophisticated taste. His personal experience was of being welcomed rather than shunned as an outsider.[5]

Mr Perry T. Jones of the Los Angeles Tennis Club was the archetype of the upper-class amateur official at home in the circles Talbert described. California was the hotbed for new tennis talent just before the war and Jones was perfectly positioned to bring young players on, as he ran the junior programme of the Southern California Tennis Association.

In 1925 Elizabeth Ryan had put him in charge of the Pacific Southwest Tournament, soon recognised as one of the major contests of the tour. Jones turned it into a fashionable social event. The upper-class patrons and other local society figures were allowed to purchase boxes on one side of the court; the Hollywood stars, looked down upon by the local aristocracy, were seated in boxes opposite. He arranged for the prominent local families to have players staying as their house guests and Hollywood celebrities and the upper crust competed to organise dinner dances, beach lunches and tours of the studios. He inaugurated a Tennis

Ball to celebrate the completion of the tournament. It was the West Coast event of the year. These initiatives generated enough money for Jones to be able to sustain and develop emerging talents and provide the financial means for them to travel to other national tournaments and even to Europe. Jones' single-minded efforts produced the finest crop of tennis players America had ever seen or would see again.

Digby Baltzell regarded him as a hero of American tennis, but even he admitted that Jones, whose mother had been a Southern belle, was 'a Victorian bachelor and a bit of a snob'. Billie Jean King crossed swords with him as a junior and dismissed him as a 'snooty sexist'; he had refused to allow her to appear in the tournament photograph on her first appearance because she was wearing shorts.

Jones himself always appeared in bow tie and tinted glasses and never unbuttoned his collar, nor rolled up his sleeves even on the hottest southern Californian day. His obituary described him as 'bridge party American, Pasadena gothic'. (Presumably this refers to the architectural style of the mansions in the wealthy suburb – although Jones sounds equally 'gothic' in a deep South, Truman Capote kind of way.)[6] Yet whatever his snobbery and disdain for women, he was devoted to tennis – the one and only love of his life.

After 1945 Perry Jones and his ilk began to appear old-fashioned. The war had changed the popular perception of social class. It had also changed the popular perception of tennis. Allison Danzig credited the war with having done away with the old stereotype of the 'sissy game', its elaborate social rules and, worst of all, the troublesome word, 'love'. Now at last tennis players could compete with the likes of Babe Ruth, Jack Dempsey and Johnny Weissmuller, because according to Danzig the effete tennis player had proved himself in battle.

Why Danzig should have imagined that tennis players would be exempt from active service or would seek to evade it is far from clear. His words merely betrayed the deep prejudice whereby even those who loved the game, as Danzig presumably did, believed it sullied by its failure to display an adequate amount of machismo.

War might make a man out of sissy tennis players. On the other hand, in at least one case the sissy game saved a war hero from post-traumatic stress. Art Larsen, post-war US champion and one of the best players of the early post-war years, took part in the D-Day landings at Omaha Beach, saw most of his regiment slaughtered and developed such a variety of superstitions and nervous tics that after the war he was unable to hold down a job. But he was able to transfer his obsessive-compulsive routines into a winning formula, although he continued to behave superstitiously on court, never treading on a line and insisting on having the same ball after every winning point.

Jack Kramer was the new transatlantic representative of manliness. As a boy he'd hoped to be a baseball player. The last thing he'd wanted to be was a sissy tennis player and he begged his mother not to tell his friends she'd bought him a racquet. This was in Nevada, but, fortunately for American tennis, the Kramer family moved to San Bernardino, California, where tennis was a big and popular game. There he was noticed and brought on by an outstanding coach, Dick Skeen. He was soon the top up-and-coming junior and once he had become National Boys Champion Perry Jones gave him the opportunity to practise regularly at the Los Angeles Tennis Club with Ellsworth Vines, then the world's best player. Kramer developed what he called 'the Big Game' and 'percentage tennis'. He was the first player to come to the net after every serve; his big serve and big volley style became generally known as the Big Game. In this, Kramer was following the theories of Cliff Roche. Roche was a club player, by no means outstanding, but he was also an automotive engineer who had worked in Detroit as a mass-production designer. As a result of this, he developed 'a theory of the game based on repetitive action'.[7]

The era of mass production in industry was now to be

reproduced on the tennis court. Henry Ford had destroyed the artisanal conception of making things by inventing the assembly line, which broke down the construction of an object into discrete parts. The predictability of mechanisation maximised efficiency and standardisation. Now it seemed that this belief in reproducible routine was to be adopted on court.

Roche stated that 'every ball should be hit in a certain pattern. The forehand down-the-line approach shot, for example, became 100 per cent automatic, since it was not a function of the opponent's position or strength. Every time the "automatic" player came into net behind a forehand, he hit for an area two feet from the sideline and three feet from the baseline. Cross-court forehand approach shots were never to be used, since, on a percentage basis they would lead to more passing shots on the return.'

Kramer and his doubles partner, Ted Schroeder, followed this plan religiously. Kramer became 'the automatic player'. He almost invariably served to the backhand, went cross court on every backhand exchange from the baseline, always hitting the two- by three-foot rectangle in the court. That he had little defensive game hardly mattered, since he was so strong on his service games and conserved energy by going all out to break his opponent's serve only when there was a real chance of doing so.

This was machine tennis. Not everyone was convinced of its superiority. A. L. Laney regarded it as 'a rather unimaginative, conventional style of play based on the theory that you will always be the attacker, never the defender. There was little or no surprise in it.' He thought that Kramer advocated this type of game because he had himself done so well by it and become an extremely wealthy professional, first as a player, later as a promoter. 'A shrewd and highly personable businessman who could wheedle reams of publicity from uninformed newspaper columnists', he used his professional tour to spread the gospel of the 'big game' he claimed to have invented. Laney was unsure whether Kramer himself really believed in his own propaganda. But Kramer seemed certainly not to know that the term had been used in the 1920s when it had described the very different all-court game of Tilden and Johnston. Nor did he seem to be aware that Maurice McLoughlin had played serve-and-volley tennis before the First World War.[8]

But Kramer was totally dedicated to his version of tennis. He believed that audiences 'pay to see the big game' and did not at first appreciate the artistry of such players as the Australian Ken Rosewall. The 'big game' was more masculine, it was a game fit for the heroes who had returned from the war and who, in casting off their uniforms, had not relinquished their warlike aggression.

On the surface (amateur) tennis during the 1950s and early 1960s continued smooth and bland. The Kramer generation of Americans was displaced by Australians, who dominated the men's game. They created an aura of uncontroversial good sportsmanship. Frank Sedgman in particular, with his clean-cut good looks and quiet personality, seemed the ideal of what a tennis star – or any sports star – should be. The on- and off- court demeanour of the Australians set a standard of conservative restraint that was taken for granted. They were trained by the redoubtable Harry Hopman who, as Davis Cup captain, created the most dominant Australian cohort ever. Lew Hoad, Ken Rosewall and Rod Laver were sublime tennis players who never hit the headlines for any other reason than their game. Like other sportsmen of the period, they did not become mega-wealthy celebrities with an international lifestyle to match. They did not appear on every giant hoarding to advertise watches, cars or banks. They just played tennis. Hoad and Laver were the great all-round players; Rosewall was the genius of stroke play. Laver twice won the calendar slam – all four major tournaments in one year – the only player ever to have done so. Yet not everyone was enchanted by their tennis. Peter Wilson of the *Daily Mirror* described them as 'magnificent robots' instead of 'living personalities'. Resentful of their total dominance, he deplored Hopman's 'conveyor belt system' and 'iron curtain' regime: players were not allowed to be interviewed or to express their views on any subject; they were not to go to the cinema or take a girl out without Hopman's permission; and minor misdemeanours, such as the wrong use of cutlery, resulted in fines.

Like their American rivals, they had left behind the glamour of the Riviera time, but they arrived too soon for the glitz of celebrity tennis. Therefore what remains of them can be gleaned largely from old newsreels and the still photographs that capture them in frozen motion. They fitted with the self-effacing, polite and unobtrusive side of the decade in which they excelled as they swept across the smooth green surface of 1950s tennis in their all-white gear.

Yet that smooth surface was deceptive. It could not go unremarked that no sooner had a new champion won a brace of major championships, than he or she would disappear into the ranks of the professionals. Jack Kramer was of the view that 'as the 1950s wore on it was possible for very average players to become great amateur champions'. Perhaps the polite crowds at Wimbledon did not notice at first, but elsewhere in the world interest in tennis was on the decline. For the 1954 Davis Cup at White City Stadium in Sydney, temporary stands had to be built and there was a turnaway crowd of 238,000. A decade later it was difficult even to sell the 12,000 permanent seats. In early rounds of the French and Australian championships, crowds sometimes numbered only in the hundreds. At Forest Hills finals the stands would be only half filled. Profits were falling at Wimbledon too.

Eventually even the Wimbledon fans noticed. In 1958 the *Daily Sketch* mounted an all-out attack on Kramer, who was seen as the villain ruining tennis:

KEEP AWAY FROM OUR KIDS KRAMER
WE DIDN'T GROOM THEM FOR YOU

Wimbledon starts today. Sitting in the stands will be immaculately dressed, suave, plausible Jack Kramer – Public Enemy no 1 to amateur lawn tennis.

In ten years his Hollywood smile and million-dollar cheque book has skimmed the cream off the amateur game.

Now the man who was born in money-mad Las Vegas again brings Wall Street to Wimbledon.

We can't keep him out. It wouldn't make much difference if we could, for money talks and Jack's a whale of a talker.

He has weakened the American and Australian game and is now after new blood! For his circus must have a yearly transfusion. BUT KEEP OFF OUR KIDS, KRAMER![9]

To the British who packed Wimbledon every year, but who took little interest in the professional circuit, it might seem that Kramer was an unwanted intruder. The Wimbledon hierarchy knew otherwise.

15

Gorgeous girls

HOW WAS WOMEN'S TENNIS to fit into this picture? The top women players of the 1930s, culminating with Alice Marble, Wimbledon winner in 1939, had based their games on that of the men's. Helen Jacobs had pioneered the wearing of shorts on court. The women's game had developed in strength and power.

World war had brought women to the fore in all areas of life. It had encouraged, indeed necessitated, a massive movement of women into the workforce and into jobs traditionally reserved for men lost to the draft. There had been an upheaval of gender roles. Women had won the war not only on the home front, but in the forces, in the munitions factories, in the aerospace industry.

In California, for example, Lockheed and other companies recruited women at such a rate that by 1943, 42 per cent of the total workforce in southern Californian aviation was female. 'For a few brief years,' writes historian Kevin Starr, 'it seemed as if a major social revolution were occurring in American industry, the introduction of women into the workforce on an increasingly equal basis.'[1] Hitherto unheard-of forms of collective provision in the shape of subsidised cafeterias, child care and flexible shifts were introduced.

Such arrangements did not long survive in peacetime. The gains made during the war in terms of economic opportunities and moves towards equal pay, not to mention collective child-care provision, were withdrawn.

Conservative currents questioned whether the female emancipation of the war had not been at the expense of family life and child development. The turmoil of war had resulted in too many illegitimate births, too many extra-marital affairs and too much deviant sexuality. There were fears of the spread of venereal disease and of juvenile delinquency. A flourishing gay culture had developed in San Francisco. After the turbulence of war, the re-establishment of traditional relationships between men and women became a priority. Homosexuality was further demonised by its association with the British Soviet spy ring, two of whose members, Guy Burgess and Anthony Blunt, were gay.[2] Even the more general fear of the spread of Soviet-style totalitarianism could be cast in gendered terms, so that Soviet women were commonly depicted as battleaxes deprived of lipstick and nylons.

These beliefs were often justified in terms of a crude version of Freudian theory. Heterosexual relationships in marriage were the standard for psychological maturity. Homosexuality was not merely disapproved of but often punished; male homosexuality was illegal in the United States and Britain and discouraged everywhere. That the powerful voices of conservatism were often those of medical men meant that deviant sexualities were transformed from being sinful into forms of mental illness.

Japan, which had been a tennis-playing country – for male players, at least – before the war, was overwhelmed by defeat. Prostitution became a massive growth industry; on the other hand, the constitution imposed by the Americans insisted on a new democratic equality for all, including women, at least in theory. In Germany, the many widows and unmarried women had no choice but to work, first clearing the rubble, later laying the foundations of the 'economic miracle' of the fifties, only to see themselves then pushed back into the home. In France, the influence of the Catholic church and fears of national decline led to the encouragement by the state of large families and although women were now granted the vote, the situation described by Simone de Beauvoir in her exhaustive investigation of the position of women, *The Second Sex*, was far from encouraging. In Britain, the Beveridge Report, published in 1942 and hailed as the blueprint for the new welfare state, was very clear on the position of women: 'The attitude of the housewife to gainful employment outside the home is not and should not be the same as that of the single woman,' wrote Beveridge. 'She has other duties ... In the next thirty years housewives as Mothers have vital work to do in ensuring the adequate continuance of the British Race and of British Ideals in the world.'

In the United States the postwar mood was if anything even more conservative.

The Freudian ideal nevertheless differed from prewar morality because it promoted sexual fulfilment for women as well as for men and it was popularised with contradictory effect. The very fact that sexual behaviour began to be discussed more openly revealed the existence of discontent and a widespread desire for more and better sex and began to challenge the ideal of marriage as a permanent and unalterable state.

In addition, while authorities of all kinds preached a conservative morality, the expanding entertainment industries and advertising promoted sexual daring and excitement. The display of women's bodies played a noticeable part in the popular culture of film, music and mass fashion. Not least on the tennis court.

Teddy Tinling had enjoyed a special place in the tennis world since the 1920s. He was tall, good-looking and a talented player himself, often described as 'flamboyant'. A close friend of Suzanne Lenglen, who often asked him to umpire at her matches, he acted as a kind of go-between, a communicator or 'call boy' between the players and the officials and administrators at the various Riviera tournaments and Wimbledon. In 1937 Wimbledon offered him 'what was really an apprenticeship as the future secretary of Wimbledon', but by now he was a successful Mayfair dress designer. In spite of the social – and tennis-related – attractions of the Wimbledon post, it offered little money. Tinling declined and felt that from that moment his 'previously cordial relationship' with the Wimbledon hierarchy began 'an irrevocable slide toward mutual antagonism'.[3]

After the war Tinling turned his attention to women's sportswear. He blamed Alice Marble for the 'masculine' dress style of the new generation of American women players, Margaret Osborne duPont, Louise Brough, Pauline Betz and Pat Todd. They wore knee-length pleated shorts and short-sleeved shirt-blouses. This style was consistent with the military fashions of the war years, but in stark contrast to the nostalgic style introduced by Christian Dior in 1947.

Popularly named the New Look, this style was widely held to represent, as Teddy Tinling expressed it, 'an international hunger for a return to femininity and sexual attraction'. Tinling was determined to bring femininity back to the court and believed this was an advance for the women players. 'I felt that by looking like modern-day Amazons, the sports girls were renouncing their birthright.'[4]

He first attempted to flout the all-white tradition (which, he says, was not then an absolute rule) by designing a tennis dress with a coloured hem for the British player Joy Gannon (afterwards wife of British number one, Tony Mottram) for her first Wimbledon appearance. The following year Hazel Wightman, Wightman Cup captain, had any hint of colour banned from the matches to be played between the American and British teams. Hazel Wightman and Tinling, were, however, in agreement that women players should wear dresses, not shorts.

Tinling's campaign reached a climax with the notorious incident of Gussie Moran's lace knickers. Moran had played in the exhibition matches organised by Bill Tilden during the war, but had retained her amateur status and in 1949 was set to play at Wimbledon. Good-looking and, as Tinling puts it, 'curvaceous', she asked him to design her tennis wear. She would have liked a touch of colour, but, since this was now banned, Tinling conjured up a dress in a new fabric, knitted rayon, trimmed with satin. To go with this dress, he added a pair of lace-edged knickers.

The storm created by the knickers provided a foretaste of a 1950s popular culture of prurience and voyeurism. Gussie first wore them to a warm-up exhibition at the grand Hurlingham Club, the day before Wimbledon began. Men lay flat on their stomachs to catch a glimpse of the undergarment; photographers appeared from nowhere demanding that Gussy smash, serve, and stoop for volleys so that they could produce shots of the vital underwear. This continued at the Wimbledon championships. Gussie became too embarrassed to bend down to pick up balls. She was continually besieged off court as well as on. She managed to get to the women's doubles finals, partnered by Pat Todd, but her feminine outfit hardly helped her play and the reigning top pair, Louise Brough and Margaret duPont, won easily. The scandal and tabloid coverage horrified the amateur officials at Wimbledon and Teddy Tinling was effectively banned from the sacred portals.[5]

Jack Kramer signed Gorgeous Gussie shortly afterwards to play in an exhibition event in Cleveland, Ohio. It was a failure, because Gussie was the big name, but for the wrong reasons. Her game was not fully developed when she became notorious for her underwear and the uproar stalled improvement. Also, although Gussie had a good figure, she was not, after all, exceptionally beautiful, but audiences expected a film star when what she wanted to be was a tennis champion. So whether or not Tinling had struck a blow for women's tennis, he had fatally damaged Gussie Moran's chances of becoming a tennis star.

The panties remained front-page news in newspapers and magazines on both sides of the Atlantic for weeks. Indeed, they became so famous that Alice Marble wrote in disgust a year later of the way in which on the lecture tours she gave throughout the country, the question she was most frequently expected to answer was what she thought of Gussie's panties.

Tinling's design was a symbolic moment in the recasting of gender in the sport after the war. If the male tennis player was now to be a he-man, freed at last from the taint of effeminacy by Kramer's power game, correspondingly women tennis players were to emphasise their femininity. This was entirely consistent with the conservative ethos of the post-war 'free world'.

Tinling claimed he was striking a blow for women and against the 'stuffiness' of the Wimbledon hierarchy, and that Gussie's lace panties – and the 'peekaboo' broderie anglais-trimmed shorts he made for her the following year – had 'unleashed a tide of fashion progress'. He claimed that the controversy had greatly increased the popularity of tennis as a spectator sport. By sexing it up he'd done tennis a service.

Frank Sedgman might also have had his outfits designed by Teddy Tinling, but masculinity was the unquestioned norm from which women unfortunately, although necessarily, deviated. So while men's shirts and shorts – by now the norm – went unremarked, women players were always intensely scrutinised. Not everyone agreed that Teddy Tinling's push for femininity at all costs was a victory for women. In 1953 Laurie Pignon of the *Daily Sketch* wrote: 'The more I see of women's tennis at this year's Wimbledon, the more convinced I am that it is not now a crowd-drawing spectacle. The dancing and pirouetting around the baseline, the bits of lace and pieces of satin all look very attractive but ... assuming it was tennis the customers wanted, it was the men who gave it to them.' It seemed more like a seedy example of male prurience and its exploitation by the popular press than a triumph for women's tennis.

Across the world the tennis hierarchies were exclusively dominated by men. For the moment, however, there were no more lace-frilled knickers. Maureen Connolly interested audiences solely for her tennis. It seemed as if Gorgeous Gussie had been a brief aberration.

Yet a haunting unease beneath the placid surface of post-war tennis was reflected in three films, all made in the early post-war period. These directly confronted some of the underlying problems that disturbed the game and its promoters.

Ida Lupino's 1951 feature, *Hard, Fast and Beautiful*, addresses the fraught relationship between the amateur status of the player and the commercial pressures that had been bearing down ever more heavily on ordinary Americans since before the recently ended war. The story concerns a young woman player and the moral contradictions involved as she tries to work her way up through the game. A part of this is the exploitation of the woman player as sexual spectacle, a long-established ambiguity in the game, and which the Gorgeous Gussie incident highlighted. Also at issue is the relationship between the promising player and an over-ambitious parent, in this case a mother, but, most power-fully, the film exposes the absence of economic opportunity for women at that period other than through the exploitation of their sexuality.[6]

A second film to question women's status in sport is *Pat and Mike* made in 1952. In this, Katharine Hepburn reprises her madcap tomboy persona as a player of tennis and golf, who seeks to escape the overbearing influence of her patronising boyfriend. In an early scene, for example, he objects to her wearing trousers when playing golf with some important business friends. Later there are scenes of her playing on the professional circuit (recast as an amateur tournament) with Gussie Moran. (There is a rather sad moment when Gussie does what has evidently become a standard move at the beginning of a match, giving a little twirl to show off her knickers.) The film, which features 'Babe' Zaharias in the golfing sections, ends happily when Mike, the heroine's coach, has built her confidence and convinced her she can win – somewhat undercutting the feminist message of the film, since she still relies on the support and encouragement of a man.

In *Strangers on a Train* (1951), based on a novel by Patricia Highsmith, Alfred Hitchcock slyly exploits the other secret in tennis, darker than 'shamateurism' or the sexual peekaboo of women players. The film opens as the camera follows two pairs

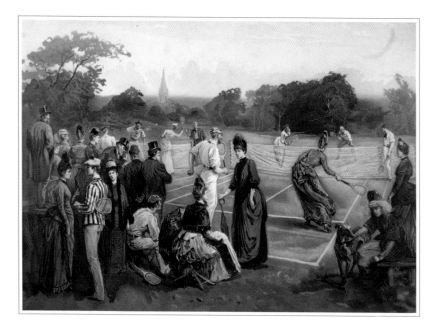

'Lawn Tennis' by Henry Sandham, 1887: the early years of the American game

Pas de quatre from the original production of Serge Diaghilev's 1924
Riviera ballet, *Le Train Bleu*

Tennis as art: 'Tennis' by Vicente do Rego Monteiro, 1928

'Tennis' by Percy Shakespeare, 1937: the 'golden age' of club tennis

Cigarette smoking, tennis and flirtation were often linked in advertisements
in the so-called 'golden age' of tennis between the two world wars

Billie Jean King's entry onto court for 'the battle of the sexes'

John McEnroe in argument with an umpire

Martina Navratilova resurgent

The Serena Williams serve in 2010

After losing the 2012 Australian Open final to Novak Djokovic, an exhausted
Rafael Nadal has to make a speech in front of the suits

Jo Wilfrid's Tsonga's trademark victory leap

The Roger Federer backhand

Still from *Pat and Mike*, directed by George Cukor in 1952.
Gorgeous Gussie poses with Katharine Hepburn

of feet crossing a station and boarding a train. Once on board, they meet under a table – accidentally ... perhaps. The camera moves up to show Guy Haines, a tennis star, and Bruno Anthony. Bruno is excessively friendly and over the course of their shared train journey, he sets out the plot that is to entangle the innocent sportsman: they are to exchange murders. At first the improbably good-looking Guy treats this as a joke, but he rapidly becomes entangled in a nightmare when Bruno strangles Guy's estranged wife, who is refusing to divorce him.

Guy, is of course, unwilling to honour his side of the 'bargain'. Yet he does actually want his wife out of the way so that he can remarry and this secret desire leads him to behave so suspiciously that the police become convinced of his guilt.

The plot thus functions as a metaphor for the shameful secret of unacknowledged homosexuality. Guy's guilty feelings and his behaviour symbolise the guilt of the closeted homosexual. The mesmerising performance of Robert Walker as Bruno transforms the psychopath into a living embodiment of homosexual panic and paranoia as he creepily insinuates himself into the tennis player's life as his friend, only to pursue him vindictively when Guy refuses to murder Bruno's father. Bruno's theatrical manner and his relationship with his indulgent mother hint at his queerness and it was probably no accident that Hitchcock chose to make Guy a player of the 'sissy' game. Ironically, Farley Granger, playing the hero, was bisexual and had had at least one sexual relationship with a man, about which he is quite open and unashamed in his autobiography, saying that it seemed like the most natural thing in the world.[7]

It was to be some years before issues concerning gender became front-line tennis news. Meanwhile, the problem of money was rapidly becoming intractable.

16

Opening play

IN 1959 DAVID GRAY, TENNIS CORRESPONDENT to the *Guardian*, described a lacklustre Wimbledon that had 'hardly set the Thames on fire'. Two years later, in 1961, he reported another frustrating tournament, in which, 'compared with a golden year like 1949 the standard of play was not particularly high'. He noted ominously that 'Wimbledon is still closed to Mr J. Kramer's company of champions-cum-lawn-tennis-businessmen'. Profits at the All England tournament were decreasing and no one could be blind to the way in which the professional tour was eating into the amateur game.[1]

Gray's frustration arose from the failure the previous year of the International Lawn Tennis Federation to pass a motion that would have paved the way for open tournaments in 1961. New rules would have limited expenses-paid play abroad to 150 days a year and laid down clear and strict rates for subsistence payments. The President, the Duke of Devonshire, advised the members to accept them, asking the rhetorical question: 'How many people can afford to play lawn tennis for love nowadays without a private income?' But the distinction between amateur and professional remained and the proposal pleased neither those who felt that unless players were fully professional – permitted to earn as much as they could throughout the year – the drain into the professional ranks would merely increase; nor those who wished to defend amateur status at all costs and feared losing control of the game to promoters bent primarily on making a profit.

The motion had been lost by only three votes, and on all sides there was dismay. Gray felt that 'it seems that several large and influential nations – Britain and France are honourable exceptions – are quite happy to go on for years talking and theorising, but taking no positive action to prevent abuses and invasions of the laws governing expenses'. So matters rumbled on unresolved until the summer of 1967.

The pro tour previously run by Kramer had always been tough. As had the Tilden group in the 1930s, the tour usually travelled through the night – hundreds of miles from one stop to the next across America – in order to set up the mobile court in time for the next match. Because the tour started in December, after Forest Hills, this often meant bad weather – driving through snow – although after the mid-1950s jet travel began to be possible, for the players at least. It was, confessed Kramer, a lonely and hectic existence. 'Many of the guys ended up divorced.' And it wasn't as if the tour was a sure-fire money maker. It was necessary to play five matches a week for ten weeks in order to make a profit; and if well-publicised matches with big names pulled in a lot of money, the tour also sometimes found itself playing in school gyms and makeshift halls and barely breaking even. By the late 1960s it was languishing. It was insufficiently publicised and besides, audiences grew weary of seeing the same players beat one another time and again in matches that were essentially meaningless; and the players were ageing and had grown stale.

To add to its difficulties, in 1967 a new promoter, David Dixon, from New Orleans, started a fresh tour, World Championship Tennis (WCT), or the 'Handsome Eight'. He enlisted the help of Dallas oilman, Lamar Hunt, who had already had success in the world of American football. By signing up the Wimbledon champion of that year, the dashingly moustachioed John Newcombe; semi-finalists Roger Taylor, the UK's number one, and Niki Pilic from Yugoslavia; plus Cliff Drysdale, the leading

South African player, he convinced Herman David, Chairman of the All England Club, that the writing was on the wall.

On 14 December 1967 the British Lawn Tennis Association (LTA) voted to abolish the distinction between amateur and professional players. It was the immense prestige of Wimbledon, then and now considered the most important and most 'traditional' tournament of all, that permitted its officials to take such a radical decision. The proposal was then taken to the International LawnTennis Federation (ILTF), where a number of countries, including the Australians, opposed the move. The Soviet Union also supported the continuation of amateur status. State officials in the Eastern bloc had an iron grip on the game and may have felt that a professional tour would challenge their power. Amateur status also benefited their players, none of whom was absolutely of the top rank, by removing the strongest opposition and increasing the chances of their player winning a major.

However, the hard-won support of the United States saw the measure accepted internationally. In 1968 the first open tennis tournament was the British Hard Courts Championship at Bournemouth. This was followed by the first open Wimbledon.

Some months before that, in February 1968, the WCT (the Dixon–Lamar Hunt tour) staged its inaugural event in Kansas City. David Gray thought the disagreeable and unglamorous location 'made Wolverhampton [a dreary, Midlands industrial town] look like Athens'.[2] But this was the new commercial approach to the game, and aimed to turn it into a popular sport more like baseball or football than the old 'sissy' affair. On a converted ice rink, the players squared off, watched by an audience that barely filled a sixth of the arena. It was freezing cold, both outside and in. The Astroturf that had been laid didn't fully cover the ice surround, so players kept slipping. A new system of scoring, based on the cumulative table-tennis system, was used. The players wore garish colours instead of white. Rock'n'roll 'tennis dances' entertained the crowd between the matches.

To the traditionalists all this was a hideous form of sacrilege.

Yet the audience was made up of 'the usual solid, middle-class American tennis crowd' and the tennis itself, when it was exciting and tense, 'won', David Gray felt. It wasn't that the new razzmatazz was insignificant – far from it – but, Gray believed, the game itself was strong enough to transcend the new promoters.

In June came the first open Wimbledon. Thirteen former champions played in the main events. Don Budge and Bobby Riggs appeared in the veterans' draw.

At both Roland Garros and Wimbledon, 1968 seemed to be a marvellous year. 'A huge family quarrel had ended and we were all brothers and sisters again,' wrote Richard Evans. The mood was one of jubilant celebration. There were epic matches, such as that between Gonzales and Charlie Pasarell, described in Chapter 3, and it was the old pros who came out on top. Rosewall won in Paris and Rod Laver at Wimbledon.

The euphoria did not last and was followed by several years of turmoil and uncertainty. Herman David and the All England Club, having made their radical gesture and risked Britain's expulsion from the ILTF and the Davis Cup, lapsed back into negativism, fearing Lamar Hunt as a bogeyman who wanted to take over the game, including Wimbledon, completely. No one had worked out how tournaments and tours were to be organised. The attitude of the amateur officials who ran them was unremittingly hostile. They still clung to their privileges and their control of the game. Some – perhaps most – were genuinely worried about 'opening the temple to the money changers' as one official put it. They cited the 'amateur spirit', the sportsmanship that they feared would be lost, although 'shamateurism' itself was the very opposite of that ideal.

At the end of the sixties amateur players were controlled by amateur national associations and the professionals by one of two groups as the game was splintering between the rival tours: the old Kramer tour, subsequently taken over by the former player, Tony Trabert and by 1968 known as George MacCall's National Tennis League (NTL); and Dixon's new WCT. The promoters would not allow 'their' players to enter events at which players from the rival tour appeared. This meant, for example, that despite the perceived good will, NTL players entered at Roland Garros in 1969, but not those signed up by the WCT. There were still numerous tournaments that only amateurs were entitled to enter. There were also 'registered' players who depended on their national federations and could not play in 'pro' events, but were entitled to receive prize money at open events. Finally there were a few freelance professionals, notably Lew Hoad, whose back troubles had taken him into semi-retirement. The whole situation was chaotic and confused.

By 1970 three men were beginning to work out what had to be done: the Davis Cup captains of France and the US respectively, Philippe Chatrier and Donald Dell, and Jack Kramer himself. Kramer's idea was for what he called a 'Grand Prix' with a fixed schedule of tournaments, a ranking system based on the awarding of points and an end-of-year event for the top eight players.

This system became the brainchild of the ILTF, but had to contend with the growing success of the World Tour Championships, which soon incorporated the NTL tour under the direction of Lamar Hunt when Dixon withdrew. With the help of the ex-British Davis Cup player, Mike Davies, as his executive director, Hunt was beginning to develop a properly organised tour, largely along the lines Kramer had suggested. Players would be signed with proper contracts to play a given number of tournaments and a points system would be introduced to create rankings. The whole thing would culminate in an end-of-year championship in which the eight best players would square off.

In 1971 this WCT world tour was taking shape. Even in the United States, where tennis had a low profile by comparison with other sports, it aroused significant interest. Televised by NBC, intense dramatic matches launched the game into the American consciousness in a new way. However, the tour clashed with the major established 'amateur' events of the tennis season. For example, to the annoyance of Philippe Chatrier, the WCT players did not show up at Roland Garros in 1971, because they had embarked on their (very successful) tour in the US. The following year the players bypassed the US Open.

The ILTF continued its open hostility and this threatened to develop into all-out war as they limited the number of tournaments in which professionals were allowed to play. The greater the success of the WCT, the more fearful and hostile the old guard became. In July of that year the ILTF passed a resolution that would ban all WCT players from tournaments from January 1972.

Mike Davies brought in Teddy Tinling to try to open dialogue between the warring camps. Given Tinling's skill as a communicator, this kept the whole project alive, but sports columnist J. L. Manning, for example, sneered: 'How sick can a game be when it needs a dress-designer to solve its problems?'[3] – and Tinling's intervention solved nothing. However, in 1972 the ILTF president Alan Heyman came to an agreement with Hunt whereby the WCT tour would operate in the first months of the year and from May the ITLF Grand Prix would take over.

The players themselves had done well out of the years of dissension as Hunt began to build a new tennis with television, which brought a growing audience and lucrative sponsorship deals. Yet they had no say at all in how the game was to be run. As amateurs they had been controlled by their various national associations – Australian and American players, for example, were not even allowed to leave their country without permission from their national associations. As professionals under contract to the WCT they had equally little room for manoeuvre. Now that the ILTF and Lamar Hunt's WCT had combined, they would be, they felt, completely powerless.

For years there had been talk of a players' union, but it was only now, in the face of a monolithic employer, that the Association of Tennis Professionals, the ATP, was finally formed. As the drama of the final of the US Open between Ilie Nastase and Arthur Ashe was playing out at Forest Hills West Side Tennis Club, a group of players met in one of its lounges to form their professional association, with Jack Kramer as its executive director, Cliff Drysdale as its president and an eleven-member board that included Arthur Ashe, Stan Smith, Niki Pilic and British players Mark Cox and John Barrett.

Kramer spent the winter talking with amateur officials all round the world. He explained that the motives of the new organisation were not antagonistic and that the players wanted everyone to work together in harmony. But the seeds of conflict remained, not least in the overlapping scheduling arrangements, and sooner or later there was bound to be a conflagration.

The spark came in May 1973. The Yugoslav national federation expected their number 1, Pilic, to play in a Davis Cup encounter with New Zealand, but this clashed with a WCT event at which he was contracted to appear. The head of the Yugoslav tennis federation, General Korac, who happened also to be Pilic's uncle-in-law, claimed that Pilic had given a categorical promise to play, but Pilic maintained otherwise and was able to prove that his promise had been conditional. Korac nevertheless suspended him for nine months. The ILTF, who would normally have rubber-stamped the suspension, agreed to a review under pressure from Philippe Chatrier, who wanted Pilic to play at Roland Garros, but although the suspension was reduced to one month, this would still prevent Pilic from playing at Wimbledon. The fledgling ATP had supported the Yugoslav from the outset and this was their big test.

Support rapidly began to build for a players' boycott of Wimbledon and any other tournament from which Pilic was barred. The ILTF maintained a hubristic disbelief that the players would actually be prepared to sacrifice the most important tournament in the world, but the players held firm and the hubris turned to fury. For the British press – and the public – the only important thing was Wimbledon and once again, as in the late 1950s, Kramer was portrayed as the greedy bogeyman bent on destroying it. He was no longer welcome as a BBC commentator alongside Dan Maskell.

The ATP attempted to take out an injunction against the ILTF, but a British judge refused to grant it, further provoking the fury of the press. Pilic crumbled under the pressure, offered to withdraw his name from the draw and flew home, but Kramer and his supporters knew that this was a fight that had to be won if the ATP was to have any credibility in the future. Players were under pressure from their national associations to ignore the boycott. The British members of the ATP board eventually voted to play, as did Stan Smith, the reigning champion, but they did not command a majority and the boycott remained.

The ATP assured its own future by remaining resolute, but there were casualties among the players: for example, Roger Taylor, the British player, a semi-finalist at Wimbledon, who had joined Dixon's 'Handsome Eight' and was indeed tall, dark and handsome. His father had been a miner and a staunch union man. Now the son was put under huge pressure to support Wimbledon and break the boycott, which he eventually did – the equivalent of crossing a picket line. He was never the same player afterwards. Rosewall supported the boycott and thereby renounced what was probably, now that he was thirty-eight years old, his last chance of winning Wimbledon, the one trophy he had never held. Stan Smith, winner in 1972, nobly refused to defend his title in spite of having voted against the boycott. He too, never recovered his previous form.

Strangely, as it seemed to the ill-informed British public, the Eastern Europeans were instructed by their various national associations to play; and they did. Ilie Nastase from Romania, losing finalist to Stan Smith the previous year and recent winner at Roland Garros, should, on paper, have won the tournament, but did not and also faded subsequently. Jan Kodes from Czechoslovakia won a devalued championship, defeating the Russian Alex Metreveli in the final. There was a widespread assumption that the underrated Czech would never even have got to the final in a normal year, but he redeemed himself at the US Open, where everyone played and where he again reached the final, only losing to former Wimbledon winner John Newcombe.

The success of the ATP Wimbledon boycott led to the formation of a professional council to run what had now become a world-wide sport – even if the All England Club, and to a large extent the British public refused to recognise this. The Men's International Professional Tennis Council (MIPTC) was to consist of three ATP representatives, three ILTF members and three members representing the tournament directors. The council was to elect its own chairman. Richard Evans became ATP press officer. In this new position he was to play an important role in the modernisation, organisation and restructuring of the game and, with the arrival of the computer, saw the creation of the points system that would rationalise the ranking and seeding of the players. Amateur officials could no longer act in the patrician manner of Perry Jones of the Los Angeles Tennis Club, treating players 'like cattle' and maintaining the obsolete distinction between the grand members of various exclusive clubs and the 'mere' professionals.

Yet, as most of those who lived through this turbulent period acknowledged, there was loss as well as gain. In a sense, both sides had been right in their assessment of the situation. The amateur game was out of date and clung to a model of sportsmanship that had lost its meaning, it was class-ridden and snobbish. On the other hand, big-time, big-money professional tennis *did* mean a different kind of game, a game tailored for television audiences who were by no means tennis experts. It *did* open the door to the 'money changers' who in future years would chase profit at all costs.

Those who recorded those years could look back at the amateur era with justifiable nostalgia on two counts. There had been tremendous comradeship among the groups of players who toured the world together in the jet age. They were friends off court even if they were rivals on. This sense of camaraderie was especially highly developed among the Australians. Harry Hopman had welded his team with a strict training programme, but had also built the sense of a team whose members supported one another. A poignant example was Roy Emerson's offer in 1968 to take six weeks off in order to help his mate Lew Hoad get fit and prepared to play Wimbledon. Emerson was a Wimbledon champion himself, one of those slightly less outstanding players who had benefited from the continual haemorrhage of players to the professional ranks, but he was willing to reduce his own chances of winning again by helping his great buddy to a magnificent comeback, although in the event Hoad didn't take up his offer. Kramer's pro troupe in the 1950s had also been a band of brothers, a travelling posse away from home for weeks and even months at a time, reliant solely on one another for companionship.

The South African Gordon Forbes travelled with his sister, also a top player and his doubles partner, and described a joyous amateur life of friendship and fun. It was true that by the 1950s, indeed before the war, the amateur game was no longer amateur, that it was unfair, snobbish and pompous. Yet there was another side to it, as Forbes recalled.

> They were so simple, those little English tournaments, so utterly artless. Home made if you like … club houses of old brick and inside all the woodwork nearly worn out. Floors, tables, bashed-up little bars. In the change-rooms, wooden lockers, wet floors and nice old smells, musty as the Devil … they were open hearted and they allowed ordinary people to play them. Everything was absolutely fair and square.[4]

David Gray, too, remembered the magic of these old-fashioned tournaments, and especially the last ever played at Hoylake, Cheshire in 1967. The matches were played on public courts in the early evening with local players and international stars mucking in together. There were then no corporate sponsors, only the leader of the local council for John Newcombe to thank when he won the tournament, hot on the heels of his victory at Wimbledon; there was no corporate hospitality with invited guests called to a champagne lunch just as the big match of the day was hotting up, only a refreshment tent with tea and sandwiches, staffed by

volunteers. (Even in the twenty-first century the Eastbourne tournament has retained a little of this atmosphere in its small, grassy
grounds, its tents and its folding chairs from which to watch international players at close range.)

When Forbes was on the tour he encountered a riot of
eccentric personalities. Although most of the players were 'reasonably sane', notably the incorrigibly normal Australians, there
were dozens of 'colourful lunatics'. The Dane, Torben Ulrich,
for example, who was a jazz clarinettist as well as a top tennis
player, sported the then unheard-of decoration of a beard and
moustache and indulged in deep, incomprehensible philosoph-
ical conversations with his friend Don Candy, whose speciality
was surreal engagements with linesmen. Above all there was Art
Larsen, with whom Forbes once played doubles, in the finals of
the year-end Paris tournament. Forbes heard several different
stories about the reasons for the American's superstitions; perhaps
he had not, after all, witnessed the slaughter of his whole platoon
on D-Day but had been in a plane crash or trapped in a burning
tanker; but his superstitions were certainly real, so that he might
look round for eagles in the middle of a point, might have to tread
or not tread on the lines or get stuck in a doorway blocked by an
invisible barrier. None of this impeded his wonderful play.

Tennis also remained a white man's game. In all the comings
and goings of the late 1960s and the struggle to modernise tennis,
women appeared on the court, but were wholly absent from the
negotiating tables. The man who triggered the 1973 boycott,
Niki Pilic, was a five-star male chauvinist, who proclaimed that
'woman is made to serve husband'. Pilic was hardly unusual in
his dismissal of women and in a sense he was empirically correct.
Wives were there to support their husbands. Kramer's wife, who
brought up five boys with Kramer often absent, appears in the
history of these years only in the clichéd role of wife-as-shopper
maxing out her husband's American Express card if his obsession
with tennis became too vexing. Philippe Chatrier's wife, formerly
the British player Susan Partridge, was only mentioned when she

'appeared occasionally to refill the men's glasses'. (She eventually tired of the role and the Chatriers divorced.)

But this was the 1960s. Women were absent not only from the power centres of tennis, but from every boardroom. It is true that films sometimes portrayed women with a career, Doris Day in *Pillow Talk*, for example, but she was, after all, merely an interior decorator. That was not a serious profession and therefore thought to be feminine enough for a woman (or a queer).

Gordon Forbes' otherwise thoughtful and delightful tennis memoir illustrated the assumptions of the time with painful clarity. His sister Jenny was his mixed-doubles partner when they won the tournament at Roland Garros, but he discussed the tennis of no other women players. Instead he wrote of the variety of their looks, from the beauties to the 'cart horses', as his fellow player Abe Segal gallantly described the less attractive. Forbes described their sweat, their smells and whether they made good lovers; of their tennis there was barely a mention.

Meanwhile Arthur Ashe had won the US Open – an historic first for a non-white player. Kramer had refused to let his group tour South Africa, because the apartheid state had denied Pancho Segura a visa, on the grounds that he was not 'white'. (Segura came from Ecuador, but played for the US and was a world number 1 in the early 1950s. In 2012 he was interviewed on his ninetieth birthday by Bobby Riggs.)

With the open era under way, new tensions came to the fore.

17

Those also excluded

B UILT INTO THE NINETEENTH-CENTURY sporting ideal was an unquestioned assumption of the superiority of the white Anglo-Saxon race.

Until the Second World War tennis in the United States was almost entirely segregated.[1] That African-Americans played tennis at all was due to the existence of a small black middle class. In an interview in 2000, black tennis coach, Branch Curington, recalled that 'Tennis was always considered a rich man's game. All the tennis was channelled through private country clubs. The black folks who started playing tennis were mostly teachers, maybe a few ... doctors. Some wealthy black families had tennis courts constructed in their yards. The so-called elite blacks tried to play tennis because it was a social thing to do. Those who played tennis didn't care anything about working people or helping anybody with tennis unless you were in that social environment.'

African-Americans were playing tennis by the 1890s and the American Tennis Association, the ATA, was set up in 1916 when the numerous black tennis clubs, mostly on the Eastern seaboard, got together to create a national organisation and circuit for their players. The first national championships were hosted by the Monumental Tennis Club in 1917 in Baltimore. In the 1920s and 1930s Ora Washington played on the circuit devised by the ATA and by 1939 there existed 150 black tennis clubs with

28,000 players; and thirty-five sectional and state tournaments. A tennis tradition was developing in black colleges. A minority of African-American men played tennis at white colleges and these players, who had the best exposure to serious, high-level tennis, benefited from good coaching, sharp competition and modern facilities. Some even captained college tennis teams, for example Richard Hudlin at the University of Chicago, who was the first black captain in the top ten colleges. Richard Weir was another talented black player between the wars; he was team captain at City College of New York for three years. He was one of two players who attempted to challenge the racist stance of the USLTA, when in 1929 he was refused entry to the Indoor Junior Championships. The National Association for the Advancement of Colored People filed a formal grievance in the hope that this would force the USLTA publicly to defend its policy. This would have exposed its racism; however the grievance was disallowed. (Years later Weir did finally win a title at a USLTA championship – the Senior Indoor title in 1956.)[2]

The promising African-American players of Weir's genera-tion had no chance of becoming star players in the white tennis world. Instead, a number contributed something more valuable in African-Americans' long-term progress in tennis by becoming coaches. One prominent coach was Dr Robert Walter Johnson, who coached Althea Gibson. Johnson was the son of a successful African-American businessman and trained as a doctor. He started to play tennis in his thirties and had a clay court built in the garden of his home in Lynchburg [sic], Virginia. He became one of the most important figures in the development of tennis for African-Americans when he began to train promising youngsters who would not otherwise have been able to develop their game.[3]

In the 1950s Arthur Ashe was his protégé, attending his training summer camps from the age of nine until he was sixteen.

'The black players and coaches of the 1940s and 1950s trans-formed professional tennis by opening doors for players of later generations. They challenged the racism in both the game and society in order to participate in an exclusive sport. Racism remained within the structure of the game, however, and class snobbery continued to permeate it even among blacks.'[4]

In 1940 Don Budge played an exhibition match against a talented black player, Jimmie McDaniel. The match was sponsored by Wilson Sports Goods and played at a black club, the New York Cosmopolitan Club in New York City. The windows of the surrounding apartment blocks were jammed with spectators and a local paper reported that 'the colour line was erased, at least temporarily, for the first time in the history of major American tennis'.

After the Second World War things gradually changed. Players seem to have been less prejudiced than the amateur officials. The African-American player Oscar Johnson was accepted into the draw for the National Indoor Championships in 1948, after having initially been refused, and commented that while the officials had been hostile, 'I had no trouble at all with any of the players. In fact a [white] guy from Texas asked me to be his doubles partner and we reached the semi-finals.' And Althea Gibson attested that when she was the only black woman in all-white draws, the other players, who were genuinely friendly, made her feel 'right at home'.[5]

By 1950 sports were beginning to breach the colour bar – in men's basketball and baseball, for example. Althea Gibson reached the final of the National Indoor Tennis Championships, but no black player had ever been invited to play at Forest Hills. Alice Marble wrote to *American Lawn Tennis Magazine* to challenge the USLTA, pointing out that if Gibson was a challenge to the top white women players, then it was for them to face that challenge, and that to disbar her was to judge her by the colour of her skin, not her ability.

Althea Gibson did play at Forest Hills, but while integration in sports may have been inevitable, it did not follow that prejudice

Althea Gibson and Angela Buxton playing doubles at Wimbledon
in 1956

had been eradicated. In the mid-1950s, by which time Althea
Gibson was the dominant women's player in the world, at least
one commentator insinuated that her place at the top was due
only to the departure of the great post-war generation of players,
Louise Brough, Margaret duPont, Doris Hart and Shirley Fry,
and by Maureen Connolly's departure through injury. Little Mo's
premature retirement was significant, but the others were past
their prime and such speculative comparisons seem invidious. At
Wimbledon Gibson lost to Shirley Fry in the 1956 quarter-finals,
but she triumphed over the British player, Christine Truman, in
1957 in the semi-finals. Understandably the crowd was partisan
during this match, but then, when she destroyed the American,
Darlene Hard, in the final, 'the centre court raised only an
apathetic cheer as the Queen presented the trophy'.

   She played doubles with Angela Buxton. Buxton was her
friend and – significantly – was one of the few Jewish women on

the circuit. At Wimbledon, suggested one journalist many years later, they were 'an oddity'. Scottie Hall of the *Sunday Graphic* went further, describing the crowd's bias against Gibson in the quarter-final she lost to Fry as shameful. It had, he felt, robbed her of a match she deserved to win. It wasn't that anything was whispered, and certainly not shouted: 'It was just an atmosphere, tight-lipped, cold ... an unspoken, unexpressed but felt anti-Gibson atmosphere.' Another reporter made a similar point: 'To pretend that Miss Gibson is just another player is to bilk the truth. She is the first coloured player ever to invade a game that is riddled with snobbery ... it was very noticeable that the crowd ... did not applaud the Gibson girl.'[6]

Nor was it just the British crowd. Scottie Hall heard an American at the Wimbledon Press bar sneer: 'So Joe Louis became a champ. And what happened? Nigger boxers came out from under every stone. Same thing if Gibson walks away from here with a tennis pot.'

He was wrong. During the tennis boom of the 1970s more black American players did come forward, but lack of money and failure to find sponsors continued to prevent many talented youngsters from getting to the top. There were no more black Wimbledon champions until the end of the twentieth century when the Williams sisters triumphed, although Zina Garrison reached the women's final in 1990 and MaliVai Washington the men's in 1995. Yannick Noah, discovered by Ashe in the Cameroons, won the French Open in 1983, and the first decade of the twenty-first century saw James Blake from the United States and the French players Jo-Wilfried Tsonga and Gael Monfils reach the top echelons of the game, but Wimbledon and Flushing Meadow still awaited another black men's champion.

Althea Gibson was fated to belong to a transitional decade, the decade before open tennis ended the old amateur system. Tennis did not reward her with the wealth enjoyed by later top players and her old age was dogged by ill-health and poverty.

The next African-American player to make it to the top,

nearly ten years later, faced a changing culture and a changing situation. Arthur Ashe was fortunate in arriving on the scene just as opportunities were opening up. Born in Richmond, Virginia, he experienced the racism of the American South as a boy, but by 1963 when he was chosen to play for his country in the Davis Cup, there was also a new consciousness of racism. There was a growing civil rights movement and traditional attitudes were being challenged. So although he was the first black American Davis Cup player, his right to be there was not in question; in 1968 he was part of the winning American team. That was also the year in which he won the first US Open championship. In 1970 he won the Australian Open, but his most famous victory was his defeat of Jimmy Connors in the Wimbledon final in 1975 at the age of thirty-two.

The players were on bad terms. Ashe had fully supported the founding of the ATP; Connors refused to join, although he benefited from its existence: 'he never helped in our ongoing struggles with the national and international governing bodies', said Ashe. Furthermore, Connors refused to play in the Davis Cup, which Ashe felt was unpatriotic. In response to Ashe's open criticisms, Connors filed a lawsuit, which was pending at the time of the championships. Jimmy Connors was by far the favourite for the title that year at Wimbledon. When Ashe won in four sets, the legal proceedings were dropped.

Ashe bestrode the transition from amateur to professional tennis. He was known as a consummate 'gentleman' of the game. That could be interpreted as stereotyping Ashe as the kind of soft-spoken, polite African-American whom the white folk could accept because he did not openly challenge them. But Ashe was no Uncle Tom. Refused entry to South Africa on account of his colour, he attended demonstrations against the apartheid regime and in 1985 was arrested outside the South African embassy in Washington. In the 1970s he wore his hair in the popular afro style; after his win over Connors at Wimbledon he punched the air with his fist – though this was probably not to emulate the black power gesture made by black players at the 1968 Mexico Olympics. Yet at the same time he remained a product of the 1950s, courteous and sportsmanlike in the traditional mould.

This was due to all he had learned from Dr Johnson, who emphasised good manners. Ashe was later to say that his mentor had realised that in the segregated South of those days, tournament directors were liable to seize on any excuse they could to eject a young player from a tournament. Therefore any sign of bad manners, let alone a temper tantrum on court, was to be avoided at all costs. Ashe and his peers were taught 'first of all, when you walk onto the court you have to be impeccable in your appearance … you were to be the most courteous guy – you know, faultless person – one could find.'[7] This training led Ashe to the conclusion that 'how you played the game was more important than whether you won or lost'.

Commentator Peter Bodo felt that he suffered from the 'black man's burden': that then, and to some extent even today, any outstanding black personality will still be seen as representative of and speaking for his whole race. He also suffered from not seeming radical enough because of his old-fashioned manners. He was therefore paradoxically in the position of being a principled activist who was for a large part of his career viewed as lukewarm in support of the advancement of his race because he worked diplomatically behind closed doors, and as a member of the old elite tennis establishment because, bookish, aloof and private, he was so different from the raucous new stars of the seventies, Connors and Ilie Nastase.[8]

Ashe suffered poor health. A heart attack in 1979 and two operations were followed in 1988 by brain surgery, during which doctors discovered that he had contracted AIDS from contaminated blood during an earlier operation. It seems to have been only then when he went public about his illness and became a campaigner around the disease until his death four years later at the age of forty-nine that the American people fully took him to its collective heart as a true hero.

The open era and the radicalism of the 1970s did not result in African-Americans, or for that matter non-white players from other countries, appearing on the professional tennis circuit in large numbers. In a more race-conscious time there was still covert prejudice. Black Americans, Afro-Caribbeans in Britain and the indigenous people of Australia, for example, suffered dispro-portionately from poverty and lacked the opportunity to even acquaint themselves with an expensive and complicated game requiring equipment, specialised venues and regular coaching.

Evonne Goolagong was an extraordinary exception. The daughter of an aboriginal sheep-shearer, she was noticed by a local (white) resident when she peered through the netting at the local courts. He invited her in to play. News of her talent reached Vic Edwards, a tennis coach in Sydney, who took her on and had her live with his family as she completed her education. She won seven grand-slam singles titles, the last in 1980 at Wimbledon, the only mother to have done so in the open era.[9] She remained an exception and with the gradual decline of tennis in Australia her triumphs did not empower other potential indigenous players.

When John Wilkerson started a free tennis clinic in Houston at MacGregor Park in 1974, this was a fairly unusual initiative. His two most successful students were Zina Garrison and Lori McNeil. Yet the general trend during the last decades of the century was for the development of tennis academies, which, while they did not exclude blacks, were likely to have been too expensive for the majority of aspiring black kids. In any case, boys in particular saw a more promising pathway in basketball, boxing and other sports in which non-whites were already more visible.

It was in the United States that racial issues in tennis were most noted, because of the particular African-American history in that country. If there were no black players in Europe between the wars, this was because Europeans to some extent exported racism to the colonies over which they ruled. There had always been non-white citizens in Europe, but no significant ethnic middle class had developed in any country, apart from well-established Jewish minorities. But Jews, too, were unwelcome in many tennis clubs.

In the imperial Raj Indians were likely to appear on court as ball boys, apart, that is, from wealthy rajahs, for whom the game was an ingredient in their international lifestyle and who were as likely to be spotted on the Riviera as Russian princes or English dukes. Cricket, as a team game requiring less equipment and which could be played on waste ground, was able to take root among the general population and achieve winning popularity, but tennis was too complicated and exclusive to achieve a mass following.

However, when the British departed they left behind a number of tennis clubs and an Indian middle class who could and did play. The Brahmin Ramanathan Krishnan reached the semi-finals at Wimbledon in 1966 and led the Indian Davis Cup team that reached the challenge round, losing to Australia. Krishnan was an inspiration to Vijay Amritraj, growing up in Madras (Chennai).

Many ex-pats had stayed on in India after the end of British rule and in Madras they kept the Madras Gymkhana Club flourishing. Vijay's parents played mixed doubles at the club and as soon as they were old enough Vijay and his brothers learned tennis there too. It was, remembered Vijay, all very British. There would be tea and scones on the lawn and dancing in the evening. The walls of the main salon were hung with honours boards engraved with the names of past presidents of the club. 'Not until the 1950s,' he recalled, 'could one find a name that was not obviously British.' But in his parents' day the number of ex-pat members was on the decline.[10]

Amritraj became a top-twenty player in the early open era days and led the Indian team on a successful run to the Davis Cup final. Unlike some of his more introverted fellow players, he enjoyed the lifestyle and 'was always ready to put myself out for sponsors by attending parties ... a little effort goes a long way in this corporate-minded world'.[11] His success led, like others before him, to the movie industry. He was 'movie mad' and started his own cinema company, and he reckoned that many sports stars were tempted by film and received offers, only to find that they couldn't actually act. Amritraj was more successful than most, landing a big supporting part in the Bond film *Octopussy*. This was thanks to the fact that he knew the wife of the producer of the Bond movies, the late Cubby Broccoli (whose father invented the vegetable, according to Amritraj). Even this, however, did not lead to an acting career. He did land some parts on Indian television, but they were not as rewarding and the final straw was when he had to play an undercover cop in drag (to infiltrate a prostitution ring).[12]

Non-white players often suffered not only from generally negative stereotypes, but also from what might seem the more positive stereotype: that they are 'naturally' athletic. Whatever the evidence, or lack of it, for any inherent ability, the result has often been that in childhood and adolescence black children or children of mixed race may be pushed in the direction of athletics rather than academic excellence at school.

Racism in sport was certainly not confined to tennis and continued to be a problem into the twenty-first century. In tennis it was complicated by issues of class, but it would be fair to say that in this, as in so many other ways, sport in general and tennis in particular did no more than reproduce attitudes in the wider society. Yet because it was such a middle-class game, it was even harder for individuals from immigrant or ethnic minority groups to participate; a classic case of the way in which class also shaped the destinies of 'minority' groups.

18

Tennis meets feminism

PREJUDICE AGAINST WOMEN IN TENNIS took an entirely different form from that experienced by non-whites. The problem was not that they were excluded, but the very opposite: that they were integral to it, at the centre of the game. In the old amateur days tennis was not yet regarded as a lifelong career for men and certainly not for women. On the contrary, their time on the courts could be enjoyed as a sparkling prelude to their real-life calling as housewives and mothers.

In the 1950s and 1960s exciting women players maintained the interest of the crowds. In 1958 the glamorous Brazilian, Maria Bueno, partnered Althea Gibson to the women's doubles title at Wimbledon. The following year she won the women's singles title. The grace and dancing quality of her all-court, serve-and-volley game made her a crowd favourite and over the course of the next half-decade she won Wimbledon twice more, defeating the Australian Margaret Court in 1964. She also won four US singles titles, the last in 1966. Besides Margaret Court, her most significant opponent was Billie Jean King, who defeated her in a close-fought Wimbledon final in 1966.

In her feminine mini dresses Maria Bueno seemed the very spirit of the early and mid-sixties when the rising hemline appeared to symbolise a new spirit of liberation. It was mistakenly assumed that the exposure of the female body in revealing

garments signified a blow for social progress and women's emancipation. But soon women began to protest that it looked more
like exploitation than empowerment.

In 1963 Betty Friedan's *The Feminine Mystique* created a
sensation. Here was a writer telling the world that the American
Dream was a nightmare for women, especially for those educated
women who, instead of finding fulfilling careers, were pushed
back into a suffocating domestic regime. The book launched an
international debate on the status of women. Women formed
discussion groups. As the Vietnam war hotted up so did the opposition to it, but student radicalism exposed the prevailing sexism
of society, even among supposedly progressive men, and by the
second half of the decade women's liberation was no longer a
discussion group; it was a movement and a revolt. That Billie Jean
King triumphed on the tennis court at this political moment was
to change women's tennis.

She has been described as a 'liberal feminist', interested in
equality and equal opportunities within the existing society. She
was neither a 'radical' or 'cultural' feminist – one who saw relationships between women as part of a revolutionary change in
existing society – nor a socialist feminist, rejecting the whole
economic system. On the contrary 'Money is everything in sport,'
she said, 'it made me a star.'[1]

She was shrewdly ready to embrace the 'permissive' atmosphere of the late 1960s and use it to popularise tennis, as the
sport in which the human body, and especially the female body,
was most consistently displayed for long periods. 'Tennis is a
very sexy sport, and that is good,' she maintained: 'The players
are young, with excellent bodies, clothed in relatively little. It
offers the healthiest, most appealing presentation of sex I can
imagine and the sport must acknowledge that and use it to our
advantage.'[2] She pointed out that while the appearance of players
was important in all sports, it was especially so in tennis, since the
fans were so close to the players. Actually, they were not always
close, it was rather the relentless focus of the camera and the long

duration of matches, and of course, for female players, the fact that they were women.

King's father was a fireman, her mother a housewife. She learned tennis on the public courts of California and her mother made her tennis outfits. She was good enough to play at the Los Angeles Tennis Club, still in the sixties ruled by Perry T. Jones, and it was there that her confrontation with Jones, described earlier, took place. In 1961 at the age of seventeen she won the Wimbledon women's doubles title partnered by Karen Hantze Susman (who had been coached by Teach Tennant). The unseeded pair beat the top seeds and third seeds along the way. Two years later Billie Jean reached the singles final, to be defeated by Margaret Court. The report in the *New York Times* described her as 'the bespectacled tomboy from Southern California' and rated her 'the liveliest personality to hit the international circuit in years. She has courage and she has colour, a combination rarely found in tennis today.'[3]

In 1965 she married Larry King, who became her manager and chief support. He never expected her to do other than continue playing tennis. Journalists, on the other hand, who described her as a 'bouncy housewife', were fond of asking her when she was going to retire – the implication being that it was time to settle down to her true job as wife and mother.

The greater her success, the more galling became the issue of shamateurism. In 1967 she made a series of statements on its corrupt nature, and with the open era coinciding with a growing and vociferous women's movement, Billie Jean became a force for female equality in the game. In 1968 she won the Wimbledon singles in the first open tournament, but while the men's champion, Rod Laver, received $4,800 in prize money, hers was $1,800.

For Billie Jean, as for many feminists, equal pay was crucial to gender equality. Without her own income no woman could be independent. Marriage had long been a 'career for women' because it offered the best chance of security and material ease.

Yet it had always been *insecure*, since it was dependent on the goodwill of the husband. In unequal marriage money was power and this power was held by the man. So for King to campaign for equal pay on the tennis circuit was entirely consistent with the demands of feminism; it was not merely mercenary.

She embraced open tennis, but open tennis in 1970 did not embrace the women's game. On the contrary, promoters claimed that there was no audience for it. Men were being paid more than before, but women were being paid less and the number of women's tournaments was in decline. War was declared when Jack Kramer, who was now running the Pacific South West Open tournament, offered a top women's prize of $7,500, while the men were offered eight times that. Kramer was perfectly frank. It was only fair that men should receive 80 to 90 per cent of prize money or expenses because it was the fans not the promoters who were prejudiced against the women players – that is, they didn't want to watch women's tennis, or so he maintained. Men should also be paid more because they played more games and more sets than women.[4]

Kramer's defence of his position appeared in his autobiography, published in 1979, by which time women had equal prize money at the US Open and were much closer to equality at Wimbledon (although only in 2007 was prize money there fully equalised). To Kramer this was 'simply ridiculous'. He claimed that far from being 'a crusader against women's tennis' he was merely being realistic. To his first two reasons against equality he added a third: that women were simply not strong enough to play the aggressive game, with the result that the duller defensive game would always dominate women's tennis.

Many male players of the time agreed with him. Fred Stolle told King to her face that 'No one wants to watch you birds play anyway. They're not going to *pay* to watch you birds play.' But it was Stan Smith who really let the cat out of the bag when he told the UK *Daily Mirror*: 'These tennis girls would be much happier if they settled down, got married and had a family. Tennis is a

tough life and it really isn't good for them. It defeminises them
… they become too independent and they can't adapt to anyone
else, they won't be dependent on any man. They want to take
charge, not only on the courts, but at home.'[5]

These comments waved a red rag to Billie Jean King. She and
her doubles partner Rosie Casals approached Gladys Heldman.
Heldman had edited the influential magazine *World Tennis* since
1953 and had promoted and supported women's tennis throughout
the 1950s and 1960s.[6] At the centre of the tennis world, she was
the logical person to approach and she swiftly showed her resolve
by devising a women's tournament in Houston to be played at
the same time as Kramer's Pacific South Western tour. Joseph
P. Cullman, the CEO of Philip Morris, donated $2,500 to this
eight-woman tournament, which got unprecedented publicity
for women's tennis backed by Virginia Slims. ('You've come a
long way baby' was the advertising slogan for the cigarette in the
1970s.) Its success was such that Mrs Heldman was able to set up
a whole tennis circuit for the women. Eventually the tour was so
successful that it merged with the USTA (previously the USLTA),
but for some years ran in rivalry with it.

The success of the tour was down to the exciting women
players then coming forward; besides Billie Jean, there was Rosie
Casals, the emerging Chrissie Evert and Evonne Goolagong. Evert
reached the semi-finals of the US Open in 1971, aged sixteen and
a half. Blonde, pretty and feminine, she was the perfect poster
girl for the new professional women's tennis; and women's tennis
became part of the tennis boom of the 1970s. In 1973 Evert
reached the finals of the Rome tournament, losing to Goolagong;
of the French Open, losing to Margaret Court; and Wimbledon,
losing to King. But she would go on to win many finals.

Billie Jean's biggest PR scoop was the notorious match
staged between her and Bobby Riggs, winner of the 1939 men's
Wimbledon singles. This event has been remembered and
described many times as a sensational contest and a huge boost
for the women's game. On 20 September 1973 a crowd of 30,472

crammed the Astrodome in Houston, Texas to watch the ill-matched pair, joined by over fifty million who saw it on television. It was also relayed to fifteen countries outside the United States, but its main impact was in America itself.

Like the Kansas City event that had heralded the open era, the event proclaimed a future for tennis of razzmatazz and unrepentant vulgarity. This match, known as 'the Battle of the Sexes' and/or 'The Lobber versus the Libber', was to propel tennis into popular culture. Mindful of the disdainful manner in which Perry Jones had treated her, Billie Jean was as keen as the most macho of the tennis top guys on a 'less sissy' tennis and despised the snobbery with which it was still, she felt, tainted.[7]

Riggs, like Billie Jean, had been an object of contempt to the tennis elite, because, as Herbert Warren Wind put it, 'he had such a large supply of whatever is the opposite of charisma'. He was the son of an evangelical preacher; he was short, he was abrasive, he was usually described as a 'hustler' or a 'scoundrel', and he was above all a gambler. In 1939 he had laid down a bet of £100 that he would win all three of the Wimbledon events in which he played: singles, men's doubles and mixed doubles. The odds were three to one against his winning the singles, with the doubles at six to one and the mixed at twelve to one. He did win all three and made £21,600 (equal to $108,000 dollars), then a very large sum.

Riggs agreed with Kramer that the women players simply did not deserve the money they earned, so inferior was their play. In May 1973 he challenged Margaret Court to a match. Played on Mother's Day, it went to Riggs, who won easily, 6–2. 6–1. At the age of fifty-five he bamboozled Court with his 'girl's game' – taught him by Teach Tennant, who had encouraged him to offset his short stature with finesse, guile and tactics.

Given the ease with which he had dispatched Mrs Court, Billie Jean knew she would have to take Riggs on. One might have thought the Wimbledon winner would have been the favourite against a man of Riggs' age, but she went into the match as the underdog. After her triumph at Wimbledon she had flopped at

Forest Hills, retiring in the third round from a match she was losing. Riggs, by contrast, had become very fit for his match against Margaret Court. He may also have been the favourite from sheer prejudice: the belief that a man was always going to be stronger and better than a woman, whatever the difference in age. Ironically, though, the contestants did not fit the gender norms of the day. A man in the audience wore a T-shirt inscribed with 'BJK wears jockey shorts' and she was said to 'play like a man' by contrast with Riggs' girly game.

The event was preceded by 'ten days of incessant hoopla and drumbeating' and when it came was 'part circus, part Hollywood premiere, part television giveaway show, and all bad taste', thought the old guard *New Yorker* writer, Herbert Warren Wind. Billie Jean was carried into the arena on a litter by male attendants 'wearing hot-pink, fuchsia and white plumes', while Riggs was wheeled in by showgirls as he reclined in a litter. Both entered to the tune of 'Anything you can do I can do better' from the musical *Annie Get Your Gun*.

The commentating for the television audience was consistent with the raucous atmosphere and the scripting of the event as a contest of gender and, even more, as a challenge to 'Women's Lib' itself. Originally the lead commentator was to have been Kramer, but King vetoed him. Instead a more neutral figure was chosen, but was backed up by Rosie Casals, King's doubles partner, who made belligerent anti-Riggs comments from the start.

Billie Jean won 6–4, 6–3, 6–3, but to Warren Wind the mystery was why Riggs abandoned his normal game and instead played his opponent's serve-and-volley game, at which he was inferior. But, ridiculous as the whole event might seem, it was of huge symbolic importance for King to win. Riggs may not have been too disappointed, however, since they both made a lot of money from the event, as did the promoters and, in the long term, the game itself.

There was one figure courtside – among all the celebrities and sports stars – who attracted the attention of reporters, a 'willowy blonde', who, said *Newsweek*, 'sits worshipfully at courtside during [Billie Jean's] workouts, oversees her diet and weight programme and attempts to shield her from most journalists'. This was Marilyn Barnett, Billie Jean's long-time lover; but it was not until some years later that Billie Jean's relationships with women were to erupt in scandal.

The Houston event brought feminism and sports together. There was often an underlying hint of lesbianism on the women's tennis circuit and at this time lesbianism was a central – and divisive – issue for the Women's Liberation Movement: it was an absolute taboo in tennis.

Personal relationships on the tour were changing. In earlier, more innocent times, it had been taken for granted that the wives of top tennis players must play a traditional wifely role, whether graciously or not. Some marriages did not last the course, as social attitudes relaxed during the later 1950s and the 1960s, but many did.

Women players could get married and retire. Even if they continued to play, as Margaret duPont did, they were not free agents. Margaret duPont's husband, an oil man, never allowed her to compete in Australia, because he suffered from breathing problems, needed to be in California in the winter to alleviate these and wanted his wife at his side.

The couple later divorced and Margaret duPont found a new life for herself with Margaret Varner Bloss. They had reached the Wimbledon doubles finals together in 1958, losing to Althea Gibson and Maria Bueno. Later they bred thoroughbred horses in El Paso, Texas. (DuPont died in 2012.) She was part of the post-war generation that included Gussie Moran, when it seemed that three possible roles were offered to women tennis players. Gussie Moran was pushed into the role of glamour figure; many women retired into domestic life – although Lenglen, Helen Wills Moody, Helen Jacobs and other top stars did not; and the third, but never mentioned, possibility was to form relationships with other women.

We know little of the romantic inclinations of most of those
players who never married, or even if they had any. Lottie Dod,
Wimbledon women's champion in 1887 at the age of fifteen (and
still the youngest woman ever to win there), who moved on from
tennis to golf, cycling, archery and mountaineering, appears to
have had at least one intense friendship with another woman,
which ended in a quarrel so bitter that their differences 'were
never resolved',[8] but it is fruitless to speculate as to the nature
of their feelings. No openly acknowledged lesbian relationships
'sullied' the tennis courts until the 1980s. If men's tennis had been
dogged by the slur of effeminacy, women playing tennis had for
the most part avoided the accusation that they were too butch –
although Coco Gentien remarked bitchily of Elizabeth Ryan that
'she was always accompanied by a friend even more masculine
than she was, the Irish croquet champion, Florence Walkerleigh,
who looked like a kind of enormous turkey'.[9] More usually, the
presence of women on the court had from the beginning been
perceived as possibly a dangerously erotic spectacle for men.

Their very presence had raised the question of whether the
sport was appropriately masculine because sporting activity is a
significant part of masculine identity. By contrast, a too-sporty
woman 'brings into question the "natural" and mutually exclusive
nature of gender and gender roles. If women in sport can be
tough minded, competitive and muscular too, then sport loses
its special place in the development of masculinity for men. If
women can so easily develop these so-called masculine qualities,
then what are the meanings of femininity and masculinity?'[10]

It may have been an open secret within the sport that Billie
Jean King had close relationships with women, but it was not
until her former lover sued her for 'palimony' in 1981 that the
general public was made aware of this – and King lost all her
advertising endorsements within twenty-four hours. Marilyn
Barnett had been a hairdresser when she met Billie Jean, who was
a client at the salon where she worked. She became officially Billie
Jean's secretary and unofficially her lover. After the relationship

ended Marilyn claimed a settlement from her former lover on the grounds that she had contributed significantly to her career and success. Despite the publicity, King was still reluctant to acknowledge the importance of the relationship, which she referred to as 'a very private and inconsequential affair'. (She did not 'come out' completely until 1997.)

This was not simple cowardice. Her relationship with feminism was very important, not just to her, but to the game and to her efforts to obtain financial equality in the sport between men and women. So her reluctance to be openly lesbian can be understood as part of an attempt to protect the sport she loved from the slur of deviancy, lest this should damage its popularity as well as hers.

Long before gossip, innuendo and outright revelation spewed out all over the tabloids and later across the web, the connection between women's sport and same-sex relations had been a submerged theme. Just as there was a chicken-and-egg question whether blacks excelled in sport because they were somehow genetically programmed to do so and were therefore that much more different from white people, or whether they entered sports because other avenues of advancement were closed to them, so a similar question was posed in relation to women. Were some women attracted to sport because they were potential lesbians or were lesbians more suited to sports than heterosexual women?

Women participated in sports in growing numbers throughout the twentieth century, but women's sport was never taken as seriously as men's and attracted comparatively little press and broadcasting coverage. It could therefore, paradoxically, be a haven for women who were not interested in marriage, family life and traditional gender roles, whether they were gay or not.

Peter Bodo regarded professional tennis as a boon for them. He commented ambivalently that lesbians constituted a distinct constituency in tennis. The anti-traditional life on tour suited them, he felt, and it became, at times, almost a world unto itself.[11]

So the sport that was considered insufficiently masculine because women participated, later came to be seen as encouraging too much masculinity in its women players. Partly because there was so much stigma in being a muscular, masculine woman, players such as Chrissie Evert worked even harder on being and appearing feminine.

To label a woman athlete as a 'dyke' was a means to discredit her and her achievements, because a lesbian was not a 'real' woman. In this view sexual deviance goes hand in hand with female athletic prowess, suggesting that there is something wrong or transgressive about women's desire or ability to play sports.[12]

The controversy would recur. For the moment the 1973 Houston contest was a turning point in the convergence of sport and entertainment. The definition of 'entertainment' might be far from what Perry T. Jones, Julian Myrick or indeed Dan Maskell would have wished, but it was to dominate the rest of the decade, not least on account of the new personalities in the men's game and the very new way in which they behaved.

PART THREE

THAT'S ENTERTAINMENT

19

Bad behaviour

A N EARLY SYMBOL OF THE CHANGES that shook the tennis world was the abandonment of white. By the 1970s the wearing of white on a tennis court had come to symbolise the stuffy, snobbish aspects of the game. All very well on grass and lawns, but tennis wasn't being played on grass much any more. Coloured clothing, as Tinling had believed in the fifties, was perceived as more up to date and more expressive of the individual.

Yet the reason the all-white rule was eventually broken had more to do with television and profit than player power or hatred of tradition. The large and growing audience for televised tennis complained that when players wore white it was difficult to tell them apart, so in 1970 coloured clothing was permitted for the first time at the US Open. Wimbledon was the only significant tournament at which white remained mandatory; as a result the wearing of white became pure symbol, signifying 'tradition'.

The television audience was an important part of the 'tennis boom' inaugurated by the open era, particularly in the United States. It brought new wealth to top players, promoters and agents and to racquet and sports clothing manufacturers. The number of amateur players grew exponentially, building on the efforts throughout the 1950s, not just of the black coaches, but of sports enthusiasts all over America to bring tennis to a wider community. Local instruction groups were organised at schools and on public courts, encouraged by a growing understanding of the importance of fitness for health. The number of tennis players in the United States had grown from around five and a half million in 1960 to double that number ten years later and to twenty million by 1976.[1]

Sales of tennis balls, racquets and magazines more than doubled. Tennis courts were laid, tennis camps were organised and soon tennis academies appeared. France, Spain and West Germany also promoted the game, with a network of clubs, tournaments and tennis schools; but tennis in Britain, its birthplace, lagged behind.

There was growing discord in the wider world as well as within tennis throughout the 1960s. An international generation not formed and marked by the experience of two world wars grew increasingly impatient with the imposed rigidity of social convention and a democratic deficit that left them without a voice. In Britain clashes between rival youth subcultures, Mods and Rockers, in 1964 were elevated into what sociologist Stanley Cohen termed a 'moral panic', blown up by the popular press into a major crisis of authority. The Rockers, with their Teddy boy outfits, leather jackets and motorbikes; and the Mods, with their effeminate Italian suits and scooters, were demonised as a threat to the orderly fabric of 'normal' society. These groups had no formed political agenda. By contrast, students rioting on campuses all over the United States, not to mention rioters in the ghettoes, certainly did. Across Europe the demand for social change was equally obvious. In 1968 *les événements* in Paris almost toppled the French government. Disaffection culminated in the Baader-Meinhof Group or Red Army Faction in West Germany and the Brigadi Rossi in Italy. These reacted with violence to societies perceived as sclerotic, corrupt and semi-fascist. The state retaliated in kind.

The paradox of the 1960s and 1970s was that these 'golden years' of Western prosperity were a delusion, a dream dissolving into a phantasmagoria of declining economies making ever greater promises. By the early 1970s Keynesian welfare capitalism was no longer working; women's liberation, gay liberation, black power, Marxism and Maoism created a sense of turmoil amid demands ranging from the just to the utopian to the insane.

It was as if the world had become an unending psychedelic experience. There was ecstasy; but the economies of the West were having a bad trip. The fabric of its cities was falling apart. In New York arsonists reduced the South Bronx to a smouldering ruin, the city was nearly bankrupt, a multiplicity of dangers from rats to drug dealers ravaged streets strewn with rubbish, along with the mentally disturbed who had been ejected as asylums shut down. Governments, authority, were losing control. Anything might happen.

It might seem a far cry from bank robberies and bombs in Europe or rioting students in America to an altercation with some luckless linesperson on Wimbledon's Centre Court, yet such incidents were miniature explosions of the same sense of injustice, the same rejection of established authority, the same breakdown of control. Open tennis itself was a gauntlet thrown down to the snobbish amateur establishment and no one should have been surprised that youthful defiance appeared in the sporting arena.

The old guard was horrified. Dan Maskell, by now a fixture in the Wimbledon commentary box, watched the tantrums aghast. It was bad enough that Roscoe Tanner, the man from Lookout Mountain with the monster serve who had taken Borg to five sets in the 1979 Wimbledon final, had *permed his hair*, as Maskell told BBC viewers in a shocked undertone. 'Oh I say!' was his strongest reaction to untoward events on court, but there was no doubt about his utter disapproval of the young Turks. In 1973 he had had no time for the ATP strike action; indeed he had had a run-in with Arthur Ashe at Queen's Club about it. Ashe had finally ended the discussion 'by storming out of the room'.

Dan Maskell had by 1980 achieved the status of 'national

treasure' (or its equivalent, since that patronising accolade had not yet been invented), but actually he was a King Canute, helpless before the rising tide of the new tennis. For by 1980 tennis was being transformed from its light and airy traditions into a *television show*. In retrospect, believes sports writer Tim Adams, it can be recognised as one of the first examples of reality TV on British screens. Alan Bennett, the playwright (and himself today a 'national treasure'), became aware of this at the time, convinced, as he wrote in his diary, that it was exactly what Wimbledon wanted. The Championships were about money, they had sold out to TV and the psycho-dramas of bad behaviour delighted the television viewers. Therefore, all the talk about sportsmanlike behaviour, or its absence, was pure English hypocrisy.[2]

Digby Baltzell equated the open era with the 'decline of civility'. He lamented the passing of the amateur 'unspoken code of honour'. Baltzell's heroes were Arthur Ashe and Stan Smith, the 1972 Wimbledon winner. They were 'college graduates reared in the gentlemanly traditions of amateur tennis' (even if Stan Smith, a devout Christian, had not been at all gentlemanly about women players). How different from the 'college dropouts' that ruled the courts in the seventies.

True, Bjorn Borg left school at the age of fifteen – his teacher told him he knew nothing – because the new tennis was beginning to demand fulltime commitment from an ever earlier age; but it was inaccurate to label John McEnroe a drop out. He was a model student at his prestigious private school, Trinity, in Manhattan and got a scholarship to Stanford University. He did indeed drop out after one year, but this was because he was playing tennis so well that it seemed obvious he should pursue it full time. Besides, it wasn't college dropouts who were causing chaos and mayhem at universities across the Western world; it was the children of the elite.

In its origins the youth rebellion was an outbreak of idealism. Open tennis had promised a break with hypocrisy, a new transparency and new opportunities for players who didn't come from the 'four hundred' of America's upper class or the college system, or, in Britain, the middle-class world of tennis clubs and private schools. These hopes were not fulfilled.

Moreover, the political and social sides of tennis, the exclusionary aspects, which needed to change, were conflated with aspects of the game itself, above all its 'sissy' image. In order to obliterate that slur, tennis had to become 'raucously authentic'. Baltzell understandably asks why raucousness equates with authenticity, but authenticity was what the 1970s was all about. The idea was to 'tell it like it was' and if this involved raucousness, that was because the truths being exposed were not always pretty.

Peter Bodo was a rookie reporter when Ilie Nastase and Jimmy Connors entered the stage. He and his journalist companions, he freely admitted, 'didn't properly understand or appreciate the tennis ethic', but were 'bewitched not by the game of tennis and the things that it traditionally represented, but by the antics of Nastase and the punk, iconoclastic fury of Connors ... and we took silly pleasure in charting the battle between the conservative and revolutionary factions in tennis.'[3] They rooted for the 'revolutionaries' because they considered them more 'real' and more 'honest' – in other words, more authentic.

To be authentic was to express your feelings. 'Shout it loud, I'm gay and I'm proud' was just one example from those times of 'letting it all hang out' – of acknowledging and speaking your 'real' feelings, your 'real' desires and your 'real' self. With that in mind, good manners were easily perceived as yet another form of inauthentic hypocrisy. The British stiff upper lip had been one of the most advanced forms of concealing your feelings, an exquisitely polite façade to disguise your contempt for most of the human race, but, once also a mark of stoical bravery, it was now transformed into a form of emotional constipation and a living lie. Any expression of emotion was a good thing. In a caricature of Freudian theories, throwing a tantrum on a tennis court somehow equated with the cathartic release of unconscious conflict. The tennis 'poker face' worn by Helen Wills Moody, the refusal of Bill Tilden ever to mention an injury that cost him a match and the courtesy to linesmen advocated by Cramm, were no longer admired.

In *Towards Zero*, published in 1944, but set in the 'golden' thirties, Agatha Christie had advanced a damning commentary on good sportsmanship. Her protagonist, Neville Strange, is a topflight tennis player and consummate sportsman. He had never reached the final at Wimbledon, but had 'lasted several of the opening rounds and in the mixed doubles had twice reached the semi-finals'. But as a friend explains to Neville's new wife, Neville had never been true championship class, because 'he's too good a loser ... always the complete good sportsman. I've never seen him lose his temper over losing a match.' 'Of course not,' replies his wife, 'people don't.'

'Oh yes they do,' insists the friend. 'Tennis stars who damn well snatch every advantage. But old Neville – let the best man win and all that. God, how I hate the public school spirit.'

The significance of this becomes apparent only with the dénouement, when Neville is unmasked as a crazed killer. 'He played the part of the good sportsman you know. That's why he could keep his temper so well at tennis. His role as a good sportsman was more important to him than winning matches.' In the end, though, his ability to mask his feelings is revealed as a fatal fault. He suppresses his jealousy of his first wife, but the emotion eventually erupts in the form of murder and psychosis.[4]

Perhaps it was better to express emotions. Repression was dangerous. To give vent to anger and frustration could bring catharsis. Rage or outbursts of despair were also more entertaining than the stiff upper lip; and the new professional tennis was first and foremost a form of entertainment.

The word 'entertainment' derives from two Latin words, *inter* and *tenere*, literally to 'hold among', and includes the idea of hospitality and agreeable communication in the sense of conversation or chat. There is no exact equivalent in French, where the word *spectacle* is sometimes used, or in German, where *Amüsement* or *Unterhaltung* might be equivalents, *Unterhaltung* also meaning conversation. So entertainment implies a light-hearted event put on to amuse and communicate with an audience. 'The entertainer's only real mandate is to captivate and amuse,' Peter Bodo rightly points out. 'No code of conduct or value system applies: in fact, the entertainer often thrives on flouting such conventions.' It implies mischievousness.

Commentators do repeatedly refer to tennis as entertainment, yet it seems too light a word for a sport – or perhaps any sport – in which the spectacle is so intense. In every close-fought sporting contest something more than mere amusement is at stake. Nor, for that matter, is it likely that artworks such as Wagner's *Ring Cycle*, Dostoyevsky's *Crime and Punishment* or Orson Welles' *The Third Man* would be referred to as 'just entertainment'. Something more serious in terms of the emotions both of audience and performers is involved (even if we don't quite know what it is) and the same is true of sporting spectacles. The narrative of a match, as of a fiction or a film has depths that the word 'entertainment' cannot reach. On the other hand, there have been tennis players who undoubtedly were entertainers, Borotra being the classic example. By today's standards his behaviour was disgraceful, but the audiences of his day adored him because they found his antics amusing. He made them laugh.

By the early 1970s, the similar antics at which the Romanian Ilie Nastase excelled were no longer considered funny, certainly not by the new authorities now getting a grip on the professional sport, and nor indeed by the perpetrators of such antics, who took themselves very seriously. Bodo described a match at the US Open in 1976 when the Romanian was up against a German, Hans-Jürgen Pohmann. Disputed line calls and protests to the umpire were only the beginning. Before long the crowd got involved in the fight, throwing coins and crushed paper cups on to the court to show their disapproval of his complaints. 'In the second set, after Nastase made a ruckus over another line call, all hell broke loose. Nastase freaked out and spat at spectators, threatened courtside photographers and trotted out every vulgar gesture and obscenity in his formidable repertoire. The crowd responded ... with gusto.'⁵

Behind Nastase stood Ion Tiriac. Since they came from what was probably the most repressive of all the East European regimes, it is understandable that to these men success in tennis and the money it brought would have represented more than wealth and enjoyment: it was the passport to escape from the Ceaucescu regime, or at least the freedom to travel the world, denied to their compatriots. Theirs was a no-holds-barred style of play that included every trick in the book.

Herbert Warren Wind described Tiriac in sinister terms. Wreathed with rumours that he might have belonged to the secret police, he was 'straight out of Eric Ambler', an escapee from a spy thriller with hair like Brillo pads and a Transylvanian moustache like Fu Manchu. Yet he was a great tennis player, who later coached the Argentinian Guillermo Vilas, the Frenchman Henri Leconte and the German Boris Becker. Becker remembered him as an important and formative figure in his career and valued his support, although they eventually parted company. And Tiriac remained a significant figure in the sport in the new century, running the Madrid ATP tournament (and courting fresh controversy in 2012 when he had the usual clay replaced with a faster blue variety that suited neither Novak Djokovic nor, more importantly in Spain, Rafael Nadal).

Nastase was exceptionally talented, a natural for the game. He lost a close five-set final to Stan Smith at Wimbledon in 1972. (Surprisingly Stan Smith, with straight blond hair, a thin moustache and an old-fashioned cricket sweater, was not the crowd's favourite. The Wimbledon spectators, for all their reputation as sticklers for manners, preferred the clown to the gent.) But later that year Nastase defeated Arthur Ashe at the US Open to win his first major tournament, and he won at Roland Garros in the following year. He was world number one from June 1973 to the following summer.

Why his behaviour was so outrageous and sometimes bizarre (he was known as the Bucharest Buffoon and, in the British tabloid press, as Mr Nasty) was mysterious. He seemed unable to control his own outbursts. Amritraj, who played him a number of times, felt the Romanian 'needed someone to sharpen his blade for him before he could get down to the serious business of carving up his opponents with all his rapier-like skill'.

The Indian player found that 'playing Mr Nice Guy proved to be a definite tactical advantage', so he always attempted to 'defuse the time bomb ticking away on the other side of the net'. The simplest way was to acquiesce whenever Nastase questioned a line call (which he did frequently). 'I killed every argument stone dead by the simple expedient of giving him the point. That took the wind out of his sails completely. Suddenly there was no one to argue with. As soon as I conceded a point the umpire was calling the score in his favour and that was that.'[6]

Some players, Tilden and Nastase among them, thrived on theatrics and drama, but temper tantrums probably hindered rather than helped most players. Perhaps in Nastase's case they made little difference. Either way, raging on court was now all the rage.

Like Nastase, Jimmy Connors never held back. He came from the wrong side of the tracks in East St Louis, Illinois and was raised by his mother and grandmother. It was his mother (and later Pancho Segura) who taught him tennis, which he 'played like a girl', that is to say he had a 'flat, all court, all purpose game', including a two-handed backhand, then less ubiquitous than today. He had minimal backswing and a pretty flat stroke and he hit forcing balls from the baseline, which meant that he needed to take the ball on the rise and keep the pace on it by keeping it flat. His was, he said himself, 'basically a women's game', but with added power. With this game Connors was able to dominate both baseliners and exponents of the serve-and-volley power game.[7]

He and Nastase formed a demonic partnership with their gross-out antics as the new 'entertainers'. Connors' mother would sit impassively courtside while her adored son screamed obscenities and massaged his genitals. In press conferences he would masturbate the mike. In retrospect he admitted that he'd behaved like an animal – an animal with rabies. Bodo described him as the ultimate 'punk' (although in fact he wore an outdated Beatles haircut).

Punk was a music style and a subculture of alienation, in which the body became the site of an aesthetic of defiance and revolt, never better described than by sociologist Dick Hebdige, who pointed out that the punk style of dressing was like Marcel Duchamp's 'ready-mades – manufactured objects which qualified as art because he chose to call them such'. This was Vivienne Westwood's 'confrontation dressing'. The gruesome, the cheap and the trashy mocked all notions of modernity, taste and prettiness. Notions of sexual normality were rejected in favour of 'the illicit iconography of sexual fetishism', the forbidden and the deviant. It was, however, 'in the performance arena that punk groups posed the clearest threat to law and order'. They subverted the conventions of entertainment, specifically in breaching the boundary between audience and performer.[8] Thus when Nastase and Connors brought the spectators into the drama this was a distinctly punk tactic, whether they realised it or not.

The punks' style spoke alienation and youth rebellion. It could be interpreted as infantile angst, the teenagers with their safety pins and mess reconfigured as angry babies (as John McEnroe was indeed sometimes described). It nihilistically attacked all establishment proprieties.

Yet tennis was sport; and while it was one thing to savage the 'establishment' and disrupt television programmes, there was something bizarre – indeed surreal – about the attempt to subvert a game *while still playing it*. Avant-garde artists such as Duchamp who in 1919 declared that a urinal was a work of art, wished to destroy 'art' altogether or dissolve 'art' back into 'life'. But Nastase, Connors and McEnroe had no intention of destroying tennis itself or querying the very concept of 'sport'. On the contrary, McEnroe wanted to play the perfect game.

It was perhaps the promoters, the agents, the corporations such as Nike that wished to change the game. The players just loved tennis. That made the freakish and hysterical dramas played out in the seventies even more bizarre.

The frustration and fury of the tennis rebels exposed not the similarity of tennis to art, but the significant difference from it. The difference was in the contest. This is to state the obvious, but, like the medieval jousting tournament or the Spanish bullfight, the tennis spectacle was simultaneously art *and* contest. So whereas when Nureyev danced, he had a free field on which to display his virtuosity and the beauty of his art, the tennis player was condemned to force his brilliance *against* an opponent. It is from this that tennis (more, I would argue than other individual sports and certainly more than team sports) derives its tension: the unremitting pull between the art and the fight. So, while a performance of transcendent music is something deeper than 'entertainment', tennis is ultimately *darker* than entertainment, containing within itself an inherent contradiction and thus continually in thrall to frustration and paranoia.

When Connors and Nastase brought the audience into the conflict, this was nevertheless an 'avant garde' move and by the end of the 1970s the crowd at least in the US, was out of control. In one notorious match at Flushing Meadow in 1979 Nastase was drawn against McEnroe in a second round match of the US Open. This, said Richard Evans, gave tennis 'its first real inkling of what it was like to be a sport for the masses'.[9] The crowds came looking for a fight and they got one. The trigger, as usual, was a dispute over umpiring and gamesmanship. It was also a test of the recently introduced penalty system, probably unfamiliar to the hyped-up crowd, whereby the umpire could dock a player of a point, then a game, then finally default him for improper behaviour. This now happened. Nastase was first defaulted, then reinstated and 'for seventeen minutes chaos reigned' as the crowd became a howling mob.

On this occasion Nastase seems to have been the guilty party, but McEnroe soon created his own one-man moral panic. Nastase was a showman. When McEnroe was on court the drama seemed less about recreating a seventeenth-century bear fight and more about performing an Existentialist drama of man's lonely search for perfection. 'Hell is other people,' the most famous line from Jean-Paul Sartre's play *In Camera*, seemed perfectly to describe McEnroe's continual battles against the officials, which played out as a drama from hell, with McEnroe playing a mixture of victim and devil.

McEnroe raged against authority on courts all over Europe and America, but it was in Britain that he became the 'Superbrat' of the tabloid press and the infantile teenager the crowds loved to hate. In his insightful short book about McEnroe, Tim Adams pointed out that Wimbledon on the cusp of the 1980s was still run by the old amateur hierarchy, led by Air Chief Marshall Sir Brian Burnett, flying ace, war hero and aide de camp to the Queen. His own 'aides de camp' came from the same mould. Some were unhappy or at best ambivalent about the change to open tennis although their club had spearheaded it; and as many of them had spent their lives in the officer class of the armed forces, any challenge to authority was entirely alien to them.

Unfortunately for McEnroe, it was just at this time that the new brash culture of the tabloids was getting fully into its stride, led by Rupert Murdoch's 'Soaraway *Sun*', transformed a decade earlier from the newspaper Murdoch had purchased – the respectable, left-of-centre, trade-union-friendly *News Chronicle* – into a startling rag that provided turbo-fuelled celebrity gossip. It was a right-wing paper masquerading as a friend of the people. It pandered to prejudice and trampled on privacy, but its language was colourful and engaging and it and other tabloids specialised in punning headlines, making fun of McEnroe with a cascade of nicknames: the Merchant of Menace, Super brat, McBrat, the Incredible Sulk. At this period hair and dress still had the power to shock, especially when linked to 'bad behaviour' and it didn't help that McEnroe's combative personality was somehow expressed in his wild frizzy curls barely held in check by a red hairband.

It was not only the tabloids that whipped up hostility against McEnroe. One broadsheet even argued in 1981 that the tennis player was responsible for the race riots that swept Britain that year. Yet the press did not entirely reflect the mood of the public. Letters of support appeared not only in the leftish and liberal paper the *Guardian*, which might have been expected, but also in the spiritual home of disgusted colonels from Tunbridge Wells, the *Daily Telegraph*. When it ran a damning editorial about the player, who had only just left his teens, the paper was forced to print a whole page of letters disputing their condemnation. One correspondent wrote:

> I feel very sad when I contemplate what is happening to young McEnroe … He is a very rare, indeed a unique talent, amounting to genius, which I fear is to be crushed out of existence by a small-minded, rigid tennis establishment. What is his crime? He smashed a ball into some netting behind the court … As for the crowd, their savage baiting of a defenceless youth makes me feel quite sick. No wonder he is goaded into petulance. Should we not treasure a unique talent … rather than simply destroy it? [10]

And a straw poll run by one paper found that at least half its readers were rooting for McEnroe, not Borg, before the famous 1980 Wimbledon final.

When he walked on to the Centre Court to play that final he was greeted nevertheless with a chorus of booing. Yet it often seemed as if his outbursts were not deliberate gamesmanship, but rather erupted from the same nervous tension as his continually twitching movements between points, tugging the shoulder of his shirt, touching his hair, twisting his racquet and tying and retying his shoelaces, and that all of it was part of the electricity within, the abnormally sensitive hairsbreadth reactions, that he was just wired up to a tighter point than the average human being.

It should have been plain to see that a player so highly strung was liable to explode when the inevitable frustrations of a match became too tense. It was especially the case with McEnroe because, intensely competitive though he was, for him the match was not just about winning. It was about *playing the perfect stroke, the perfect game, the perfect match*. And that, of course, was impossible, even were he to win. Hence what seemed to be his continual rage – his hatred of himself as much as or more than hatred of his opponent. And as was also the case with Bill Tilden, it was his rage that produced his great tennis. At least at first.

In the early days his method owed less to obscenity than to pithy comments of biting irony and contempt: 'Mr Incompetent!', 'chalk flew up', 'you're a disgrace to mankind!', 'I'm so disgusting you shouldn't watch – everybody leave!', 'the pits of the world!', 'you're sitting there like two bumps on a log', and most famous of all: 'you cannot be serious'. Journalist Steve Tignor called him 'the Rimbaud of tennis ranters' and it did seem that his endless rage expressed some existential disillusionment with life and its promise.

> Once, if I remember it well, my life was a festival where all hearts were opened ... One evening I sat Beauty on my knee – And I found her bitter – and I reviled her. I armed myself against justice ... I succeeded in banishing from my spirit all human hope. I strangled every joy with the wild beast's unremitting leap.

This was Rimbaud, but it could have been Johnny Mac. It was as if there was always an emptiness in winning. After he became number one in the world the feeling was ashes in his mouth: 'I'm the greatest tennis player who ever lived. Why am I so empty inside?' He was distraught when his chief rival, Bjorn Borg, retired, suddenly and prematurely, at the age of twenty-six. Nothing was ever the same again. McEnroe won Wimbledon in 1981, finally defeating Borg. He bested him again at the US Open. At the end of that final Borg drove away from Flushing Meadow and from tennis for ever. McEnroe won both Wimbledon and the US Open twice more, but no one could replace Borg as the perfect opponent and McEnroe himself never won a major tournament after the age of twenty-five.

Bjorn Borg surrounded by fans in 1975

Borg was always cast as the hero to McEnroe's villain. Against the spirit of tennis at the time, he was the classic baseline returner. He depended on speed, athleticism and accuracy. He hit his forehand with an unusual, extreme grip and it was he who popularised the two-handed backhand. Many spectators preferred the then dominant serve-and-volley 'power game', but the relentless rhythm that Borg brought to the court was matched by his icy Swedish personality. Nastase referred to him as 'the Martian', but he was more like the Iceman, a god from Valhalla, a Viking God, the Angelic Assassin. 'A silent man with a headband for a halo, Borg was renowned for his icy precision and improbable, back-from-the-brink victories ... With his ... inhuman consistency and impenetrable reserve on court, there was an air of mystery, of the uncanny, surrounding everything Borg did.' His myth grew.

It was said 'his heart rate was thirty-five (it was between fifty and sixty). He slept ten hours a night in freezing cold hotel rooms … His racquets were strung so tight they popped in his hotel room while he was sleeping … He had ice in his veins …' [11]

But at first he had been Teen Angel. Schoolgirls at Wimbledon had for years raced round the complex, brandishing their autograph books. Coco Gentien had described them in the 1950s as 'a swarm of flies'. Twenty years later they had become emboldened by the permissive society and wore micro-skirts instead of acres of New Look cotton, and on his first appearance at Wimbledon in 1973, Borg was mobbed and wrestled to the ground by the swarm. With his bow legs and narrow, foxy face, his eyes set close together, he was not, objectively speaking, particularly good-looking, but his long blond curls and air of unreachability sent teenagers crazy and his close fitting Tachini shirts with a faint green pinstripe represented a European style of elegance.

The following year Wimbledon officials attempted unsuccessfully to prevent a repeat performance. This time it was his police protectors who got knocked to the ground. He was the perfect foil to the turbulent, pasty, irascible McEnroe.

So the tennis soap operas of the 1970s played out in a spiral of transgression, anger and despair. The dramas were hardly in the spirit of Wimbledon, but Baltzell had a point in blaming the new US stadium at Flushing Meadow for some of the 'decline in civility'.

The US National Championship, which became the US Open after 1968, originally played at the Newport Casino, Rhode Island, had moved in 1925 to the West Side Tennis Club at Forest Hills, a garden suburb of New York City. Forest Hills Gardens was a genteel and elegant environment suited to tennis between the wars. Its architect was Frederick Law Olmsted Jr, son of the designer of Central Park, and the suburb followed the style of the English garden cities, Letchworth and Hampstead Garden Suburb, designed by Barry Parker and Raymond Unwin and based

on the utopian principles of Ebenezer Howard. The architecture
was in the Arts and Crafts tradition, reminiscent of rural cottage
architecture. A concrete stadium was built in the 1920s, but Forest
Hills retained its grass courts and its 'air of civility' until the early
1970s, when the grass was replaced first with clay and then with
asphalt. By that time, the height of the tennis boom, the tournament and its spectators had outgrown the venue and it was
decided to relocate the tournament to a new stadium.

The National Tennis Centre at Flushing Meadow was built
on what had once been a gigantic rubbish dump. It was located
under the flight path of all planes from nearby La Guardia
airport. Its main court was an enormous concrete bowl, the
highest seats of which were located so far from the ground that
the spectator might as well have been watching a colony of ants
far below. Herbert Warren Wind went out with some cronies
to inspect it during the building and was not impressed. He was
reasonably happy with the court surface, but he and his friends
could not understand why such a site had been chosen and were
'bewildered that no effort had been made to turn it into a fine
functioning tennis capital', but rather were 'content to accept
the cheap, carnival midway milieu that has emerged'. This was
supposed to be the new, populist, egalitarian tennis, but despite
the raucous crowds, the new tennis public wasn't significantly
different from the old, especially as the tennis boom came to a
halt in the mid-1980s.

Flushing Meadow remained a concrete-and-metal ziggurat,
defiled with Coke stains, discarded chewing gum and garish advertising. There were night matches under a blaze of electric lights.
And all around festered New York City at the end of the 1970s,
legendary for its muggers, its murderers, its drugs, its madness
and its hedonism. Gay men were having a *Walpurgisnacht* orgy
in the city's many clubs, unaware of the disease that was about
to descend; disco dancers burned the night away on the wings
of cocaine (Vitas Gerulaitis, another blond tennis player, Borg's
friend, winner of the Australian Open, twice semi-finalist at

Wimbledon and dedicated disco and party animal, was said to wear his gold coke-cutter razor blade round his neck when he played).

Things hadn't changed much when writer David Foster Wallace spent a day there in 1996. He described the beery, unbuttoned daytime crowd at the top of the bleachers and the corporate, logo-bearing types in the decent seats near the courts, but what fascinated him most was all the under-the-counter, illicit and semi-illicit commerce that went on at the periphery of the stadium all day and evening: the selling of weed, bribes for special passes, food passed out to waiting cabbies, exchange of black-market tickets and even prostitution.[12]

As Warren Wind had predicted nearly twenty years earlier, this tournament – and the whole sport of tennis – was now, ultimately, all about money. Bad behaviour did not stop short at the tramlines of the tennis court. The snobbish amateurs were finally being pushed out of their position in the game. But the men who replaced them – and they were men – were not and did not represent the masses; they constituted a new breed of elite businessmen in a new, celebrity environment.

20

Corporate tennis

THE 1980S WAS THE ERA OF THE 'information revolution', dominated by US capital as it went global. Ted Turner's CNN (Cable News Network) and new media in general transmitted American popular culture far beyond national boundaries. In itself this was not new – jazz, dance, blue jeans and Coke had long held sway. Basketball had been spread from America to many countries by the YMCA missionaries of the late nineteenth century. Now, however, sport assumed a new domination as the last frontier of heroism.

The company most successfully to exploit the possibilities of international advertising opened up by global media was Nike. Nike was cofounded by Phil Knight with Bill Bowerman. Knight had begun his business life by selling foreign-made sports shoes from the back of his car. His rise to stellar success was fused with that of basketball star Michael Jordan. The 'tick' logo of the company and its motto, 'Just do it' were cunningly associated with athletic performance and this was transcendentally identified with Jordan, the black athlete who in 1985 appeared in a Nike commercial in the firm's trainers. The image was of Jordan in flight like a bird and this produced the impression that his Nike shoes had 'something to do with his agility and grace'.[1] The Nike commercial 'Jordan flight' was played and replayed and Michael Jordan became Air Jordan, the Nike guy who could fly, the Nijinsky of sport.

Phil Knight exploited the vision of sportsman as American hero, and the secret of his success was that he harnessed that belief in heroism to the acquisition of goods. Soon Nike spread far beyond trainers. It represented the fusion in the 1980s of sport, entertainment and culture generally. The Nike Town stores were 'pure retail theatre'. The Chicago store was a 68,000-square-foot space much more like 'an athletic shoe and sports museum than a store – with a basketball court, white statues of Michael Jordan and other Nike athletes, giant tanks full of tropical fish and Nike imagery built into every wall and even the floors. As soon as Nike Town opened during the summer of 1992 it became the single most popular tourist attraction in the Chicago area.'[2] Who cared if Nike's employment practices in its Asian factories were far from progressive?[3]

In this era of sporting endorsements Nike captured many sports stars. In particular it used the 'controversial' tennis personalities, John McEnroe and Andre Agassi, to project its anti-establishment image. ('Nike is McEnroe's favourite four letter word', ran one ad.) From the beginning of the open era tennis players began to wear garishly coloured T-shirts and shorts as part of the project to revolutionise tennis and transform it into a red-blooded spectacle more akin to football or baseball than its own dainty past. Nike became the most successful purveyor of the new tennis fashions; the German firm, Adidas, remained a close contender.

Nike was fashioning sport into the collective vision of the masses. It had turned a pair of shoes into a fetish. Possession of this talisman would transform the owner into a *different person*: a winner, a hero. The sporting life, the sporting spectacle was a form of salvation.

Nike emerged at a time when capital was being reorganised and was symptomatic of the growth of a globalised economy. Capitalism had to expand continually. Its logic paid scant regard to national boundaries; it was always international. Faced in the 1970s with overproduction, stagnation and a falling rate of profit, the Western world moved from an ailing welfare capitalism to the neo-liberal model. This rejected the Keynesian regime of state intervention, wage regulation and (ultimately) social democratic participation in favour of the casualisation of labour in a deregulated society in which the market had free rein; and resulted in the greatly increased power of business corporations, particularly in the financial sector. Neo-liberals convinced politicians that the free market was not only a better wealth creator than one hampered by the state, but that it also distributed wealth more effectively as the enrichment of those at the top trickled down to everyone else, increasing wealth and wellbeing in all sections of society.

Workers protested, but ultimately they were defeated. Societies became more divided and the gap between rich and poor widened as social solidarity diminished in the face of the increased power of big businesses to control all aspects of their operations, including conditions of work for employees, in order to generate increased profits, ultimately for shareholders. Tennis followed the trend and it is to this tendency that 'corporate tennis' refers.

Turmoil continued behind the scenes as on court. There were rows within the Association of Tennis Professionals (ATP); there were rows between Lamar Hunt's World Championship Tennis and the Men's International Professional Tennis Council (MIPTC). In the mid-eighties attempts were made to establish a system of payment for players that would reward those lower down the rankings as well as the top stars. These included an aborted effort to organise a pension fund. But as Jack Kramer pointed out, 'the big stars and their agents wanted to freelance like movie stars and the average players wanted socialism, a welfare tennis state' and in the process they weren't looking after the game.

A series of contentious ATP directors struggled to institute and enforce new rules. For example, players were required to enter a stipulated number of events over the course of a year, a rule that is said to have hastened Bjorn Borg's premature exit from the game. Meanwhile, the WCT's dispute with the MIPTC lasted all through the 1980s. Towards the end of the decade the WCT was eclipsed. The MIPTC was also under threat.

This organisation had endeavoured to carry out the vision of Philippe Chatrier, one of the most significant figures in the postwar game. French junior champion in 1945, Chatrier had reached the last sixteen at Wimbledon in the vintage year of 1949. In 1953 he had founded *Tennis de France*, which became an influential publication. In it he had advocated open tennis throughout the 1960s, when he ran the prestigious Club du Lys in Paris. There he developed the ideas that as president of the Fédération Française de Tennis (FFT) he later put into practice nationally, promoting a system of club membership, tournaments and training. This included support for the creation of tennis courts and clubs by local communes, lowering the cost of active participation all over France. He also promoted the opening of tennis schools from 1971 and 'tennis studies' in the following year and restructured the regional tennis leagues. He was thus the architect of the extremely successful development of tennis as a popular and more democratic sport in France. He was also chairman of the International Tennis Federation from 1977 to 1991.[4]

During these boom years for tennis, membership of the FFT grew from 311,000 to 1.3 millon. And Chatrier's ideas brought results. France won the Davis Cup in 1991, 1996 and 2001; and in 2012 had five male players in the top thirty and ten in the top hundred, more than any other nation except Spain. However, the only French grand slam winner in the open era was Yannick Noah in 1983.

Chatrier's vision of tennis was a solidaristic and democratic one. The MIPTC expressed both these views and his vision of a tennis not completely dominated by money. Acknowledging the importance, indeed the necessity of agents and sponsors, he nevertheless wished for money to be put back into the sport at local and club level and he therefore wanted money to be controlled by local, national and international federations rather than by private commercial operators. During the 1980s he was embroiled in the struggle to prevent the powerful management companies, in particular IMG (the International Management Group) and Proserve from taking over the game.

In 1987 Hamilton Jordan became chief executive of the ATP. He did not come from the tennis world, but was a veteran political fixer, who had propelled Jimmy Carter to the White House. Under his leadership the ATP waged an ultimately successful battle against the MIPTC and the ITF (formerly the ILTF). In 1988 the ATP split from the MIPTC, which was disbanded the following year. Chatrier's vision had been defeated.

The MIPTC had operated with representatives from the players, the ATP, the tournament directors and the ITF. Henceforth the ATP would become the ATP Tour and would run the yearly tournament circuit. The ATP was now no longer a players' union, but a corporate organisation, dedicated to the commercial success of the sport. Each of the four grand slam events, however, would still be run by the ITF.

As an ordinary ATP member Vijay Amritraj first read in *USA Today* that IMG had been awarded the marketing and television rights for the tour. The deal was worth $50 million to the ATP over three years, but many feared that IMG had taken over. McEnroe, for example, is quoted by Amritraj as reacting with: 'It's not our tour … How can it be our tour when we don't have any input? We've just exchanged one bunch of guys in blazers for another bunch and they don't give a damn what we think.'[5]

As a popular and emollient figure, Amritraj was chosen as the president of the ATP during this stormy period, but he believed the merging of the ATP with the tournament directors was a mistake and that a joint venture would have been better: 'Many people do not realise exactly what happened to the ATP since it broke away from the MTC and formed [its] own tour with the tournament directors … the ATP has, as an independent players' union, ceased to exist … the players have only fifty per cent of it.'

Key was the role of Mark McCormack, to whom credit should be given for the invention of modern sports management.

Originally a lawyer (and, according to sports journalist Mihir Bose, a distant descendant of the eighteenth-century philosopher David Hume), he played golf and persuaded Arnold Palmer, the big golf star of the 1950s, to join his sports management business, which eventually became the International Management Group and now IMG. This was so successful that the company was soon expanding into hotel ownership, charter airlines, insurance and property development. In 1990 *Sports Illustrated* named him as the most influential individual in the sporting world. In 2001 he bought the Nick Bollettieri tennis academy, by which time IMG had for a long time effectively been running tennis.

McCormack moved into tennis as the game embarked on its years of turmoil. In spite of having led the charge for open tennis, Wimbledon retained its air of tradition and purity. It was beginning to seem a little passé, however, and the Americans at least seemed hopeful at this time that the US Open in its new, brash venue would soon overtake the British championship as the most important tennis event of all.

Notwithstanding its image, Wimbledon was quick to elicit the help of McCormack, who contracted IMG to organise Wimbledon's television and video licensing. In 1983 Buzzer Hadington, formerly the general manager of the sports firm Slazenger, was elected as chairman of the Wimbledon Committee of Management and, determined to prepare the tournament for the twenty-first century, he encouraged IMG to market the tournament for all it was worth by emphasising its traditional ethos while actively promoting corporate hospitality.

Strawberries and cream and plastic glasses of Pimms were sold in industrial quantities. In 2005 Ralph Lauren designed new uniforms for ball girls and boys, linesmen and umpires; a dark blue and cream combination reminiscent of a Great Gatsby image of the 'golden years' between the wars. Wimbledon, in other words, had become a 'brand'. This brand concealed its late-twentieth-century transformation into a gigantic commercial behemoth, because it cunningly combined a pastiche of its 'tradition': (a restriction on advertising around the court, the wearing of white, the loyalty to grass) with all the adjuncts of the contemporary game.

The commercial success of the sport *as spectacle* was of critical importance since by the end of the 1980s the tennis boom was over. Active participation in the sport declined: in the US there were thirteen million fewer players in 1994 than there had been in 1978.

The decline in numbers of club and casual players had several possible causes. Firstly, tennis was a relatively complicated game, requiring expensive equipment and location. A group of boys could play football on any wasteland site and all they needed was a ball. Tennis, by contrast, was individualistic so that a whole group of friends could not play it together in quite the same way. At the upper end of the social scale its popularity may have declined as golf became the game of choice for the upper classes.

In the new world of corporate, neo-liberal tennis, sponsorships and television became key. This was to have a major impact on the players and not only in terms of vastly increased wealth. Television demanded a tennis tailored to commercial breaks. Yellow balls replaced white ones, partly because they showed up better on the TV screen. There were further changes in the game that were to have far-reaching effects.

John McEnroe's domination of the tennis courts bridged the 1970s and 1980s as did his angry outbursts. His first great triumph was, paradoxically, the 1980 Wimbledon final, which he lost in five sets to Borg and which included the famous tie break at the end of the fourth set, which McEnroe won 18–16.

Tim Adams felt that the two Borg–McEnroe finals, 1980 and 1981, marked a watershed in tennis because 'this was the last time when genuine subtlety and guile, the attributes that McEnroe preserved', could fend off Borg's 'obdurate power hitting', which was soon to become the way tennis was played.[6]

In 1984 McEnroe played eighty-four Grand Prix and Davis Cup matches and lost only three. He lost at Roland Garros to the new Czech tyro, Ivan Lendl, but he crushed Connors at Wimbledon and defeated Lendl at Flushing Meadow and at the January 1985 Masters Cup. But by January 1986 the combination of his increasingly hysterical and foul-mouthed outbursts and his marriage to the former child film star, Tatum O'Neal, were destroying his tennis.

The public was probably unaware of the extent of his unhappiness as his marriage broke down, doomed by Tatum O'Neal's Hollywood life and McEnroe's endless travelling. An embarrassing exit from Wimbledon on the unpopular Court Two was followed by defeats in the United States and finally humiliation at the hands of the unfancied Brad Gilbert at Madison Square Garden at the end-of-year Masters Cup (today, the World Tour Finals). Four years later, at the Australian Open in 1990, after early round matches in which his game had apparently returned to its old brilliance, he was finally defaulted in his match against Mikael Pernfors for shouting obscenities at the tournament director. In 1992 he managed to reach the semi-final at Wimbledon, losing to Andre Agassi, but this was his last hurrah and effectively his career was over. He was later to find a second career as a brilliant commentator, a role for which his verbal dexterity was ideally suited. He also captained the American Davis Cup team for a number of years.

Spectators and commentators at the time interpreted his anger as symptomatic of the new, uncivilised tennis, but, counterintuitively, his first biographer, Richard Evans believed it might possibly be an inchoate response to the changes that were coming. It was not at this point clear how much the corporate mindset would change the game itself, but McEnroe, Evans suggested, was at heart 'the true amateur sportsman' and would have far preferred the camaraderie of the amateur sporting world with its code of honour than the cut-throat professional circuit.[7]

In any case, even if the behaviour of Nastase, Connors and the rest was often ugly, obscene and at the same time childish, it was covertly welcomed as adding to the entertainment value of the new tennis. It was shocking. It was news. This was what mattered most, now that tennis had become big business – as Alan Bennett had drily observed.

Once, eccentric personalities had flowered on the tennis court. McEnroe and his misbehaving fellow players were probably the last great eccentrics of the game. The stuffy officials and equally the sports journalists seemed not to notice that attitudes in society were becoming more relaxed. The use of swear words increased; sexual behaviour that would once have resulted – for women at least – in exile to outer darkness as an unmarried mother or a mistress 'living in sin' was now tolerated and even defended. The AIDS crisis of the 1980s initially brought vilification to gays, but eventually resulted in their much higher profile and greater social acceptance.

Seemingly oblivious to all this, politicians – and sports officials along with them – continued to fulminate against moral decline, blind to the paradox that it was precisely the new neo-liberal economics they had so eagerly embraced that had brought about this latter-day Sodom and Gomorrah. The ardent promotion of a consumer society in which everything could be bought and was a matter of 'choice' was resulting in a general change in moral attitudes. 'Choice' was a form of relativism. 'Choice' extended to morality; homosexuality, single parenthood, Christianity, became simply 'lifestyles'.

'Choice', however, was confined to consumption. Work in the corporate world, by contrast, was regimented, rule-bound and undemocratic.

On the tennis court, the moral code tightened up. Too much swearing and shouting ceased to be entertaining. By the second half of the 1980s outrage, defiance and eccentricity were no longer in fashion.

This new corporate tennis was no longer a game. As it turned into big business, it became a gruelling form of *work*. And now there emerged from Eastern Europe the player most fitted to embody the image of the new tennis player in the corporate age.

Borg, a wonderfully naturally gifted athlete, had made fitness central to his game, which was constructed around his ground strokes and return play. He had popularised the ugly, two-handed backhand, considered a more efficient and less vulnerable even if less versatile stroke than the single hander. But it was Ivan Lendl who most clearly exemplified the new priorities of the 1980s. He developed the serve-and-return game to a new level. He came from a sporting family in Czechoslovakia during the socialist period; his mother was a top tennis player herself. He arrived in the West in 1980 at the age of twenty, but despite his talent and promise, he was for a long time known as a 'choker' and had lost four major finals before he finally defeated John McEnroe at Roland Garros in 1984, after having been two sets and a break down.

Lendl was tall and not particularly graceful and in youth his skull-like face gave the impression of an inhuman and humourless player. He had to work fanatically to become an eight-slam champion. Amritraj paid tribute to this, with respect and admiration for Lendl's work ethic, but contrasted the Czech to the more naturally gifted Nastase and McEnroe. While it would take either of them an hour to perfect a stroke, Lendl would have to work on it for eight hours or more. He was, said the Indian player, a machine.

Lendl transformed tennis into hard labour, producing a game built round his powerful and consistent serve and his relentlessly accurate and powerful ground strokes. Lacking speed and flexibility, his volleying was his weakness – the main reason he never won Wimbledon. Above all he was tough. This robotic image fitted – even if accidentally – with his origins in a totalitarian country. David Foster Wallace felt that watching him was like watching Leni Riefenstahl's homage to Hitler, the film *Triumph of the Will*.

Lendl's work ethic exemplified the way tennis was developing from the 1980s on. As work, tennis became a specialised form of activity for which training from an early age was required. A 1980s generation of very young players testified to the way in which tennis was becoming a way of life from early childhood. Students at the tennis academies that were springing up were, or at least some critics alleged, not getting an education at all, but were becoming one-dimensional tennis robots. Arthur Ashe alluded to this when he commented that the players had 'given up fun for the money' and that the next generation would be 'practising twelve hours a day and sleeping the other twelve'.[8]

Specialism had been at the heart of the modern industrial system since its origins in the nineteenth century. The wealth of Victorian Britain had been achieved by the mass manufacture of an ever increasing range of goods, to be produced in a standardised form, in the largest quantities possible and disseminated rapidly all over the world. Speed, measurement and power were the watchwords.

By these standards tennis, like everything else, would be judged, and the game was inevitably moulded not only by the sports individuals and institutions that promoted its development, but also by the industrial mindset, which valued efficiency above all. Ergonomics, time and motion studies, input and output, the general application of mathematical reason to promote the greatest possible profit from more and more activities, would increasingly be applied to sports as to everything else, with the paradoxical result, as Gillmeister put it, that although sport was the 'typical outgrowth of idleness' it was to be governed by the ideology of the work ethic, of efficiency and continual improvement.

The German sociologist, Max Weber, described this unique system as bureaucracy. Bureaucracy replaces a system based on paternalism, personal patronage and other more informal means of organisation. Prior to the development of capitalism, affairs of both business and state had been carried out 'through personal trustees, table companions or court servants … commissions of power are not precisely delimited'.

This was how the traditional amateur tennis clubs and tournaments had operated. The voluntary officials and organisers had exercised power through their personal relationships, the classic 'old boy network'. It could work very effectively, as with, for example, the carefree atmosphere at local tournaments described by Gordon Forbes, or it could be arbitrary and autocratic as was the case with Julian Myrick's treatment of Alice Marble.

Bureaucracy by contrast runs on a system of clearly stated rules as opposed to personal favours and/or custom. Bureaucracy met the demand for absolute efficiency in large-scale manufacture and other enterprises by means of the control of every aspect of a given process from start to finish. Predictability is crucial and predictability leads to the quantification of everything, wherever possible. Everything has to be measurable. One example of this is the obsession with statistics found in sports.

This quantification was codified and institutionalised by Frederick W. Taylor, who introduced methods of work to replace artisanal production based on time-honoured customs. All aspects of work could be broken down into its discrete parts, capable of being performed by unskilled workers. Since each worker is no longer in charge of a complete task, hierarchical management becomes necessary in the interests of coordination. Individuals are not left to their own devices to figure out solutions to problems, but have to observe the rules and are penalised if they fail to do so. Efficiency is achieved at the potential cost of undemocratic forms of control.

The minutely accurate management of time became crucial in bureaucracy. Taylor's time and motion studies optimised the time that needed to be taken for a given task. The autonomy of the worker was reduced and more and more aspects of the work process could be standardised to achieve greater efficiency and therefore productivity. This was the method further developed by Henry Ford.

During the course of the 1980s tennis became Taylorised too. The new bureaucrats of the game had taken over.

Computer rankings, drug tests and a by now well-established code of conduct were sucking the controversy out of tennis. A code of conduct was set up in order to control the perceived bad behaviour displayed in the 1970s. Instead of an 'honour' system where players controlled their own comportment based on shared values of sporting comradeship and *politesse*, a system of rules was imposed by managers and officials, that is, those in power.

A computer-based ranking system was set up, so that participants could be more rationally placed in tournament draws and more accurately seeded. The number of seeds was increased, which further standardised the game and made for fewer upsets. This points system was in turn based on participation in a mandatory number of tournaments. The system had contradictory effects. The ranking system was fairer than the old system based on the judgements of officials. On the other hand, it made the fight for rankings more intense, especially in the lower ranks and among the juniors. It also favoured a more uniform tennis in the sense that it rewarded consistency rather than flair; and there was later to be a number of female players who reached the number one position without winning a major, but who appeared unfailingly in the later stages of every tournament. At one time, a low-ranked player who beat an opponent in the top ten received a points bonus, but this was discontinued.

All sorts of stipulations regarding the conduct of a match were introduced. Failure to participate and conform to these and other rules resulted in penalties of various kinds. An example was the rule, which hit the headlines in 2013, that a player was not to take more than a certain number of seconds between points. This rule was instituted when rallies tended to be much shorter than they became in the new millennium, and, as circumstances changed, was not strictly observed, if at all. However, in 2013 a decision was made to enforce it, as the delays of certain players, notably Novak Djokovic and Rafael Nadal, were perceived as particularly flagrant, their time-wasting amounting at times to gamesmanship. There was even a suggestion to place a large clock on court so that spectators as well as players would be aware when a transgression took place.

Scientific rationalism was increasingly applied to the training of sportsmen and women. 'Modern sports are characterised by the almost inevitable tendency to transform every athletic feat into one that can be quantified and measured. The accumulation of statistics on every conceivable aspect of the game is a hallmark,' writes Allen Guttmann.[9] Efficiency and calculability became as important in sports as they had been in manufacture. With this comes further scientific management both of the players and of their environment and equipment.

Standardisation was a desired feature in the manufacture of many goods. All biscuits in a packet, for example, should be exactly the same. The bureaucractic system was based on the belief that this was best achieved by rational systems. The rational use of manpower was to result in efficiency, calculability, control and predictability. Sociologist George Ritzer called this the 'McDonaldisation' of society.[10] It is not just that the processes of production are standardised; the products themselves are also standardised, so that you can eat exactly the same McDonald's hamburger anywhere in the world.

By the 1980s McDonaldisation was spreading to the world of leisure and sports. Partly as the result of new technologies, tennis was being McDonaldised too.

21

Women's power

YET THESE WERE GREAT DAYS for women's tennis. In the twelve years from 1975 to 1986 either Chrissie Evert or Martina Navratilova topped the rankings almost without interruption. They crested the wave of women's tennis that Billie Jean had fought so hard to bring about and theirs was exactly the rivalry for which the powers in the game longed. These were players with personality.

There was Evert, who was a child prodigy but enjoyed an exceptionally long career in tennis. At the age of sixteen in 1972 she was given a wild card to the US Open and reached the semi-finals. She didn't retire until 1989 and her last major success was in winning at Roland Garros in 1985, beating Navratilova after a string of defeats at the hands of the Czech.

The crowd loved Chrissie Evert, so blonde, so slender and so feminine. She could be pigeonholed as the Ice Princess, with careful make-up, plaited hair and crisp pleats in her charming outfits. Her tennis was the perfect contrast to Martina's explosive style. Evert was sometimes apologetic about her metronomic tennis and conceded that it was not much fun to watch.[1] This sort of tennis was not showy and did not translate as well onto TV as Billie Jean's volleying or Martina's aggressive style. Viewed live from courtside on the other hand it was possible to appreciate the nuances of her cleverly angled shots, changes of pace and the

Chrissie Evert: the perfect poster girl for Open Tennis

disguise she brought to the court because her back-swing never varied. Mary Carillo, a friend of McEnroe (together they won the mixed doubles at Roland Garros in 1977) observed that it was a mistake to think that Evert did the same thing over and over again. On the contrary, the gradual variation of her strokes would move her opponents imperceptibly from their ideal contact point until eventually she would take the opportunity to hit a winner.[2]

Her control and demure demeanour came from her strict Catholic upbringing. As she grew into her tennis career she rebelled to the extent of getting engaged to bad boy Jimmy Connors (but called the wedding off eventually) and she was influenced by the older women on the tour, moving to feminist positions on abortion and abandoning on-court make-up. She was no clone. But she remained ever graceful and ladylike in this brash era of in-your-face defiance and her marriage to the handsome blond British player John Lloyd seemed like the perfect match.

It wasn't. Lloyd had reached a career high of twenty-three in the rankings, but the demands of their dual careers inevitably clashed. Soon Lloyd had tumbled to 356 and he humiliatingly appeared in an article in *World Tennis*, 'Best in a Supporting Role', along with the wives of Connors and Borg and Rosie Casals' dog. A further humiliation occurred at the US Open where Connors, Chrissie's former fiancé, beat him 6–0, 6–0, 6–2.

There was turmoil in Navratilova's life too – and far more dramatically. In Eastern Europe sport provided opportunities unavailable in many other kinds of work and it carried special prestige. Navratilova's talent was quickly noticed. The problem was, as throughout the socialist bloc, that the state supported sports as a source of international prestige and legitimation and the sports hierarchy felt it necessary to control its players completely. True, players in the West had to toe the line to a certain extent, but the whole atmosphere in Czechoslovakia was particularly repressive, especially after the Prague Spring and Russian invasion of 1968.

Martina Navratilova was already a well-known player when she made the difficult decision to defect, a cloak-and-dagger affair accompanied by the fear that she might be kidnapped and returned to her homeland under duress. Once she was safely settled, the freedom of the United States and the temptations of the consumer society went to her head. She gorged on junk food and chocolate, put on weight and went on spending sprees. She suffered meltdown in matches and her love-life became a thing of scandal. Her tennis, however, was a glorious contrast to Evert's, the perfect foil, a hustling serve-and-volley game, 'choppy and harsh, percussive, frenetic, more of a jackhammer style ... hitting these approach shots, just chipping and charging and she'd sweep into shots, sort of take in the court as she ran in, lifting volleys off her feet'.[3]

She was the opposite of the ultra-feminine Chrissie. She was – or was stereotyped as – an iron curtain Amazon. She had defected – yet the taint of communism clung to her. Unlike Billie Jean, she was fairly open about her relationships with women, first with the golfer Sandra Haynie and then with the feminist novelist Rita Mae Brown. Brown introduced Martina to a world of culture she'd had little time to explore and embedded her more deeply in the women's movement of the period. The trouble was that the writer despised sport. The conflict of careers and lifestyles eventually sundered their relationship – just at the time when Evert, too, was grappling with problems in her marriage.

Martina's relationship with the basketball player Nancy Lieberman was far more productive from the point of view of her tennis. Lieberman judged tennis to be sissy because it wasn't a contact sport. Basketball involved pain (as if tennis didn't). But, appalled by her new lover's casual attitude towards practice and training, she resolved to transform her approach. She cured Martina of the ambivalence towards tennis that had grown up in her days with Rita Mae Brown and soon had her in the gym and on the running track. Like her Czech compatriot, Lendl, Navratilova became the fittest athlete on the women's tour and this really launched her extraordinary run of victories from 1982 to 1986, a period during which she won twelve majors.

She pioneered the help of gurus, nutritionists and physiotherapists, and benefited from the work of her coach, the transsexual player Renée Richards. Of course the very existence of a transsexual on the women's tour was controversial, but the period was one in which many taboos were being challenged and by the end of her career Martina Navratilova was acknowledged as a heroine of the game.

Yet her triumph involved struggle, not least with the enduring ambivalence of the sporting public towards the body of the female sports star. As a child, Martina was frequently mistaken for a boy, reached puberty very late and was troubled about her own body. She tried to look more feminine but continued to feel that it was difficult, if not impossible, to overcome the image of a muscular female body as monstrous or freakish – a problem that went far beyond women's tennis, even if it was especially problematic on the tennis court.[4]

Yet the styles of the 1980s moved away from the sexualisation of the female players' bodies, to the displeasure of sportswriter Peter Bodo. Court wear for both men and women became baggier and more billowing, but, using an argument identical to that advanced by Tinling thirty or more years earlier, Bodo bemoaned women's loss of femininity. Even Gabriela Sabatini, considered the most beautiful woman player of the late 1980s, looked awful in separates, Bodo decided, the loose shirts worn with skirts or shorts that did not 'skim' the body. He longed for the traditional tennis dress in which all a player could do was 'look divine' and saw the 'androgynous' trend as 'defeminising' women.[5]

In 1979 a new teenage star, Tracy Austin, beat both Evert and Navratilova to win the US Open, the youngest player ever to lift the trophy. She won a string of important matches against Evert and the following year was ranked number one in the world. She won the US Open again in 1981, but suffered a succession of injuries and by 1983 her career was effectively over. Children were learning tennis from an early age, so this wasn't surprising. Agents were hungry for emerging talents and tennis academies were keen to develop them. And, like Suzanne Lenglen, these precocious teenagers were typically coached by ambitious fathers.

Jimmy Evert and George Austin maintained a distance from their daughters' tennis careers, but a cohort of overbearing dads followed. Andrea Jaeger was coached by her father, Roland, a club player, and became the ultimate precocious teenage tennis prodigy, turning pro at the age of fourteen and being ranked number two in the world in 1981, aged sixteen. She reached the final of the French Open in 1982 and of Wimbledon in 1983, losing both times to Navratilova, but a serious shoulder injury ended her career in 1985. This was widely ascribed to 'burnout', but in an interview with the *Daily Mail* in 2008 she described her tennis life as fundamentally unsatisfying from the beginning, because in such an individual sport a player has to be completely selfish to reach the top. In addition, her father was an overbearing disciplinarian. She was not interested in the money and celebrity that the sport offered, because the life was so lonely and joyless. She hated the competitive atmosphere at the top level and got into trouble at Wimbledon by hanging out in the locker room reserved for the lower-ranked players, who seemed to be enjoying themselves so much more than the top stars.

The occasion of the *Mail* interview was that Jaeger had just become a Dominican nun, a life she found far more satisfying and fulfilling than the debilitating life on the tour, which had disillusioned her and which she had despised. (Lili de Alvarez, Margaret Court and Mary Pierce all became deeply religious post tennis; during the 2012 Australian Open Mrs Court, now an evangelical pastor, was pronouncing against gay marriage.)

Whatever the difficulties behind the scenes, Martin Amis, writing at the end of the Navratilova / Evert epoch, believed that the women's game was more interesting than the men's, and more fun to watch. The men's game seemed to have become 'a power struggle of outsize athleticism, machismo and foul temper'. The women's game was powerful too, but slower, 'so that the amateur has time to recognise the vocabulary of second-guessing and disguise'. It was subtler than the men's game.

He felt that Steffi Graf's tennis was unbelievable with its speed, balance and intense athleticism, but in one respect she couldn't compete with another star of the early nineties, Gabriela Sabatini, the pin-up of the period. Teddy Tinling observed that although Sabatini might look like Marilyn Monroe (she didn't, being dark and Latin) she walked like John Wayne, but Amis likened her to a human racehorse.[6]

In his eulogy of Sabatini, Amis wrote that it was essentially her beauty quite apart from her talent that terrified her opponents – because tennis was 'above all an expression of personal power' and, so far as the women's game was concerned, personal power flowed inextricably from the looks of the player. This succinctly summed up the pleasures and problems of the women's game.

Vorsprung durch Technik

T HE VERY EXISTENCE OF LAWN TENNIS depended on technological development: the lawnmower, the lawn roller and
vulcanised rubber. The first two provided the smooth surface of
the court; the third provided a ball that bounced, unlike the 'real
tennis' balls stuffed with rags and covered with leather.

The industrial revolution brought about technological
advances in every field of human endeavour. Following the
initial mechanisation of labour processes, science, engineering
and design continually speeded up and exponentially improved
the making of objects of daily use; medical science increased the
capacity and resilience of the human body. Traditional ways of
doing things were no longer accepted. Methods and practices were
subjected to continual examination and reflection and continually
retested and improved. In tennis, this meant that over time the
courts, the balls and above all the racquets were transformed. Nor
did it stop there. The players' very bodies underwent alteration.
Meanwhile outside the arena itself technology radically reconfigured the circumstances in which the game was played.[1]

The arrival of the jet engine and accessible air travel made
possible the development of the contemporary tour. In the 1950s
and 1960s, some top players did not travel to Australia for its
Major. Tennis only became an endless circling of the globe with
the introduction of long-haul flights. By the twenty-first century

the tour lasted over eleven months of the year and entailed long and repeated absences from home for players. Tennis became a war of attrition not only on the court, but also off it, a sport demanding the dedication of a holy adept, a life completely subordinated to the game, a perennial pilgrimage from one shrine to the next.

Television was a further transformative technology. It bent the game of tennis to its will, recasting it to suit the huge global audience for all sports. Some of the finer points of play might be lost on screen (which is not the case with, say, snooker) whereas power and speed were readily understood. Attempts were made to fit tennis matches into TV schedules, although the indeterminate length of matches was an obvious problem for programme organisers. The tie-break helped, but the game was resistant to further rule changes, the abolition of the serving 'let', for example, to speed up matches still more.

Doubles play, other than at club level, was downgraded. Doubles play is entertaining to watch, demands a variety of strokes and often involves quick-fire volleying at the net, but there was less and less room for it in the TV schedules, which always privileged men's singles. Over the years five-set matches were reduced to three until today the five-set doubles match no longer exists except at the majors. At many other tournaments two sets are followed by a super tie-break to settle matters, like a penalty shoot-out and equally unsatisfactory.

The construction of racquets underwent continual innovation. There were early experiments with steel racquets before the First World War and into the 1920s, but as they could not be strung with natural gut, their development was limited. Changes in the construction and strength of the wooden racquet were essentially contingent upon developments in the aircraft and later aerospace and Formula One industries. For example, in the 1930s scientists developed a synthetic resin to be used to bond together the frames of Hurricane and Spitfire fighters and this was adapted to bond together six thin strips of different types of wood to produce a much stronger racquet.[2]

The British player Frank Donisthorpe experimented with a larger racquet-head in the early 1920s. He later worked for Dunlop, where he developed the first oversized racquet in the 1950s. In the same decade Dunlop also started to try to develop strings made from nylon instead of natural animal gut.

All of these changes finally came together in the development of a new, lighter, much more powerful graphite racquet with a larger head in the 1980s, and the abandonment of the wooden racquet. The forerunner was an aluminium racquet, the Prince 'Classic'. This, granted a patent in 1976, was developed by Howard Head, who had previously revolutionised skiing with the introduction of fibreglass and metal skis. This racquet had an enlarged head and nylon strings; it met the need, during the tennis boom, for racquets that could be more quickly mass-manufactured and which also made playing tennis easier for the neophyte as the 'sweet spot' in the centre of the racquet was larger.[3]

The graphite or carbon fibre racquets are made with 'up to 200,000 strands of carbon fibre … impregnated with epoxy resin and rolled under great pressure into a sheet form. The resin acts as a bonding agent to the fibres and increases their resilience. The finished sheets … are folded at different angles and cut into pieces ready for manufacture.' This material is placed into moulds to produce the racquets, which are then strung with 'luxilon' polythene strings. Some of the top players use a mixture of gut and artificial strings, but for most racquets nylon strings are the norm. These 'do not have the responsiveness or shock-absorbing qualities of the expensive natural gut' and may therefore also take extra toll on the player's body.[4]

In the late 1990s a new form of 'modulus' carbon fibre four times stronger than normal carbon fibre was introduced and this allowed for the production of an even lighter racquet that was nevertheless stiffer and stronger. The new artificial strings were even more important in making possible a much higher degree of spin. These new power racquets brought about the contemporary game. The much greater power and spin from the back of the court rendered net play hazardous. By 2010 a version of the clay-court baseline game had become almost universal, even at Wimbledon.

The physical demands of the game increased; as the ball was hit harder, the players had to run further and faster and their response times and reactions had to be speeded up. The balls used became heavier and slower and thus the game was fundamentally altered. Rallies and matches were now longer – sometimes much longer – and this led to suggestions that five-set matches should be abolished, even at the majors.

Court surfaces, where further significant changes were made, played a role in this. Until the 1960s three of the slams were played on grass, and the French Open was played on clay. There were many hard courts; there were also indoor courts, often with wooden floors, sometimes with carpet, which were very fast. With the arrival of the new mass tennis, grass was phased out. This was not simply, or primarily, because turf equated with 'tradition'. That was the symbolic role of the grass court, but more impor-tantly, grass was expensive to maintain, requiring manpower to nurture it. Already in the mid-1920s Tilden foresaw the demise of grass courts for this reason. And – if anything worse from the managerial bureaucratic point of view – grass was unpredictable, for it was impossible to eliminate all possibility of a bad bounce. There were those, of course, who continued to believe that grass-court tennis was a superior game, because the unexpected bounces necessitated more improvisation and versatility. Peter Bodo believed that the Australians had done themselves a disser-vice by abandoning grass, which suited their game. But besides being the most expensive surface to maintain it was unsuited to the many climates in which tennis was now played.[5]

In the 1990s the fast grass court presented a further problem in that the new, powerful graphite racquets rendered the serve an unanswerable weapon; matches could degenerate into serving contests. Where grass remained, therefore, above all at 'traditional'

Wimbledon, it was slowed down by the introduction of a different grass, 100 per cent perennial rye, introduced at Wimbledon in 2000. At the same time a harder and denser soil was introduced. In 2002 Tim Henman – a serve-volleyer and the leading British player at the time – spoke out against this move, but the slower grass was retained, with the result that after 2000 serve-and-volley play became much less common, even at Wimbledon.

In an interview in 2012 the head Wimbledon groundskeeper, Eddie Seaward, insisted that the grass itself was not slower and that the ball still came off the ground at the same speed. However, as the ground itself was harder, the ball bounced higher. The previous year Martina Navratilova had criticised the slowness of these and other courts and noted that the balls had also become much heavier. She favoured a reduction in the size of the racquet head; and throughout the first decade of the twenty-first century veteran players begged, without success, for the return of a faster game. McEnroe even felt a return to wooden racquets would be an improvement.

The natural grass court surface is the most forgiving for the human body. Clay, which traditionally produces a slow game, is also less punishing than the hard courts that increasingly became the standard surface at tournaments and in public parks and many clubs.

A hard-court surface was chosen for the new tennis centre at Flushing Meadow. Herbert Warren Wind described it as 'a rubberised acrylic cushion, on an asphalt base, called Decoturf II'. It had two things going for it. It was 'an all-weather composition that required practically no maintenance', and it was slower than grass but faster than clay. He described its composition of eight layers, which could 'be adjusted by changing the composition of the texture layers, the two layers that lie beneath the top two layers, which determined the colour'. He added that: 'Much more significantly, since healthy grass apparently cannot be maintained in the industrial areas of our country, it would seem that a composition court, responsive in a sensible degree to both the serve-and-volley paragons who flourish on grass and the patient baseline artists who are toughest on clay, might be the proper surface for our championships.'[6]

Like Tilden, Jack Kramer predicted correctly that hard courts would become the predominant surface, but (wrongly) that slow clay would virtually disappear. The various hard-court surfaces were slower than grass, and they were free of bad bounces. They therefore had the predictability beloved of management and fitted better with the heavier balls. Their main disadvantage in physical terms was that they were basically laid down on concrete and for this reason caused more strain and injury than natural surfaces. The heavy balls were also harder on the players' arms.

In the new century the courts became progressively slower. Peter Bodo was of the opinion that no one, not even the player himself, quite realised how much Roger Federer had been disadvantaged by the way in which the courts were becoming slower and slower even throughout his best years, creating a massive advantage for his rivals as his game was best suited to faster courts.

The game itself became more standardised. Because most surfaces were more or less the same, there were fewer variations in the styles of the top players. Once, every player had had his or her own unique style. This was no longer the case.

The technology of artificial fibres was equally important in influencing the clothes tennis players wore. In fact the real importance of Gussie Moran's 1949 outfit was less the lace-trimmed knickers (after all, sexism was as old as the sport itself) than the new rayon fibre of the dress. Nylons of all kinds were developed, but the most important new fibre was that known variously as spandex, lycra or elastene, invented in 1959. By the 1970s it was widely used in both sports and everyday clothing. New clothing was also devised to minimise or conceal sweat, to sit comfortably on the body, to adapt to the movement of athletes and maximise their freedom.

Not only their kit, but even the bodies of the players were

changed. By the millennium players in all sports were taller and stronger. In 1991 there were only six male players in the top fifty taller than 6 foot 3 (1.90m); by 2011 a height of 6 foot 5 (1.96m), 6 foot 8 (2.06m) or even 6 foot 10 inches (2.08m) for male tennis players and 6 foot (1.83m) for women was no longer unusual and there were seventeen top male players over 6 foot 3 (1.90m). At some tennis academies and other facilities for budding players, it was not thought worthwhile to develop those who were likely to remain short of stature. The continual attentions of coaches, doctors, physiotherapists, nutritionists, strength-conditioning trainers and sports psychologists with their intense application of science to the improvement of the athletic tennis body and mind was part of a vicious spiral leading to ever more 'physical' matches requiring ever more physical improvement. From the 1980s onwards, fitness, physical training and diet all became essential to the development of the top players.

New technologies for the enhancement of the human body included experiments with oxygen to boost the red-cell count of sports players to improve muscular performance. In 2013 Nadal revealed the rehabilitation schedule that had returned him to the number one position. Among the techniques chosen, 'were a special anti-gravity treadmill, which takes pressure off his legs and blood spinning platelet-rich plasma therapy (PRP)'.[7]

Sports persons have always looked to technology to improve performance. But in recent years the impact of technology has become controversial. Advanced technology separates rich nations from poor, while a tennis player on the challenger or futures circuit would be unlikely to be able to afford the treatments that rehabilitated Nadal so successfully.

In swimming, new suits had a major impact on performance at the 2008 Olympics, at which 94 per cent of gold medals went to swimmers wearing the Speedo LZR, 'created with the help of Nasa, which improved a swimmer's hydrodynamic position'. A polyurethane suit, which led to greater buoyancy, was banned the following year. One British swimmer compared these suits to the use of a performance-enhancing drug. The controversy that surrounded some of these innovations concerned where to draw the line between what is acceptable and what becomes unfair.

There was a further borderline or grey area in that it might eventually be difficult to distinguish, for example, the experiments with oxygen from the use of performance-enhancing drugs. These were always the great taboo in all sports, yet rumours continually circulated of their widespread use and from time to time a sportsman would be suspended. In 2012 the great scandal was the revelation that Tour de France multiple winner, Lance Armstrong, had consistently used performance-enhancing drugs. In 2013 this was followed by the news that several runners had tested positive for drugs.

Supposedly stringent regimes of drug testing had been introduced, but in return drugs that could not be detected were being developed by the millennium. In 2009 the Swiss sports magazine *L'illustré* cited many suspicions in an 'era of suspicion' surrounding the rumoured use of drugs by some top tennis players and noted that different nations tested in different ways, some less strictly than others. The article cited a French doctor, Bernard Montalvan, who claimed that urine tests were useless and noted the development of drugs in Spain and elsewhere that were more or less undetectable.[8] In 2012 new methods of detection were being debated, including the introduction of 'blood passports'. In 2013 several tennis players fell under suspicion.

The rational discussion of both recreational and performance-enhancing drugs is made almost impossible by the fundamentalist default position expressed both by governments worldwide and probably held by a majority of private citizens: that 'drugs' are dreadful and must never be used. The Victorians swigged away at laudanum and even gave it to their babies. Addiction to opium was then regarded as a distressing affliction rather than as deliberately wicked and evil. However, once drug taking entered the criminal justice system, moral positions hardened even as drugs and drug use proliferated.

In sport, the use of drugs in order, essentially, to gain an unfair advantage and thus to cheat, has recurred throughout the twentieth century, but the sporting world, writes sports journalist Paul Hayward, is still 'hooked on an ideal of purity'.[9] The taking of recreational drugs may be immoral or dangerous (as well as illegal), but the use of drugs in sports flouts the ideal and the myth of the sportsman as hero. It therefore becomes closed to rational discussion.

In the autumn of 2013 a police chief constable in Britain broke ranks to argue for the decriminalisation of drugs in order to remove them from the power of criminal gangs – a position that has been argued before, to no avail. Author Malcolm Gladwell defended Lance Armstrong asking why baseball players are allowed eyesight enhancing surgery while performance-enhancing drugs remain forbidden.

The suggestion that sporting heroes might use drugs remains blasphemous. Yet a special report in the UK's *Guardian* newspaper revealed in 2013 that 'levels of doping in sport are now worse than ever'. Along with match fixing and illegal betting, this was 'increasingly linked with organised crime', the tentacles of which were now 'so deeply embedded in sport that it is "inevitable" that other sports face problems as serious as those experienced by cycling'.[10] Moreover, although elaborate regulatory bodies were set up, they failed to halt or contain the spread of drugs use. The President of the World Anti-doping Agency expressed frustration and feared that 'Perhaps there is too much conservatism, too much concern for brand and reputation and not enough zeal for the task'. But in fact, the problem could never be properly addressed until the use of drugs was removed from its special moral category and discussed in a manner similar to issues concerning the special swim suit or the graphite racquet.

Tennis might be less susceptible to doping than cycling or athletics, where endurance is the key to success, as it requires a variety of talents, including hand-eye coordination, which are less amenable to artificial enhancement. On the other hand, the increasing importance of strength and endurance in tennis increased the temptation.

Yet arguably the new racquets and strings themselves amounted to as much of an enhancement as drugs. In opposing them, Martina Navratilova and others were concerned not just with fairness, but with the effect on the game. In sports in which speed is the main element, such as swimming, technological improvements have a clear benefit. In tennis the argument is more complex, and Navratilova's point was that the technology has not improved the game either for players or spectators. There is more to tennis than simply breaking a speed record and the argument in tennis is whether increased power and athleticism has reached a point at which the subtleties of the game have been sacrificed, as is argued by those who point to the monotony of long rallies and of all players having a similar game. McEnroe, for example, continued to argue that the serve-volley game (which he of course perfected) was superior to interminable clay-court-style rallies and that his own high-percentage style of play, with short back swing and anticipation was superior to baseline play.

The default setting of the powers who run the game in tennis (and other sports) seems to be an automatic assumption that new technology always equated with improvement; the mindset of technological determinism. Technological determinism supports the belief that things continually improve. This view has dominated tennis, the received view that the players of the new century must be streets ahead of those of fifty years ago.

The story of sport has always been the story of a search for endless improvement, a history of records broken and new frontiers reached. Sport incorporated uncritically this Enlightenment narrative of continuous progress. Profit, after all, necessitates continual innovation and the unending search for new markets. In sport uninterrupted technological change was central to this kind of endless 'going forward'.

Added to this is technological fatalism. Throughout the first decade of the new millennium, commentators spoke of the ever slower courts as though they were discussing the weather, as of something outside human power to alter – which really is the central point: that technology should not be rejected, but that it should be used judiciously and controlled. A recurring trope in science-fiction is the future in which technology controls human beings. It begins to seem as if tennis were approaching that future.

23

Celebrity stars

NSCRIBED OVER THE PLAYERS' ENTRANCE to Wimbledon are the famous words from Rudyard Kipling's poem 'If': 'If you can meet with triumph and disaster and treat those two imposters just the same ...'

In 1995 the British chose the poem, not for the first time, as their favourite. Written almost a hundred years earlier, its author was a lionised hero of Edwardian England. His tales of the British Raj had brought him fame and wealth. The stories had expressed great sympathy for the indigenous Indians and mixed feelings towards the British administrators in India, but by the time George V came to the throne in 1910, the year the poem was written, Kipling's was the voice of triumphalist imperialism in the Indian summer of the last decade before the whole structure began to crumble.

Kipling wrote 'If' as a guide for his only son, John. At the outbreak of the First World War Kipling saw to it that, despite John's defective eyesight, he was contentiously passed fit for service in the trenches, where, after a few months, he was killed. Kipling is said never fully to have recovered from the loss that he himself had engineered.

The poem, so widely admired, expresses the stereotypically British qualities summarised as the stiff upper lip. It is a poem to the suppression of emotion and – in the spirit of *Tom Brown's*

Schooldays – elevates physical activity over all else as the touch-stone of manliness:

> If you can fill the unforgiving minute
> With sixty seconds' worth of distance run,
> Yours is the earth and everything that's in it
> And – which is more – you'll be a man, my son.

This was the *Tom Brown's Schooldays* way of 'being a man'. Yet not everyone signed up to it, even in the midst of war. In 1917 Alec Waugh's public-school novel, *The Loom of Youth*, criticised the sporting culture, because the 'bloods' – the boys who succeeded at sports – became bullies, given free rein to flout teachers, drink, gamble and exploit younger boys sexually (shocking its readers in acknowledging the existence of homosexual relations at public schools). One of the main characters in the book daringly advocates the reading of Oscar Wilde; another objects to the British 'worship' of games. 'This athleticism is ruining the country.' At the climax of the novel, the debating society carries a motion against athletics.

In the wider world, no one voted down sports; indeed their importance continued to grow. The British Empire shrank and disappeared. The daily life of industrial man in the growing cities had nothing to do with hunting. Loss of life in the First and Second World Wars was enormous, but on a daily basis in peacetime the necessity to fight was largely removed.

The sociologist Thorstein Veblen, writing in 1899, explained the growing importance of sport in men's lives as a displacement of a 'fighting spirit' suitable to a previous age and in modernity largely found among adolescent boys. 'The addiction to sports, therefore, in a peculiar degree marks an arrested development of the man's moral nature.' He dismissed as spurious popular justifi-cations for sport: that it developed character and 'fostered a manly spirit'. What was seen as 'self reliance and good fellowship' was actually 'truculence and clannishness'. In fact, Veblen had no time for sport at all, an activity of 'substantial futility'. He conceded nonetheless that the 'ferocity and astuteness' required to excel at sport and which expressed 'a narrowly self-regarding habit of mind' were 'highly serviceable' to the acquisitive economic system.[1] Nearly fifty years later George Orwell voiced similar views: 'Serious sport has nothing to do with fair play. It is bound up with hatred, jealousy, boastfulness, disregard of all rules and sadistic pleasure in witnessing violence.'[2]

Kipling's version, however, continues to represent an ideal still enshrined in the contemporary world of sport today: the Edwardian hero, the warrior in defence of that great empire; the Bengal Lancer securing the Northwest Frontier; Gordon of Khartoum. The ideal was also that of the huntsman, for until the end of the nineteenth century reference to sports was often to 'blood sports'; the identification between the two was 'very strong and [only] ... beginning to wane at the end of the nineteenth century', writes Steven Connor.[3]

These men saved nations and secured the realm – and triumphed over Nature by killing wild animals. The anti-intellectualism popularised by Charles Kingsley and Thomas Hughes resonated with men who were forging an empire based on expropriation and intermittent violence and whose sense of moral virtue was reinforced by Hughes's version of manly morality.

Anthony Wilding, the New Zealand star of the Edwardian period, was the epitome of such heroes. They were outward-looking and often perhaps not very introspective. They possessed a purity that acted on the world. Sportsmen seemed specially made to become or represent this kind of hero. The hero's grace is in his action: in the throw of the ball, the sweep of the bat, the leap to the summit. Wherever the conquering spirit was to be found, in war, in colonising distant territories, in climbing Everest or on the playing field, it was a manifestation of these heroic characteristics.

It seems possible that the myth of the sporting hero – and it is a myth – became even more compelling as a reaction to the horrors of two world wars. The Allied aim to defeat fascism was justified, and the men of the Allied armies were hailed as heroes (and the Germans and Japanese demonised), but there was a different and disturbing reality that could not be confronted: that Allied soldiers also raped and looted, that men and officers on both sides were completely traumatised by experiences they mostly never talked about, by the killing and maiming, that war was never black and white, but soaked in blood and cruelty. In later wars – Vietnam, Iraq – the purpose and the heroism were more openly questioned. Generals were no longer national heroes in the way that Montgomery and Eisenhower had been. This made the sporting hero even more important as the symbolic bearer of the fighting spirit, of bravery and courage.

McEnroe, Connors and Nastase shocked because they departed so radically from this version of the (sporting) hero. Yet, seen at the time, as deviants and as destroyers of all sporting qualities, McEnroe and his contemporaries were the forerunners of a new kind of hero.

In the 1980s and 1990s a series of tennis stars were fated to experience what it meant to be a hero in post-imperial times. One of the ironies of being a tennis star was that although tennis remained a niche sport, its stars were among the most famous in the world, because the sport was so much one of individuals. Now that they earned such astonishing amounts of money they were class A celebrities, and in celebrity culture their private lives were becoming part of an entertainment world that went far beyond the tennis court.

In 1977 Yannick Noah won junior Wimbledon at the age of seventeen and reached the final of the Orange Bowl, the American Junior tournament, where he was beaten by Lendl. This was six years after Arthur Ashe, on a goodwill tour of Africa, had noticed him playing in Cameroon and made it possible for him to train in France. (Noah's mother was French and he had been born in France before the family moved back to Africa when he was five years old.) Perhaps as a result, he never recognised himself as a patriotic representative of either France or Cameroon, but rather as an individual supported by his family. With his exciting shots, one-handed backhand and his dreadlocks, he shot to fame when he won the French Open in 1983, beating the defending champion, Mats Wilander, in straight sets. But with fame came controversy, especially when he revealed that he was an enthusiastic dope smoker and liked sex. He also questioned the sporting purity of the tennis community by suggesting that the use of drugs was widespread (an accusation he repeated in 2011).

To the French sports world this was sacrilege and Noah was a traitor because he had dared to challenge the mythology of sport. He had questioned the sporting ideal, that the sportsman was an exemplary worker, devoted to self-improvement through self-denial and a personal life devoid of self-indulgence. Above all, the ideal sportsman must not be a hedonist.

When, in the summer of 1983, Noah lost in the quarter-finals of the US Open he claimed to be sick of the tour and moved to America to escape the adulation, attacks and controversy that had dogged him in France. But he did not quit tennis. He captained the French Davis Cup team and led them to victory in 1991.

Yannick Noah was more like a film star or a pop idol than a clean-cut sportsman. Indeed he later became celebrated in France as a successful musician and in 2005 was more famous there than the footballer Zinedine Zidane (but that was the result of his success as a singer rather than as a tennis player).[4]

The new, international hero was no longer an extrovert committed to unquestioned nationalist values. When he wept in interviews, exposing his doubts and discontent, he entered the territory of the hero whose battle was no longer with an external enemy, but an internal battle with himself. And if Yannick Noah was controversial, he had many supporters who defended him as a real person by contrast with 'tennis machines' such as Borg and Lendl.

This was to be the new template. The sportsman was no longer a hero out of Charles Kingsley's *Westward Ho!*; he was closer to Albert Camus's *The Outsider* or J. D. Salinger's *The Catcher in the Rye*. In the spotlight of the celebrity world, personal angst would be played out as transgression and scandal, only now it was off the court, not on. During the course of the 1980s and 1990s, several champions saw their lives unravel as the media played the double game of cheering them on as stereotypical sporting heroes and then turning on them when they either fell short of the ideal or simply rejected it as Noah did.

In 1985 Boris Becker, at the age of seventeen, became the youngest ever winner of the Wimbledon men's singles (a record he still held in 2013). This was not entirely surprising as he had already won the prestigious pre-Wimbledon tournament at Queen's Club in London. On his return to his home town of Leimen he appeared on the balcony of the town hall to be cheered by a crowd of thousands. That first win was pure joy. But things only got harder from then on. In 1986 he repeated the triumph, proving that he was not just a one-slam fluke, but on this occasion there was much more pressure. More was at stake. Henceforward he was a German hero.[5]

His situation indicated the potential difficulty for the stars of such an individual sport as tennis in their relationship to nationalism. By the 1980s sport and nationalism had grown, flourishing together for well over one hundred years. Fans and stars alike shared and signed up to the great imperative of sport: uncritical nationalism. Consequently Becker became the representative on earth of 1980s West Germany, which had got over the Baader-Meinhof years and was more economically successful than ever. But he didn't quite fit the image; he proclaimed radical allegiances, to Greenpeace and Amnesty International. In 1992, 'ignoring his country's euphoria over reunification, he refused to serve as ambassador for Berlin's bid to host the 2000 Olympics, saying he feared a triumphant Germany might stir its citizens' old fantasies about a master race'.[6] This fear was hardly surprising, since at the beginning of that year he had made public his relationship with the actress and singer, Barbara Feltus. Far from being happy for him, his hitherto adoring public met the news with outrage and death threats, because his lover and soon-to-be wife was the daughter of a German woman and an African–American serviceman. She was denounced as a gold-digger and 'black witch'. Boris threatened to leave Germany if the taunts didn't stop. And in fact by the mid-1990s the couple had somehow been forgiven and appeared as a symbol of the new forward-looking and anti-racist Germany. In November 2000 Becker marched with 200,000 fellow Germans on the sixtieth anniversary of Kristall-nacht to protest against rising racism in his country.

By this time, however, both Becker's tennis career and his marriage were crumbling. After his very last match at Wimbledon, the seven-months-pregnant Barbara was left at home on her own while Becker went out with his friends and found himself at Nobu, the fashionable Japanese restaurant on Park Lane, where his evening ended with a brief encounter in a broom cupboard with a waitress. The following year she claimed maintenance for the support of the daughter born as the result of this brief encounter. Becker was also in trouble with the German tax authorities.

There might seem little purpose in raking over Boris Becker's post-retirement problems, were it not that these frailties have traditionally mattered as they do not for stars of stage, screen and platform. There is a long history of transgression in relation to actors, singers and other artistic performers. To varying degrees from the seventeenth to the nineteenth century many such performers were largely barred from polite society or lived on its margins (although this was not true of the most famous British actors, who were already celebrities in the eighteenth century). A long tradition of artistic bohemianism associated even the most famous painters, writers and composers with a life outside and often in defiance of bourgeois respectability. Artistic culture, especially after the rise of the Romantic Movement, was meant to challenge social and moral boundaries. It was the artist/genius/hero's destiny to transgress. Women in particular were unlikely to achieve respectability, few were 'received' in polite society and they were not always clearly distinguished from courtesans.

The nineteenth-century sports star was very different, embodying as he did the muscular Christian ideal, and a century later the sports star was still different from other celebrity stars. For one thing, sport had become ever more central to cultural life, so central, in fact, that it was almost sacrilegious to question its value. It seemed 'authentic' because sporting contests were played out in real time and the outcome was unpredictable. 'Hence the seeming visceral, dramatic immediacy of the sports practice provides the sport celebrity with an important veneer of authenticity, that sets him apart from celebrities in other more explicitly manufactured, cultural realms.'[7]

However, the sports fans' hunger for finding out about the 'real person', while consistent with contemporary celebrity culture, came up against the traditional image of the sporting hero. Sports journalism changed to feed this hunger. In the early twentieth century, sports writers had drawn a veil over any frailties the stars might have, Tilden being the outstanding example; but by the end of the century celebrity culture led writers into making the private lives of stars prime material.[8] Yannick Noah flouted the traditional sporting-hero stereotype by talking about drugs, and Boris Becker by refusing the role of nationalistic German, just as McEnroe, Connors and Nastase had riled everyone because of their refusal to act out 'If' on court.

The hunger of the fans was thwarted by the dominating player of the 1990s, Pete Sampras, a multiple winner at Wimbledon and Flushing Meadow, a wonderful but introverted player. No hint of scandal attached to him, but now ungrateful fans began to complain of the 'boredom' of 1990s tennis; and possibly the failure of Sampras to be 'colourful' contributed as much as the dominance of serve to the boredom effect.

Fortunately a controversial rival emerged: Andre Agassi. Agassi's youthful rebellious persona was a startling contrast to the shy Sampras and did much to reconnect audiences with the game.

Agassi was one of a number of tennis players cursed with

Andre Agassi with hair in 1990

an obsessive parent. His father, a boxer originally from Iran, embedded in the child prodigy a love-hate relationship to the game. In the desert outside Las Vegas the child Andre was made to practise and play every day, and by the age of ten he was winning national tournaments. His father enrolled him at the Nick Bollettieri tennis academy at the age of thirteen; Bolletieri waived his fees because of the boy's talent. In his lively autobiography, Agassi confirmed all the doubts the tennis old guard had about the new tennis schools, describing the academy as a boot camp, or even a prison camp, with disgusting food, rickety sleeping quarters and a regime of work and more work. His description made it sound like a modern version of Dickens's Dotheboys Hall.

In protest Agassi used his appearance to shock, starting with an earring (sure sign of homosexuality, according to his father) and progressing to a Mohawk hairstyle, painted nails and finally at a public (and quite important tournament) to scruffy dungarees and eye make-up. This – to 'dress like a fag' as his father expressed it – was a major crime. The one thing he did not do – despite his alleged hatred for the game – was to refuse to go on playing tennis. That would have been the genuine rebellion – but perhaps he had little choice as he was already earning money, from endorsements as well as the sport. Moreover, he was not educated for anything else. His appearance, none the less, was enough to win him the rebel's label in the eyes of the fans and the officials.[9]

Kyle Kusz[10] read him as representative of 'Generation X', much discussed in early nineties America. It referred to a cohort of young white men in their twenties who had seemingly rejected the core American values of hard work, the raising of a family, independence and individualism. Those who condemned Generation X did not acknowledge, or perhaps recognise, that owing to the decline of the United States economy, the opportunities available to their fathers in the 1960s and 1970s no longer existed. When Agassi pranced on to the court in pink spandex shorts and a bleached ponytail, when he (apparently) tanked sets, showed no respect for the traditions of tennis and gorged on junk food, he appeared to mirror the Generation X of grunge-wearing, alienated slackers. He was simultaneously loved by the young and hated by their parents.

The relationship between Agassi the star and his image in the endorsements he garnered underlined this. Especially controversial was the ad by Canon cameras, the climax of which had Agassi lower his black sunglasses, stare at the camera and say *'image is everything.'*

At this time Agassi, still only twenty-one years of age, had reached three major finals, two at Roland Garros and one in Australia, and had lost all three. 'Image is everything' was interpreted as expressing Agassi's own philosophy – that of an individual interested only in being a celebrity and who had as a result not had the strength of character actually to win a slam.

In his autobiography Agassi, with a wit rarely encountered

in such texts, revealed that the loss of his first final in Paris might have had more to do with the hairpiece he was now wearing to conceal his rapidly balding scalp. It started to come apart on the eve of the final and had to be secured with hairgrips. With every move he imagined it landing on the clay and lying there like a dead bird: 'I can hear a gasp from the crowd. I can picture millions of people suddenly leaning closer to their TVs, turning to each other and in dozens of languages and dialects saying … : Did Andre Agassi's *hair* just fall off?'[11]

The combination of his own talent and his father's over-investment in it resulted in a determination to 'be himself' and 'take control of his own life' that only resulted in continual criticism. Why, for example, did the sports press object to his wearing denim shorts during the 1988 season, especially when they were simultaneously hailing him as the saviour of the game, 'whatever that means'? He felt it had to do with the atmosphere at his matches. Fans of both sexes appeared wearing his outfits and his mullet hairdo. He couldn't understand why they wanted to be him, since he didn't.

Once he started to win major tournaments, in 1994, the press embarked on a redemption narrative. Agassi had found the required work ethic! But a few years later when his marriage to film star Brooke Shields (whose grandfather was the American Davis Cup player, Frank Shields) began to fall apart, he slid down the rankings to 141 and was again in trouble with the public, while the press decided he was finished. But this story had a happy ending. He made a stunning comeback, ended his career as an acknowledged great player and was happily married to Steffi Graf.

Pete Sampras' seven Wimbledons and fourteen 'slams' in total excelled Agassi's late success. But in 2001 Sampras was beaten at Wimbledon and in the new millennium American tennis would not repeat its triumphs of the 1990s, when Agassi and Sampras along with Jim Courier and Michael Chang had ruled the world. This was a problem, because American audiences engaged fully with tennis only when they had their own players in the top ten.

Agassi won Wimbledon only once, in 1992. It was his first slam and it was only after that that he knew what it was to be famous, to be a celebrity. Until then, he'd thought he was famous, but he was 'only infamous'. Now he suddenly had hundreds of new 'friends' and was invited to all sorts of celebrity events and VIP rooms – he had been joined up to the Famous People's Club.[12]

John McEnroe had suffered the same unreality a few years earlier ('I was only a tennis player, after all') and Agassi's roller-coaster decade, complete with fast cars, film-star girlfriends (he dated Barbra Streisand for a season) and a recreational-drugs incident was equally a revelation of the reality of celebrity tennis. McEnroe and Tatum O'Neal had been persecuted by paparazzi; Brooke Shields was repeatedly menaced by stalkers who sent gruesome letters to the couple promising revenge and murder. Agassi's endless tennis journey, circling the globe to appear at tournament after tournament, while she built her career in Hollywood, pulled them apart – a fate also suffered by McEnroe and his wife. It was the ultimate celebrity life.

The hero had changed from noble man of action to tortured misfit. Once, the public loved and admired heroes. Figures in authority were treated with reverence – often with too much of it. From the Pope downwards, their virtue was assumed. To defer to those in authority or to those who wielded, or were perceived to wield power, extended to the stars of popular culture. But that very culture undermined deference and its darker side was the *Schadenfreude* of revealing feet of clay in the famous and an attitude to stars that mingled credulous overestimation with destructive cynicism. It is ironic that sporting figures, so burdened in terms of the values it is alleged they represent, should have migrated to this very different cultural environment. Perhaps tennis players were especially vulnerable, given that glamour had been so interwoven into the history of the game.

By the millennium the Victorian imperialist hero had long vanished from society. Yet notwithstanding the new controversial anti-heroes, the Victorian sporting ideal lingered on in the person who symbolically embalmed his ideals: the sportsman. He at least must preserve a traditional manliness that had long ceased to have any relevance to men's actual lives. In the future there might be little need for warriors; drones would do the killing. The head of the family might have become a diminished figure. But on the field, the arena, the court, a man could still be a real man.

Yet the Victorian hero had typically left sport behind when he reached full manhood. Professionalism, by contrast, converted tennis into a permanent career, as Bodo and Baltzell pointed out; another aspect of their never 'growing up'. It was, in fact, difficult, once stars became major celebrities and billionaires, for them to find another life after tennis.

In the modern era the end of a famous sportsman's career is likely to be traumatic. It is more like the ending of a politician's career than, say, a dancer's. The politician – particularly if he holds a senior position – is dumped, dismissed or voted out of power. The sportsman plays until he loses. It is not his choice; his fate is in the hands of others: his opponents. The ending of his career is especially difficult for a tennis player, who does not have a team manager to tell him when it is time to go. He is on his own and risks departing the scene in bathos and embarrassment, even shame and disaster, rather than triumph and pride. Pete Sampras managed to win a final major, the US Open, before he quietly slipped away – but he had endured some humiliating defeats before that. Borg did the opposite, leaving the game prematurely at the age of twenty-six, when he was still ranked number one. He later attempted a comeback that didn't work, ran into all sorts of difficulties and it was many years before order was restored in his life.

A great actor need never retire. True, he cannot play the male romantic leads of his youth forever, but his work can mature as he ages, with roles such as Lear and Prospero awaiting the seventy-year-old. A singer can pick the moment to retire; and afterwards her voice can still be heard. The dancer's art is ephemeral, but she or he may move on to choreography or to the director's chair.

For the sports star it is different. To have been at the pinnacle of the game, with the adulation, the crowds, the cheers and applause, the money of course and – perhaps most of all – the adrenalin, must make departure a desperate moment even for those players who are naturally introverted. And to have made millions – billions – by the time you are thirty, so that when you retire you never have to work ever again, is not the unclouded bliss it might seem. A sporting afterlife echoes with silence after the tumultuous applause has died away as inexorably as a wave recedes from the shore and the sportsperson is more ruthlessly effaced by his successors than the actor or the dancer. Tracy Austin described it as 'a kind of death'.[13]

This is also a test for the new hero: to find meaning in the tennis afterlife. Becker became a serious poker player, a game that provided some of the adrenalin high he used to get from tennis. (It is also a game that, while it lacks the physicality of sport, has several of the other characteristics of tennis: the intelligence needed, the patience and the cunning. It is also highly competitive.)

Many top players invested their wealth in business, with greater or less success. McEnroe, for example, became an art dealer and for a while, less successfully a musician. He also refused $1,000,000 to play an exhibition match in apartheid South Africa and talked of going into politics. Agassi and Steffi Graf opened a successful school for disadvantaged kids; and along with Navratilova supported progressive causes. Rod Laver's brother was a Marxist and Laver himself was a man of progressive views.[14] Lendl, by contrast, reported Bodo, was a Reaganite conservative. In the 1980s Buster Mottram, Britain's top player and son of the 1950s tennis couple, Joy and Tony Mottram, was said to support the British National Party, as a result of which members of the Socialist Workers Party followed him around Wimbledon, jeering. Cramm was an active anti-Nazi; Borotra a man of the extreme right. Becker also talked of going into politics. Marat Safin, the explosive Russian star, who won two majors (the US and

Australian) and the Davis Cup, lived the playboy lifestyle when on the tour and was famous for his racquet-smashing temper, but by 2011 had rediscovered his Muslim Tatar identity and become a member of the Russian parliament in Vladimir Putin's party. So long as they were active on the tour players were cagey about their political views (if they had any); too partisan political allegiances were unwelcome to the conservatism of the sponsors. So, when Gavin Rossdale, one of Federer's most loyal supporters and often seen in his box, was described as 'front man for Bush', this was startling, to those older fans, at least, who did not realise that Bush was a band, and didn't refer to George W., the President of the United States.

Politics is a form of theatre, but it was stage and screen that most attracted tennis players, although their successes, as we saw, were few. Politics might offer an attractive future for the tennis player, because, like sport, it is adversarial and also produces celebrities. Unfortunately it rarely offers the overwhelming applause and adulation granted the sporting hero.

Fame and celebrity were even more complicated for women players than for their male counterparts. Steffi Graf was the transcendent woman player of the open era, winning twenty-two majors and a 'golden slam' (all four majors in one year, plus an Olympic gold medal). With her brilliant footwork and powerful serve and ground strokes, she was considered by many to be the best woman player of the twentieth century. She was coached by her father from the age of three. Like a number of other tennis fathers, he was no outstanding player himself, yet like Charles Lenglen, Richard Williams – and indeed Agassi père – was determined his daughter should go right to the top. He controlled her life strictly with the result that her tennis thrived, but at the cost of her social life. He was later convicted of tax evasion in Germany and imprisoned.

Monica Seles was born in former Yugoslavia to a tennis-playing family. Monica's father soon noticed his daughter's talent and rapidly developed her into a precocious prodigy, but the relationship was a loving one and when she was enrolled at the Bollettieri Academy, she did not go alone; her whole family moved to Florida. Still, it was a bewildering environment and Monica developed a tendency to gorge on peanut-butter sandwiches to alleviate her feelings of strangeness and stress.

Soon, however, a fairy tale unfolded. In 1990 she won her first tournament, the Virginia Slims at Houston, beating Chrissie Evert in the final. That year she went on to beat Navratilova in Rome, 6–1, 6–1. She progressed to Paris where she beat thirteen-year-old Jennifer Capriati in the semi-final and Steffi Graf in the final. At the age of sixteen she had won her first slam. She celebrated the victory with her parents and a crowd of adults, including Mark McCormack, head of IMG, her agency, at the Ritz. 'It was a strange world I was living in,' she wrote, famous and celebrated, 'hanging out with high-powered people', but still watching children's cartoons on the TV every morning. The dream continued in 1991, as she won the Australian, French and US Open and reached the final of Wimbledon, where she lost to Graf. There followed two years of almost unadulterated triumph. She won her eighth major in Melbourne at the beginning of 1991. Illness and injury then sidelined her for some weeks, but in March she returned to the tour, playing a tournament in Hamburg. In the quarter-finals as she was resting at the change-over an obsessive Steffi Graf fan stabbed her in the shoulder with a nine-inch knife. At the moment she was attacked, she had bent forwards for some water; had she not done so she would probably have been paralysed as the knife could have reached her spine.

As if this were not bad enough, her father was diagnosed with cancer. He died four years later. Monica's life went into a negative spiral. Her body recovered quickly from the injury, but her mentality was shattered. At first she could not walk on to a tennis court and when she did she was self-conscious because of the weight she was putting on. She did continue on the tour as her father became more and more ill, but that compulsive travel seemed to be part of the phantasmagoria of insecurity and the sense that she had totally lost her bearings.[15]

Monica won one further major, the Australian Open in 1996, but she never really got her tennis life back again, although she formally retired only in 2008. Her story revealed in the starkest manner the brittle nature of the tennis life at the top and how the competitive imperatives of the modern game necessitated that a child be over-developed in one area of her life at the expense of everything else.

Studies of child prodigies in fields such as mathematics and music show that they often do less well than expected in adult life. Tennis was worse. Musicians and mathematicians simply emerge, but in tennis a system grew up in which agents and others actively sought out talent at a very young age, as it came to be accepted that success at the top necessitated intense training from an early age. Precocious talent was ruthlessly exploited for financial benefit. Furthermore, critics of sport have accused it of prolonging a kind of adolescence, especially for the very successful, so that they do not reach maturity in the normal way, but are sheltered and cocooned from every inconvenience and outrageously indulged – so long, at least, as they are winning.

The stabbing incident revealed the brutally instrumental nature of relationships on the tour. Footage of the moments immediately after the stabbing incident reveal that Monica's opponent did not even go over to comfort her – true, there were others around the wounded girl – but simply continued to sit on the sidelines as if waiting for the match to continue. Steffi Graf visited Monica in hospital, but could only stay for a few minutes because she was due to play in the final of the tournament. Monica had assumed that the tournament would be cancelled, but, as she explained in an interview with Tim Adams, 'one problem was it happened in Germany and was "because of" a German player'. The authorities deemed it preferable to 'almost pretend it hadn't happened'. Besides, to cancel the tournament would have cost a lot of money. A week later the players were asked to vote on whether to freeze Monica's number-one ranking for the time being. All except Gabriela Sabatini, who abstained, voted against.

Even the man who had stabbed her, Günter Parche, got off lightly. Tried for the offence of 'wounding' rather than attempted murder, he was given a brief suspended sentence on account of his psychological abnormality.

On her return to the tennis courts Seles was continually criticised for her weight. She was also attacked for her 'grunting' on every point, something she maintained had never been noticed when she was winning everything. Public opinion had transformed her from the brilliant winner to the ugly failure.

It was not easy to be a female player in the age of celebrity. Lenglen had had the freedom to flout all sorts of conventions, but, curious as it seems, sport and tennis in the late twentieth century was more conformist than in the 1920s. Female players moved within the narrow parameters of feminine stereotypes.

Anna Kournikova's brief trajectory through the game exposed anew women's perennial on-court problems. Kournikova was a sixteen-year-old Russian sensation who shattered a stereotype of Russia's female athletes left over from the Cold War; 'the image of bulging arms, square shoulders and something one step away from womanhood ... images of someone strapping and Amazonian with questionable sexuality'.[16]

Not Anna Kournikova, known as Cor!nikova to the British tabloid press. She was one of the teenage starlets snapped up at this period. Enrolled at the Nick Bollettieri Academy at the age of ten, she was signed up by IMG the following year – their youngest ever – and once she reached puberty was hailed as the beauty of the tour. She had a wonderful mane of blonde hair, a round, baby face with large eyes and lips and a button nose. Hers was the style of Hollywood beauty fashionable in an era when few leading ladies matched the strange, off-key looks of Garbo, Marlene Dietrich or Joan Crawford. Their faces, in the 1930s, had had the individuality of unexpected planes and angles. By the 1990s conventions of beauty had narrowed. In addition to her unchallenging looks,

Kournikova had a well-developed figure, used in Berlei sports bra advertisements, which proclaimed that 'Only the balls should bounce'. She was a babe: 'Watching Kournikova yields the additional thrill of seeing her tuck her second service ball into her knickers!', this one simple action alone being 'probably responsible for making a huge impact on the numbers rolling through the turnstiles'.[17]

Her dominance as a junior did not translate to the adult tour. The enormous publicity surrounding her on account of her looks worked against her. The press, who had promoted her in the first place, watched with gloating *Schadenfreude* as her results failed to live up to the hype. She reached her only major semi-final at Wimbledon on her debut in 1997 and never won a WTA title; her best results were as a doubles player with Martina Hingis. They won in Australia in 1999 and 2002 and christened themselves the Spice Girls of tennis. By the age of twenty-two Kournikova was retired with serious shoulder injuries.

Martina Hingis by contrast was a serial winner. She won Wimbledon in 1997 at the age of sixteen. She won the Australian Open three times and the French once and was also successful in doubles. She was a precision player who made the difficult look effortless. She was perceived as an intellectual player, who set up highly intricate points and played almost perfect technical tennis, able to dominate opponents because she was so much more mentally gifted than them in terms of tennis knowledge. Her game was compared to that of chess master Gary Kasparov; and McEnroe said of her that she was: 'a step or two ahead of all human beings out there on the court ... mentally she sees things virtually no one else sees.'[18]

Yet she too fell victim to the new emphasis on muscle, blown away by the raw power of Venus and Serena Williams. They showed how the women's game was also changing, demanding, like the men's, greater stamina and endurance. This took longer to develop and consequently the rankings were no longer being dominated by teenagers.

In the new century Serena Williams was to become the most successful and dominating player on the women's circuit, in spite of long absences. Extraordinarily forceful as she prowled around the court, where she was a larger-than-life figure, almost a kind of goddess, she was a new species of tennis celebrity, who aspired to act and who designed some of her own clothes (including a black leather all-in-one shorts outfit – a step too far, some felt). The Belgian, Justine Henin, was one of the very few players who could in her day dominate the Williams sisters by reason of her beautiful all-court game.

As with the men, though, the all-court game was in eclipse.

24

Millennium tennis

IN THE WEEK AFTER MARGARET THATCHER'S death in April 2013, Dan Jones of the London *Evening Standard* reprised the complaint that had rung down the years to accompany the growing global passion for sport: that money was ruining it. Thatcherite values – the supremacy of the market – had, he wrote, eroded its basic values and put a price on something 'supposed to be priceless' by turning sport into 'a business built on deregulated foreign investment, in partnership with Rupert Murdoch'.

In reality, nineteenth-century sport was from the beginning developed partly for gain and commercialised well before the First World War. Transfer fees in British football were already controversial. Cricket was a money-making proposition. Promoters were aware of an audience eager to watch matches. The word 'shamateur' was in circulation and W. G. Grace – the great cricketing hero of the period – was the biggest 'shamateur' of all, demanding backhanders and appearance fees. He 'was also guilty of outrageous gamesmanship, intimidating umpires, questioning or simply ignoring their rulings, yet was regarded as a "Lancelot" or chivalric hero by generations of worshippers.'[1]

The Situationist writer, Guy Debord, whose book, *The Society of the Spectacle*, became the bible of the 'événements' in France in 1968, denounced the commoditisation of leisure and accused capitalism of colonising all aspects of life. To view the spectacle

– in this case the sporting spectacle – as entirely alienated, as simply a form of false consciousness, as Debord did (and in the end Debord's final judgement on modern society was his own suicide), might be to exaggerate the passivity and powerlessness of the audience. Yet capitalism must continually expand, finding new markets at all costs. As a result everything must be commoditised. The tentacles of capitalism reach out to incorporate areas of social and emotional existence such as erotic love and leisure activities, which were once considered beyond the reach of the cash nexus.

In the early twentieth century the American photographer, Charles Sheeler, described the Ford factory at Red River, Detroit, as the modern 'substitute for religious expression' – and he was not alone in viewing the factory as the equivalent of the cathedral in an age of the worship of money. By 2000, however, the stadium had replaced it. The role of sport in giving meaning to life had grown almost beyond itself, the source of intense, ephemeral yet ever recycled passions and obsessions.

Only heretics rejected the faith. It was not yet as dangerous to be a non-believer as in, say, medieval Spain or contemporary Iran; but things were moving in that direction.

Those who loved tennis had always appreciated it for the ways in which it was different from other sports. It had had to change, to be professionalised, but with this, and the release of its wealth-generating potential, had come changes to the game itself that perhaps no one had quite foreseen and which few may have wanted or consciously chosen.

Corporate capital commoditised the game, squeezing it to fit the general template of sport and equally to fit the television screen. In the process it became less unique and less special.

In June 2001 a nineteen-year-old hippie with a ponytail and a bead necklace defeated reigning champion Pete Sampras in a tense five-set match at Wimbledon. The teenager was eventually to equal the American's record of seven championships at the All England Club, but on that day many spectators had never heard of Roger Federer. His victory was just an exciting 'upset' that would clear Tim Henman's passage to the championship.

The Sampras–Federer match was a classic all-court encounter; it was a botched smash that may have cost Sampras the match and it was a passing shot that sealed it. Federer would be the future of tennis in the first decade of the twenty-first century, but the 2001 match marked the ending of an old era as much as the beginning of a new one. Sampras had switched from a two-handed to a one-handed backhand at the age of fourteen, but two players trading single-handed backhands would soon be a rarity. The BBC commentators on the match, Peter Fleming and David Mercer, noted that the court near the net was much less worn than in previous years. There had been less net play throughout the tournament because the grass had been slowed down.

This was the Wimbledon that Tim Henman, the British hope, was supposed to win. Federer had defeated his main rival and Henman beat the Swiss newcomer in the next round. In the semi-finals he faced Goran Ivanisevic. The Croatian had been given a wild card in acknowledgement of his status as a three-times former finalist, but was now a player wrecked by injuries and an unfulfilled career. He had taken his third finals loss, to Sampras, so badly ('I go kill myself') that his career had gone into a seemingly unstoppable downward spiral. Soon he was playing challenger tournaments and not even winning those. ('I was playing in the car park – I had to play matches even to get to qualifying.')

Commentators began to notice as he moved through the draw and soon he was displaying his eccentricities on television. As a personality he could not have been a greater contrast to the stiff-upper-lipped Henman. After Ivanisevic revealed that part of his 'lucky' routine was to watch the same children's programme, the *Teletubbies*, every morning, a cohort of supporters appeared at the All England Club dressed as the on-screen puppets. His mother and girlfriend were banned from the players' box because women brought bad luck.

Yet with his blend of belief and disavowal, genuine emotion and irony, he distanced himself from his own fanatical commitment, speaking in interviews of the three Gorans: Good Goran, Bad Goran and Emergency Goran. Bad Goran had smashed so many racquets that once he had none left and was forced to default from a tournament.

His semi-final against Henman, like the Federer–Sampras encounter (referred to as 'the changing of the guard', the arrival of the new generation), created its own myth. A tremendous thunderstorm interrupted play when Henman had taken a two sets to one lead and seemed to have the match in the bag, as the score in the third set was 6-0; but next day, when the match was resumed, Ivanisevic triumphed. Overnight he had persuaded himself that the storm was a direct intervention by God in his favour and this gave him sufficient self-belief to win. (As a letter to the London *Guardian* put it, 'is it any wonder the world is in such a mess when, instead of concentrating on wars and famines, God spends his time watching Wimbledon?', but that raises questions beyond the scope of this book.) The British, of course, couldn't understand why God had favoured the wrong man. But God stuck with Goran during the final against the laidback Australian and fellow serve-volleyer, Pat Rafter. As he served for the match his cannonball first serve deserted him. Emergency Goran wept, prayed to God and a dead friend, and victory finally crowned Good Goran's career.

In 2002 a different Australian, Lleyton Hewitt, and a different teenager, Argentinian David Nalbandian, contested the final. Both kept well away from the net. But in 2003 a serve-and-volley display by Federer and Mark Philippousis, a third Australian, held back the future.

For time had been called on the old tennis. Determined to end the perceived over-dominance of the serve, the game's managers slowed down the courts and made the balls heavier to counter the power of the big-faced racquets with their luxilon strings that could put so much spin on the balls. At the end of the 1970s, Jack

Kramer had predicted that the baseline clay-court game would virtually disappear and that the future lay in a fast hardcourt game. He was right to foresee that grass would virtually disappear, but was mistaken in thinking the courts would be fast. In the early twenty-first century a clay-court game of long rallies adapted to ever slower hardcourts became the norm.

This resulted for the women's game in cohorts of clone-like blonde baseliners. Shortly before the 2011 Wimbledon, an article in the *Guardian* was headlined 'Why does the women's game seem a shadow of its former self?' Reasons cited were: that there had been three players ranked number one who had failed to win a slam; that the standard of play had fallen; that there was no 'great rivalry'; that there were no 'big stars'; and that women's tennis was boring to watch (a criticism made many times through the years).

Not everyone agreed. Petra Kvitova, for example, unanticipated Wimbledon winner that year, had a powerful left-handed all-court game and was no clone baseliner. Yet the perception persisted that the continuing dominance of Serena Williams, who at the age of thirty won both Wimbledon and a gold Olympic medal in 2012, in some way exposed the problems of the women's game. She was so far ahead of her rivals that in 2013 (in spite of failing to win Wimbledon) there was almost no contest. She was able to handle the technological demands for strength and endurance. Perhaps, though, these qualities did not really suit the women's game and there were many who missed the subtlety of Hingis and Henin.

The conservatism of corporate tennis – not to mention that of some of the players – continued to pursue and hamper women. When Amélie Mauresmo, openly lesbian, defeated Lindsey Davenport in the semi-final of the 1999 Australian Open, she ran to hug her girlfriend. Davenport, herself six foot two, told reporters that playing the Frenchwoman had been more like 'playing a guy'. Hingis, who defeated Mauresmo in the final, went one better by complaining that Mauresmo was 'half a man'. As

Navratilova had found, it was difficult to combine stereotypical femininity with power play. It was always a struggle and a contradiction for women and the corporate model of femininity was unthinkingly backward looking.

By the millennium Peter Bodo's wish had been granted. Women players were imprisoned in a mass-produced image of cloned femininity. Shorts had been entirely banished from the women's game in favour of a uniform of either a brief skirt with a vest top, or, more usually a sleeveless miniskirted dress that revealed the crotch during play (although some women wore cycling shorts underneath) and was essentially a skirted swimming costume.

'Modesty' had always been a contested issue for women and especially for feminists. Tennis was, as Billie Jean King had pointed out, an erotic sport and women players had every right to adorn and expose their bodies in attractive ways. What was so dispiriting about court dress in the early twenty-first century was its dreary uniformity. It was unimaginative and mass produced. With the exception of the elegant Venus Williams and, on occasion, Maria Sharapova, most women players did their best to achieve a banal Hollywood-defined ideal of female attractiveness. One British commentator referred on air to the 2013 Wimbledon winner, Marion Bartoli's lack of physical beauty. Women players took part in off-court fashion catwalk shows and were careful to wear nail varnish and dangly earrings on court and never to have short hair. With all the talk of personality and individualism, it was hard to tell players apart, one blonde teenager with a swinging plaited ponytail indistinguishable from her opponent and quite often wearing an identical outfit.

The system of clothing sponsorship, whereby Nike and other firms offered top players free outfits as a form of advertising, paradoxically recreated the original problem that led to the end of the all-white rule: that the two opponents were impossible to tell apart. The culture of individualism brought about uniformity. This was as true of the men as the women. Apart from a few exceptions at the top of the game, players squared off against each other in identical billowing T-shirts and flapping shorts.[2] Long gone was the close-fitting Fila minimalism of the seventies and John McEnroe for one, wasn't happy about it: 'the baggy shorts you see now are horrible and those sneakers that look like rocket ships ...' He believed the quality of the clothing had deteriorated too.[3]

However innovative global players such as Nike had been to begin with, by the end of the first decade of the third millennium creativity had disappeared. Men appeared in T-shirts of uniform ugliness, in garish or safely 'masculine' colours, sometimes aggressively patterned. Almost all chose from the same few designs.

The aesthetics of tennis dress had completely stalled. Something similar to what happened in mass-produced children's clothes seemed to have struck the tennis world. Exaggerated gender distinctions had to be drawn. That the colours worn carried a gendered message seemed to be proven by the uproar caused when Roger Federer wore a pale pink polo shirt at the ATP 1000 tournament in Cincinnati in 2010. 'Real men wear pink' was the new slogan hoisted by fans in response to the (perhaps manufactured) hysteria of the sports commentators.

Federer was, in other more significant ways, an exception to the trend as a tennis player. His dominance through the mid-decade was deeply counter-intuitive, given the progressive slowing down of the game. In 2009, when he won the French Open, Peter Bodo marvelled at how this could have happened in the era of the 'new', brutal tennis as typified by Rafael Nadal. Watching Federer, he felt he was watching some old, grainy, black and white film. The Swiss player was surely 'just the kind of guy the new millennium game has supposedly left behind – the kind of guy about whom we say, *Oh, he was a great player in his time, but he'd never last with the way the game is played today!*' He seemed utterly unconnected from the way tennis was now evolving.[4] Federer played an all-court game that he was able to adapt to the new conditions, but he himself spoke of his style as 'retro' and, writing in 2006, his biographer, René Stauffer affirmed that the player was 'bringing tennis back to an era when it was a game characterised by wood racquets, artistry [and] tactics'.[5]

Bodo considered Federer's supreme quality as a tennis player to be *sprezzatura*, a lightness of approach and an emphasis on artistry rather than brute power. 'Puritanical critics,' wrote Bodo, 'tend to regard *sprezzatura* as a suspect quality, a polish in manners that indicates over refinement or even feyness ... But such judgments ignore the real edge that must remain beneath the polish.'[6]

Anthony Wilding was adored by the Edwardians because he combined *sprezzatura* with the ideal of unintellectual manliness. As the twentieth century wore on, the two were increasingly separated, grace and elegance sundered from the qualities of the hero. In the open era brute force was to become more valued than artistry and a single player could not hold back the tide of history.

Thus by 2005 a new star for the new times stepped forward. Spaniard Rafael Nadal used a Babolat AeroPro Drive graphite and tungsten racquet to increase his stroke speed. Already three times French champion, by 2008 when he also won Wimbledon, he was acknowledged as the player for the future. He was, wrote Jon Henderson in the London *Observer*, 'the thickly muscled child of the changes in tennis that have taken place over the past 30 years, the antithesis of the sinewy players of the past'. Gradually, players had 'become more powerful until now, we have in Nadal the player with the perfect physique for extracting the most from the latest generation of racquets and strings'. The larger racquet head allowed for more topspin, with the result that 'the potential volleyer [was] .. now faced with a ball that is moving more quickly and dipping more rapidly'. The baseline, clay-court tennis taught in Spain was ideal for the new technology. Budding players were taught to serve to the backhand with a high bouncing ball, which negated the single-handed backhand, and any attempt to volley would be punished with a deadly passing shot from the back of the court. The double-handed backhand might be less versatile

than the single-handed, but was better at making a powerful
return off the high bouncing ball. Young players were also taught
to grunt, allegedly to improve their breathing. It was actually an
intimidatory tactic.

Public relations honed Nadal as the warrior, the animal with
intensity and heart in contrast to Federer, the cool and serene
artist, the Mozart or Impressionist of tennis. In a much-quoted
article the late David Foster Wallace wrote of Federer 'as religious
experience', a fusion of Mozart and Metallica.[7] His tennis was
balletic and aesthetic and in terms of all-court play superior to,
more versatile and more creative than Nadal's, but the Spaniard's
endurance and iron will to win was a punch in the guts that
everyone could understand.

A cornerstone of tennis rhetoric (or sporting rhetoric
generally) is the belief that fans love rivalries. Agassi was sceptical
of this, seeing it as partly a matter of PR and felt his rivalry with
Sampras was exaggerated. It was, like the Federer / Nadal contrast,
a genuine rivalry of styles, yet the idea that spectators necessarily
wanted to see the same two players battle it out time and time
again was another unexamined piece of PR-received wisdom.
Audiences wanted variety, different kinds of exciting matches
and upsets. The existence or manufacture of a rivalry, however,
could be cynically deployed to generate sales of fan memorabilia
and accessories and, it was hoped, to maintain interest in a sport
competing with others that were more popular.

Yet Federer's rivalry with Nadal was more than mere hype.
It symbolised the battle between the classical all-court game and
the 'new' tennis. Simon Barnes, chief sports writer at *The Times*
in London felt that Federer and Andy Murray were the only two
players whose game rose above the attritional baseline game of
the rest. Those were automatons who 'exchange Exocets or like
it best when the shrapnel is whistling round the baseline', but
Federer was different, 'benignly, beautifully, artistically' taking his
opponents apart and moving 'into a region where [others] simply
could not follow'.

There were many fans and commentators, however, who mistrusted elegance and beauty. Charles Baudelaire described the grim peasants painted by J-F Millet as figures whose 'bleak and deadly brutishness' made him 'feel like hating them',[8] but ugliness was to be the great aesthetic discovery of the twentieth century, continuing into the twenty-first and Nadal's achievement was to turn tennis ugly.

Nadal took the attritional clay-court game to new lengths. Snarls, animal roars and phallic arm pumping underlined the massive attack of the repetitive, machine-gun forehand as he charged across the court like an escapee from PlayStation. He did the same thing over and over again. Opponents found they could run, but could never hide. It was so monotonous it was mesmerising.

The clothing provided for the players by Nike cleverly underlined the difference as part of the packaging of stars that came with corporate tennis. Federer wore slender polo shirts and Bermuda shorts, often in subtle, muted colours; Nadal was initially 'piratical' with below-the-knee pantaloons, a bandana, and tank tops that reminded *Sunday Times* columnist Lynn Barber 'inexorably of Freddie Mercury'. Lynn Barber clearly did not take to Nadal, but what she really disliked was the iron curtain of PR that surrounded him (as it did all top players), a 'phalanx of middle-aged minders, big-bellied habitués of the hospitality tent' who 'wheel out their tired old stereotype' of what a sportsman should be. (This was not long after the Tiger Woods scandal, when, as Barber observed with relish, the PR machine 'broke down'.)[9] Nadal fans responded to her disobliging comments with death threats.

Lynn Barber found Nadal too macho to be true, but the contrast between the 'ultimate warrior' and the dandified Federer revived an echo of the old controversy of the sissy game. The Swiss star's masculinity was never in doubt – by the time he won Wimbledon for the seventh time he was the father of twins – but it was hardly the mark of a true sportsman to pay so much attention to fashion.

Roger Federer after winning Wimbledon in 2009 circles
the court in retro outfit

From 2003 to 2007 when he won Wimbledon five times in a row, Federer camped up Wimbledon's sartorial 'traditions' in long white trousers (removed for play), and white initialled blazers. In 2008 his change of style to a 1930s cricketing sweater, reminiscent of the 'golden years', generated acres of print betraying the underlying suspicion of his perceived dandyism. An article in the 2007 official Wimbledon programme described the Swiss star 'sashaying onto court' in a 'snazzy cream coloured blazer', looking like James Bond; and suggested – weirdly – that his opponents thought he ought to be wearing a pink tutu and six-inch stilettos in order to give them a chance to win.

Peter Bodo, for all his admiration, couldn't bear 'the cardigans, hair care products, runway gawking' and his friendship with 'fashion courtesans' such as Anna Wintour, editor of American *Vogue*; and in 2012 Giles Hattersley, interviewing Federer for the *Sunday Times*, concentrated on Anna Wintour's 'crush' on the star and Federer being a 'secret dandy' who admitted he'd 'got into the mood of being more fashionable' and enjoyed it. (He was wearing a Dior suit at the time.) Wintour had even taken him to a Milan catwalk show.[10]

Fans invested whichever of the two stars they adored with god-like virtues and extraordinary qualities and his rival with contemptible faults, when they could not possibly know what the players were 'really' like. All this proved was the capacity of audiences to project their desires and ideals onto these figures drenched in fame and it was a distraction from the central issue in the rivalry: the contrasting styles of play. Federer's fashion consciousness was relevant only insofar as his style of play was itself often described as 'elegant' – but by some that too was viewed with suspicion.

More acceptable was a perception of tennis that compared it to boxing, an analogy that had gained considerable traction by the end of the decade. British number one, Andy Murray, himself a boxing fan, was fond of it; and counter-intuitive as it might seem, there are similarities: a contest between two individuals, often with carefully differentiated personalities; the need for speed, lightness of foot and split-second timing; and the use of muscle and power.

The differences nevertheless remain even more striking. Boxing is a contact sport; tennis is not. The whole atmosphere of a boxing match is entirely different from a tennis match and is of relatively short duration. The boxer aims to wound; the spectacle includes blood, pain and physical damage. The qualities displayed on the tennis court resemble those rather of a comedy of manners or a dramatic tragedy in which the action is cumulative and long drawn out. The 'real tennis' player Roman Krznarik suggested it could even resemble a conversation. The history, the aesthetic and the emotional atmosphere of the two sports were and are entirely different.

But the boxing analogy stuck. Indeed, Dan Jones in the *Evening Standard* described the 2013 Australian Open final between Andy Murray and Novak Djokovic as:

A streetfight: brutal far more often than it was beautiful.
For the first two sets it was possible to imagine that this is
what the bare-knuckle bouts watched by Pierce Egan and
chums in the early nineteenth century must have felt like
… unsparing and unending, settled only when one man
was physically destroyed. Gripping, gripping, grisly, ghastly
stuff.[11]

In fact the purpose of the comparison was not to represent
some reality, but to contribute to a perception of tennis as an
extremely macho sport. The comparison with boxing had more
to do with how those who made the comparison wanted it to be
perceived than with such similarities as there might be between
the two sports.

The image of tennis as effete had been based on mispercep-
tion and on class and sexual prejudice. It was always a physically
demanding sport. Ricardo Pancho Gonzales brought up the 'sissy
game' issue with the first friend with whom he played tennis.
Everyone had told him that football and baseball were much
more demanding. His friend was indignant. 'Those are team
sports, he snapped. Tennis is different. You go it alone. NO help
from anybody. In football the action is concentrated. You wait
between plays or after a whistle blows or for a ball to come your
way. Tennis has action every second. You've got to make split
second decisions.'[12]

Yet, as Andre Agassi had said, 'image is everything'. With
the comparison to boxing came the masochistic and puritanical
elevation of pain into a virtue. After losing the 2012 Australian
final to Novak Djokovic, Nadal spoke of how good it was to enjoy
suffering.[13] This was 'ultimate warrior' Nadal, whose popularity
was always based on his extraordinary aggression and competi-
tiveness. He was the ideal hero for the new generation.

More generally, there was tacit recognition of the cut-throat
nature of the game, but the ideal of pain never shifted. Andy
Murray boasted of his training sessions at a 'boot camp' in Florida.
When he hired Ivan Lendl as his coach in 2012 it seemed to set

the seal on the idea that the punishing work ethic was essential to create a style of tennis that was all about endurance, speed, accuracy and efficiency rather than elegance, artistry and 'shot making'; the ideal was the returner's defensive game with added power and aggression. In his case, it could be judged as successful in that he won the 2012 US Open, an Olympic gold medal and in 2013, Wimbledon.

Tennis had become the modern equivalent of ancient Sparta. Spartan youths were trained to be warriors (and girls too participated in physical training and sports). Everything was subordinated to the production of the fighting animal. As children they were harshly treated and were sent on scavenging expeditions to fend for themselves, by stealing or scrounging for food, but were punished if caught. The famous story of the boy with the fox illustrated the ideal of fortitude. The boy caught a live fox, intending to eat it, but encountered some soldiers. Rather than allow them to see the fox, he hid it under his tunic where it gnawed into his entrails, but he endured this without showing any sign of the agony it caused him.

Rafael Nadal was the ultimate Spartan. *Rafa: My Story*, the most wooden, opaque and depressing of all the variable examples of the genre, is remarkable as an autobiography – supposedly a self-revealing literary form – that remains a closed book, except as a bible of the Calvinist view of sport. He came, one interviewer related, 'from a man's world – an old-world man's world ... in which a man is head of the family and family matters above all else'. Coached by his uncle Toni from the age of five, Nadal learned that the key word was 'endurance'. Some members of his close-knit family protested at the regime of 'mental cruelty' Toni imposed, 'treating his nephew with undisguised injustice in the company of his peers, while requiring him never to complain', but Nadal's immense success subsequently seemed to justify his method, even if it was at the cost of recurring bouts of injury.[14]

By 2010, the year in which Nadal won the US Open and

thereby became only the seventh man to win all four slams, the ongoing banking crisis and the critical state of the Eurozone were threatening to engulf Mediterranean Europe, including his homeland, Spain. Austerity was the new black. The European Union, dominated by Germany and the German Chancellor, Angela Merkel, united with the International Monetary Fund to insist on harsh measures to stem the debt problems and stagnation afflicting Europe. German sociologist Ulrich Beck saw this as an expression of long-term tendencies in German culture: 'Suffering purifies. The road through hell, the road through austerity, leads to the heaven of economic recovery.' This, he believed, was a typically German lesson based on Martin Luther and Max Weber – the Protestant work ethic at full throttle.[15]

Nadal seemed the perfect athlete to personify the new reality.

Yet the men marketing tennis confronted a paradox. They thirsted for 'great rivalries' and exciting 'personalities', yet in the twenty-first century they had produced a game notable for its uniformity. Uniformity, so desirable in the manufacture of silicon chips, steel hinges, screws, light bulbs and chorus girls, became a defect when applied to creative activity and play, where difference, variety and the unexpected were the desired qualities. With the strict codes of conduct and the intense specialism required for success, it was more difficult than in former times for tennis 'personalities' to flourish. Instead, PR men, assisted by the press, created myths that stood in for personality. The corporate mindset was conservative and required not only that the game be reproducible for a mass market and be tailored to attract the maximum number of customers, but that the players fit the stereotypical mould of clean-cut sportsmen. By 2010 almost all the players played a similar game on similar courts in similar clothes.

Spectators complained of players who had 'no personality', for example Juan Martin del Potro. True, the giant Argentinian moved around the court with the ponderous gait of an ox or a camel, his facial expression rarely changing. His game of huge serve and forehand, for all its skill (shown for example in his epic encounter in the 2013 semi-finals at Wimbledon, at which Djokovic only just beat him), could be too relentless and unvaried. On the other hand he was a tennis player, and described as shy, pleasant and not big headed in spite of having won the US Open in 2009. Perhaps fans had no right to demand a 'personality' as well.

Martin Amis had once taken issue with the whole idea of personality, thinking of Nastase and Connors. The older generation – the Australians and Ashe – hadn't needed 'personality' because they had 'character'.[16] But by the new millennium tennis itself as well as the players had lost its personality.

The powers in the game seemed to be convinced that spectators wanted to see twenty, thirty or even forty stroke rallies and tennis seemed destined to continue down the route taken by Nadal and the Serb, Novak Djokovic. He was described as a tennis machine, whose tennis was relentlessly efficient and athletic, but robotic in its precision. 'Athletic' meant the complete control of the player's body, and the corporate mindset wanted everything under control. Djokovic was the perfect player of corporate tennis: a tennis without controversy, predictable, repeatable, quantitative, metronome tennis. It was the game that emerged from the dark synergy of technology and the conservatism of the sponsors. So the 'modern tennis' the commentators felt compelled to exalt was a kind of *Stepford Wives* version, running smoothly, with no problems, no insubordination, no surprises: perfect tennis for the shareholders.

The grand slam finals between Djokovic and Nadal and between Djokovic and Murray lacked the genuine contrast that had lit up those between Sampras and Agassi or Nadal and Federer: serve-volleyer versus returner, shot-maker versus grinder. Even for the spectators the dominance of the defensive game became a form of masochistic punishment: endless rallies.

The 'modern game' of baseline tennis did have many critics.

Years before, Jack Kramer had pointed out that 'if you have only one style, there's nothing! Fans want to see … different styles … the best match worth watching was a good-conditioned Sampras playing a good-conditioned Agassi.' The Swedish player Jonas Björkman pointed out that the slowing down of the courts had not even, as anticipated, neutralised the big serve, which was as prevalent as ever; what it did was destroy serve-and-volley tennis. The two-handed backhand had also assisted in this process.

The conclusion of the 2012 Australian Open revealed the realities of the contemporary game. It had taken nearly six hours for Djokovic to defeat Nadal. Before the trophies were presented, the sponsors and paymasters of the event produced onto the court a procession of unfit businessmen in crumpled, ill-fitting suits (surely they could have afforded decent tailoring) who lined up and one by one proceeded to deliver long-drawn-out speeches of thanks to themselves and congratulations to one another. It was many minutes into this ritual before an official noticed that the two athletes, supposedly the stars of the event, were visibly swaying on their feet from exhaustion and offered each a chair and a bottle of water.

The ceremony demonstrated to everyone in the stadium and to everyone watching a television screen that the players, supposedly the heroes of the occasion, were actually the athletic gigolos Tilden had predicted they would become so many years ago. This was corporate tennis and the real winners were the suits.

25

The rhetoric of sport

A TENNIS MATCH IS LIKE A CRIME NOVEL, because until the end is reached the outcome is unknown, since the match happens in real time. (So the audience cannot cheat by turning to the final page.) Where the match differs from the thriller – and from real life – is that every result is only provisional, since the tennis calendar is a recurring loop of yearly events. The ATP and WTA Tours are cyclical; the results of a previous year erased by the next, reproducing the cycle of the seasons, ever different yet always the same: the eternal return. Each victory may be followed by a defeat the following week; none is ever finally decisive.

The rhetoric of tennis – sports journalism – fans the flames of the fluctuations, the mood swings, the continual change and sameness of victory and defeat week after week, like the oral mythmakers of ancient tribes who told the same stories over and over again to an audience that never wearied of them. The stories are always the same; the difference is that in sport the sameness and repetition are masked by the changing faces of the temporary gods that are the stars.

Sport is the ephemeral and the eternal rolled into one. Exaggeration is inevitably the result. 'The match' (in any sport) is always in the moment and the reporter must communicate the newness of that Now. From this comes the tendency to exaggerate, to conjure drama of some kind from even a dull match, to ward off the boredom of one-sided or defensive play. Exaggeration colours the backward look to a mythical golden age, the expectations for the future and, most of all, the glorious present.

Yet afterwards the excitement sinks into nothingness, like the air from a leaking balloon. As McEnroe observed, the sports writers were maybe 'a little too poetic' about the famous tie-break that ended the fourth set in the Borg–McEnroe Wimbledon final of 1980, when after 5-all every other point was either a set point or a match point: 'tennis points and games … may be awe inspiring at the moment, but then – except for the videotape, which really tells only a little of the story – the moment is gone. They're like poetry written on water.'[1]

All sports, but especially the mass team sports – football and cricket in Britain, baseball and basketball in the United States – were already hand in glove with the popular press in the late-nineteenth century. In Britain compulsory education and the extension of the vote created a market that was exploited by, among others, Alfred Harmsworth, later Lord Northcliffe, who founded the *Daily Mail* in 1896. The synergy between sport and newsprint grew by leaps and bounds before and after the First World War and throughout the twentieth century the sports pages were crucial to the circulation of newspapers. Even *The Daily Worker* and later the *Morning Star*, organ of the British communist party, enjoyed a rise in sales during the period when its racing correspondent's tips were more accurate than those of its rivals.

Over the course of time and significantly since the arrival of the internet, the media climate changed, first with radio, then television commentary, then the web and social media competing with traditional print journalism. By the end of the twentieth century the newspaper industry was in decline, yet sports coverage had increased as a percentage of the content of most news-papers, at least relatively, reflecting the massive presence of sport globally and nationally. As commercial corporate interests came to dominate sport, sports reportage also had a crucial marketing role since sports in the twenty-first century competed with one another for popularity, audiences and therefore profit. Journalism became a form of propaganda intended to intensify interest in sports and magnify their importance.

A. L. Laney cited the way in which a famous and controversial Lenglen match had been reported and felt that the search for novelty led to exaggeration and latent hysteria, 'furor and sensation' in the reportage of what were in reality trivial events. 'A whole nation, seemingly, became exercised over what really was a small thing, making of it an international incident.' But exaggeration was essential to sport, to encourage the belief that something sensational was happening. 'What courage! What heart!' cries the commentator as a player goes for broke in making a risky winning shot. He risked *losing the point* – well, possibly the match – but it was hardly the Charge of the Light Brigade.

That of course *is* the point. The match mimics the angst of real-life events, but screens them out. It has come to seem that sport is above politics and preferable to it. As Rita Mae Brown said to Martina Navratilova, 'sports are just to keep your mind off everything else'. That was why God preferred to watch Goran Ivanisevic winning Wimbledon when he should have been attending to world affairs; world affairs were just too intractable – and too frightening. The result is that sport generally has become a surrogate for other passions; a distraction, possibly; a safety valve, perhaps. Sport is visceral and compelling and of course depends on *results*, conveyed, most often, through the media.

Tennis was always a niche sport and the tennis column traditionally the least sought after by good, red-blooded sports writers, as Jack Kramer explained when he observed that journalists were reluctant to cover it, on account of its unimportance compared to most sports, and its sissy image, at least in the United States. The sports editor would have to strong-arm one of his writers: 'Hey, the fruits are playing tennis out at the club – you wanna go get some sunshine for a few days?', whereupon 'the reporter would drive out to the club, go through the door just like he was a member and write what a wonderful tournament it was for the 125 people who came out'.

Things were better in Europe. Neil Harman recalled that at one time all the British newspapers had a dedicated tennis correspondent. But by 2012 that day was long past and Harman himself, tennis reporter on *The Times*, was almost the only one left.[2]

The fickleness of fans? – or nationalism trumps the individual star

That was partly because in Britain, at least, other than during Wimbledon fortnight – which occupies a place in British culture that has little to do with actual tennis – the game might never be mentioned at all in British sports sections were it not for the emergence in the past decade or so of Tim Henman, Greg Rusedski and Andy Murray at or near the top of the rankings. For tennis, like all sports, is, as pointed out earlier, also an exercise in nationalism.

The Tim Henman years of British tennis were so saturated with national feeling that television commentary came to resemble an Ealing comedy of the 1950s. Henman was the lock-jawed hero with TV presenter Sue Barker (whose name had once been linked to Cliff Richard's) as the constipated English rose, while Andrew

Castle, a former British player (and now an excellent commentator), with his swept-back wavy blond hair and louche smile, could have played the role of roadhouse 'bounder' or 'cad'. When it rained, Cliff Richard of course, led the singing.

Sporting propaganda is also nationalist propaganda. It is understandable that football fans root for England (for example) when their team plays Spain, France or Croatia. It is understandable that locals support (say) Arsenal, even if the players are no longer local lads, but international stars and the club is internationally owned. Such loyalties are traditional and create a sense, however manufactured or tenuous, of some kind of community.

From the early years, national audiences wanted 'their' tennis stars to win. The Davis Cup in particular was cast in nationalist terms. Since the post-Soviet era, with the advent of stars from emerging nations that in some cases had previously not even officially existed, for example Serbia, tennis has become more and more defined along national lines; hardly surprising, when tennis, in those nations, was a crucial way out of poverty from tanking economies whose promises had signally failed. It is perfectly understandable, too, that national identities, stifled and suppressed during the Soviet period, should have burst out with greater intensity once they were released amid sectarian and bloody local wars.

The sight of national flags draped among the audience at tournaments big and small and fans dressed in flags or with their faces painted in national colours; the cohort of Lleyton Hewitt fans from Australia in uniforms of green and yellow with curly yellow wigs; of a phalanx of Federer supporters with cowbells and bears, could add to the fun and create an atmosphere of carnival. Yet nationalism is reductive. Sport acts as a vehicle for prejudices and passions that might in other circumstances seem far from admirable. Better, because it was a homage to the sport rather than a nation and was thus more inclusive, was the appearance at the 2013 Wimbledon of a group in the Centre Court audience bewigged as Borg, Ashe, Cash, Agassi and McEnroe.

Nationalist carnival could darken into the hatreds that always found an outlet in sport, even in tennis. In 2007 fighting broke out at the Australian Open in Melbourne between Serbs and Croatians, and again in 2009 there were scuffles after Croatian Marin Cilic defeated Serb player Janko Tipsarevic, while after Novak Djokovic beat a Bosnian-born American player, Amer Delic, thirty fans were arrested and one woman knocked unconscious as running battles broke out. To refer to this is not to condemn those nations, with their difficult histories, but to make a point about the double face of national identification, when pride for your own country equates with bitterness and hatred towards another. That these sentiments were stirred up and exploited in the Balkans by politicians with extremist views only serves to underline the ambivalence of such identifications.

At the same time, the status of a small country would be exponentially enhanced by the emergence of a top star who could become a source of justifiable pride. The pre-eminence of Djokovic, flanked by Tipsarevic and Viktor Troiki and of Ana Ivanovic and Jelena Jankovic lifted Serbia into a league of its own. It did not seem surprising that there was a plan for Djokovic to play the role of King of Yugoslavia in a local television series in 2011.

The power of nationalism and sport combined is a reality, but tennis, where the individuality of each player is so much on display, could have been a refreshing exception. It is perverse to view a game of such individualism through the tunnel vision of nationalism. A single player cannot represent a nation in quite the same way as a team; and it is a distortion that nationalism has come to override the game itself to the detriment of all its fascinating variations and personalities. Given the symbiosis of sport and nationalism, however, such a view may seem heretical or even deranged, because for fans not to support their country's representative is to transgress a norm. A few stars have managed to transcend local loyalties and become transnational stars: Borg, Agassi, Nadal and particularly Martina Hingis and Roger Federer (both coincidentally Swiss). Federer seemed especially prone to the 'religion effect'. French and British crowds were known to have rooted for him rather than their home-grown stars and when he arrived in Latin America for a series of exhibition matches he was greeted by a crowd of thousands; it was more like the second coming of the Beatles than the arrival of a sportsman. (Japanese star Kei Nishikori, ranked eleven in the world in 2013 was equally famous, not just in Japan, but throughout Asia.)

Sports reporters are conservative and with corporate tennis came control of the public image of the star as of everything else. Mary Carillo felt that the dead hand of management had first begun to stifle spontaneity when Chrissie Evert came into the public eye. The teenager's sheltered upbringing and her youth had contributed to the trend to protect the top players and limit the access of the press, which perhaps further drained the sport of colourful personalities. Chrissie, thought Carillo, 'was the beginning of the downfall of media access in tennis. She was so young and so shy and she needed handlers. She didn't know how to handle certain situations at sixteen, seventeen. So the tournament people, the [Virginia] Slims people – everybody – they … told her whom she had to talk to, what questions to answer. And once Chrissie got that treatment, it sort of became standard.'[3]

Certainly the press-conference ritual seldom produced any comments of the slightest interest. In the first place it seemed cruel to subject a losing player to such exposure at a moment, possibly, of bitter disappointment and that players were required to attend was yet another aspect of the controlling hand of the management. It allegedly offered the press a chance to penetrate the wall of PR that surrounded the top players, but the players themselves became cagey. Stock answers – 'I thought I played well, I'm very happy with my game' or 'he was the better player today' – produced predictable ennui. At Roland Garros in 2013 Djokovic refused to answer questions about his anticipated semi-final against Nadal, and Nadal banned questions about his suspect knees. Yet these were the only issues the press wanted to hear about.

Naturally, they were eager for news; news is the journalist's stock in trade – and raw material. The 'rhetoric' of tennis – the way it is reported, how it comes to the attention of the general public as well as the tennis-following community, and its media presentation – is, however, more than just news. It is governed by certain dogmas.

In the first place there is a narrative of continued and unending progress and improvement (in all sports, not just tennis) – the Enlightenment view, mentioned earlier, of the combined powers of reason and science to propel civilisation irreversibly forwards. The emphasis on scientific management, on continual 'improvement' – in players' physical capabilities, in the advance of technology and in the continual search for innovation in every aspect of the game, from the design of courts to the shape of shoes – understandably contributes to the view that 'things can only get better'. Players today are 'better' than those of thirty years ago: they must be because they are taller and heavier, pay minute attention to training and diet and are surrounded by an entourage not just of coach and girlfriend/parents, but of sports psychologists, agents, fitness trainers, hitting partners and celebrity supporters (it was a leg up for Andy Murray when Sean Connery and Kevin Spacey appeared in his box). They are also 'better' because they keep on breaking records. In turn, records are widely believed to keep punters interested. 'Records sell. They are part of public expectation and make commercial money' (but what money is not commercial?).[4]

The Western belief in progress has taken many hard knocks in the area of economy, welfare and well-being, but in sport generally and tennis in particular it remains unassailed, at least officially. Each new winner of a major has invariably 'raised the bar'.

As A. L. Laney pointed out many years ago, from the belief in continual progress there follows the view that each generation of players must be better than the last, leading to an unending procession of 'greatest' players. 'However unrealistic it may be, there have always been those who accept the view that once you name a player great at any period, he must be greater than all who preceded him, and to have carried the game to new heights.'[5] The eternal return of the sporting cycle and its recurring regime of competition, creates each generation as the best, the greatest, the never-before-seen.

Laney rightly did not subscribe to this view, for in reality, the idea that there can ever be a 'greatest player of all time' is a fantasy. It is quite impossible to compare Rod Laver with Roger Federer or Nadal with Lacoste in any meaningful way. In practice the tale of endless progress only succeeds in devaluing the past.

But the narrative of progress is central to the *ideology* of sport, to which tennis, originally so different from other sports, must conform and we saw how important a role technology played in reinforcing this ideology. Part of the history of lawn tennis has been the gradual imposition of these general ideals of sport and the manipulation of the game to conform to them. In addition, in the specific case of tennis it became the perceived role of journalists and the powers in the sport after the Second World War and especially in the open era to expunge its effete image and replace it with something more rugged.

Secondly, records and numbers are key. The centrality of records and the quantification of achievement is part and parcel of the bureaucracy that characterised and continues to characterise industrial societies. Sports writer Mihir Bose defended the sporting obsession with statistics as a more certain measurement of ability than aesthetic or more subjective judgements:

> Sport is often compared to an art form, but unlike other arts, it generates objective facts in the form of results and statistics which in turn create accepted rankings of individual performers … The only objective facts for other forms of the arts are sales and the earnings of artists.[6]

He qualified this astonishingly philistine observation by conceding that commercial success is not recognised as the only or main criterion of artistic merit. Indeed, if it were, the author of *Fifty Shades of Grey* would be judged a finer writer than Virginia Woolf. It might be that over time a classic author such as Woolf *would* outsell an ephemeral best-seller; but to rate Shakespeare a greater writer than Charles Baudelaire *because he wrote more words* is not a valid reason for preferring him over the French poet. It is perfectly possible to make an argument for Shakespeare's superiority, but not on statistical, quantitative grounds.

Nor do sporting records necessarily reflect a hierarchy of greatness. Aesthetic and qualitative judgements enter just as much into sports as into music or painting. Rankings of the 'greatest' players based on how many tournaments, games, matches or anything else they won omit crucial qualities of beauty, excitement and creativity.

Already mentioned and central to sporting ideology is an enduring belief in the moral superiority of sport and sportsmen. As soon as Andy Murray won Wimbledon in 2013 a rash of newspaper articles rushed to celebrate all the moral qualities supposedly revealed by virtue of his having won a tennis tournament. A similar reaction when, for example, Ian McKellen triumphed as Gandalf or Laurence Olivier as Othello would be regarded as simply ridiculous. Indeed, heroes from real battlefields are not so garlanded. There were no laudatory articles on returning generals from Helmand; and some of the soldiers seriously wounded and mutilated in the war in Afghanistan were even shunned.

In fact, Murray's efficient straight sets defeat of a flat Djokovic, perhaps still weary from his exhausting win over Del Potro, had a strange, but definite feeling of anti-climax. For so long the world had known about Britain's seventy-seven-year wait for a successor to Fred Perry. Now, however, there was the reminder that actually four women had won Wimbledon since 1936: Dorothy Round in 1937, Angela Mortimer in 1961, Ann Jones in 1969 and Virginia Wade in 1977, suggesting that there was something belittling to women in making so much of the long non-appearance of a men's champion. In addition, the euphoric celebration of Murray's win lasted exactly two days, for by Wednesday the following week Britain was plunged into the new glory of winning the first match of the Ashes against Australia and that was swiftly followed by the British win of the Tour de France. So what had been trailed as the biggest triumph for years was as ephemeral as all sporting victories.

Mihir Bose believes wholeheartedly in the moral transcendence of sport as a pure region, free, at least in principle, from the mess and venality of politics; it places ideals of effort, courage and perfection before its audiences; it promotes community feeling and collective solidarity and unites people. 'Sport is simultaneously a global language and a creator of personal and local identity. A contest in a popular sport is one of the few experiences that can be understood by and excite passions in people all over the world regardless of language, culture or intellect.' [7]

Bose rejected the argument that music is just such a global language, arguing that this is because although some musicians have a global following, 'there is no set of rules, conventions and implements ... quite the opposite'. The different kinds of music preclude universality and anyway popular Western music is 'largely a product of technology and conquest'. His argument is perverse, an absurd piece of special pleading, given that the global spread of sports was originally, as he himself charts, the result of conquest by the British in pursuit of their empire, and is today massively indebted to technology. (A concert given by exiled Malian musicians at the Barbican in London in January 2013 refuted that idea of the non-international appeal and meaning of music. The harmonies and styles were unfamiliar to many in the largely British audience, but the music's beauty and political significance could be shared without any difficulty in the context of the ongoing civil war in Mali.)

While Bose brushes aside the way in which sport divides as much as it unites, continuing the myth of the superiority of sport to all other human activities, Joe Humphreys is one of the few writers to have questioned the beneficial influence of sport as against its promotion of antagonism, racism, sexism and general intolerance. He examines the popular idea that sport has in some way replaced religion and concludes that sport actually displays many of the worst aspects of faith and 'embraced some of the unhealthiest aspects of religion: fanaticism, judgmentalism and irrationality, to name but a few'.[8] He shares Bose's view that sport in general has been corrupted by money and concludes that as a result of the vast wealth it generates sport is now taken far too seriously. But whereas for Bose the solution is for sport to get back to its original high mindedness, for Humphreys it should return to its essence; which is *play*.

This was the view of the Dutch philosopher Johan Huizinga. Play was essential to humanity and central to human life, but also an end in itself. It was a distinct sphere, saturated with myth and ritual in its developed forms, characterised by rhythm, harmony and a highly developed aesthetic quality. In classical Greek, Chinese and Sanskrit the words for 'play' and 'contest' are different, but in Latin, Japanese and European languages they are the same.

Not all forms of play are contests, but all have, or develop, a ritual function, to the extent that religions can be understood as forms of play, to which moral and belief systems have been added. For the most part, however, play is an end in itself, an enchanted realm. In play the human individual steps outside 'real life'. It is disinterested and 'stands outside the immediate satisfaction of wants and appetites ... it is an intermezzo or interlude in our daily lives. As such it adorns life, amplifies it and *is* therefore a necessity as a cultural function.'

Huizinga rejected the common tendency to explain play away. It does not serve 'some other purpose that is not play'. Unfortunately, the industrial development of Western societies in the nineteenth century acted against the spirit of pure play: 'Even in the eighteenth century utilitarianism, prosaic efficiency and the bourgeois ideal of social welfare ... had bitten deep into society.' In the nineteenth century, 'work and production became the ideal, and then the idol, of the age … Henceforth the dominants of civilisation were to be social consciousness, education aspiration and scientific judgment … [and] our worship of technological progress, which was itself the fruit of rationalism and utilitarianism … Men's dreary dress,' he observed, symbolised the triumph of the utilitarian ideal.

Huizinga points to the modern development of sport as typical of this negative trajectory. Sport at the time of his writing (his book was published in 1949) had been almost entirely divested of the true play spirit. It lacked 'spontaneity and carelessness'; none of the sporting events that became so prominent after 1945 had, he felt, 'in the smallest degree, raised sport to the level of a culture-creating activity … it remains sterile. The old play factor has undergone almost complete atrophy.'[9]

The legacy of Thomas Arnold and the book, *Tom Brown's Schooldays* he inspired, propelled sport down this road because it cast sport as not an end in itself, a play ritual, a form of pleasure, but as a *preparation for life* in its alleged character-building characteristics. This was also the 'spirit of the game', its moral validity.

The history of lawn tennis marks this move in a particularly poignant fashion. The game, more clearly than the team sports developing so rapidly towards the end of the Victorian period and far more than boxing, embodied the spirit of play. The presence of women was part of that, but it was due as well to the elaboration and artistic possibilities of the game.

Those who loved the atmosphere of more macho sports, however, despised the spirit of play they found on the tennis court and misunderstood it as 'effeminate' and 'sissy', precisely because they wholly accepted the ideals of *Tom Brown* and the view of sport not as play, but as an educational training for a life of serious work dominated by technology and science, allied to brute force. As the decades passed, the game was gradually fitted into the approved model, not because of the abolition of the amateur professional distinction, but because of the more general, gradual transformation of almost all 'play' into work and – paradoxically

– the development of organised sports as 'entertainment'.

These spectacles retain, for audiences, some element of the participation that Huizinga seems to have felt necessary for an activity to be truly playful, but the dead weight of the significance of any sport's success for those who have a financial stake in it strips out the 'irrational' aspect Huizinga prized. Meanwhile even the spectacle has become less playful. In the case of tennis, the aesthetic of the game has been increasingly subordinated to the worship of power, endurance and violence.

The sporting world could surely have managed not to have a nervous breakdown if a single sport – tennis – had been allowed to follow its own beautiful and eccentric path untrammelled by the totalitarian imperatives of conventional sporting culture. It would not have come to an end if tennis players had been indulged in their aesthetic preferences and social rituals. After all, the attempt to turn tennis into a hybrid of boxing and baseball has not propelled the game to pole position among sports; nor transformed it into a working-class one; it is still largely a middle-class preserve and it has been unfairly castigated for its 'elitism' when other sports – dressage, yachting, polo – although far more elitist, have been left alone.

26

Back to the future

IN 2003 JOHN MCENROE WON the ATP Champions Tour, the senior event, held on this occasion at the Royal Albert Hall in London. The stars of the seventies and eighties played a classical game and if they no longer played at the pace they had once commanded they nevertheless showed flashes of the old brilliance. More surprisingly, Ilie Nastase, now a little portly, tried valiantly to reprise his role as Mr Nasty, while from John McEnroe, lean as ever but with much less hair, was heard every so often the cry: 'You can*not* be serious.' But no one was shocked any more. The audience merely laughed. And somehow at that moment the spectacle became a little sad, McEnroe momentarily an old lion in the circus, twitching his tail and tickled into a half-hearted growl at the crack of the whip. What had once expressed passion and outrage was now 'entertainment'.

Sports stars are ephemeral. Lenglen, Tilden and Cramm are forgotten outside the tennis world. Once McEnroe has departed from the commentary box he too will pass into oblivion. For unlike Napoleon or Julius Caesar, or even Greta Garbo or Marilyn Monroe, sports stars are replaceable. The fiery years when McEnroe and Nastase had dominated were a distant memory. Their style of tennis had gone out of fashion. The tennis boom was long since over. The game had changed.

The world of tennis is a microcosm of the wider world. In the twenty-first century the turbo expansion of capitalism is faltering. Now it was not just Marxists who were predicting the collapse of capitalism, but economists at the heart of the enterprise. Stephen King, for example, chief economist at HSBC banking, foresaw a dystopian future in which 'nations recoil from globalisation and fight over resources, populations lose their faith in governments and in money that has been debased by attempts to revive growth'.[1]

Yet the search for growth continues, because no politician can contemplate an alternative.

Tennis like all sports is fully committed to and dependent on the growth scenario. In the words of Neil Harman, it is 'imperative ... that the sport looks further afield, secures its markets ... preparing for the rainy day that is bound to come'.[2]

The big stars and the big matches continue to draw huge crowds. The slams are sell-outs. The US Open, reported Harman, was 'New York's largest and most valued annual public sporting event, generating $756 million in "economic impact"'. It was the highest-attended annual sporting event in the world. Television audiences for tennis generally are enormous. Eighty-five million viewers watched the 2012 US Open in the US alone and it was broadcast to 188 countries.

Yet by the end of the first millennial decade it was clear, in spite of the boosterist PR rhetoric, that the ATP tour had problems. The sport generated huge TV audiences, but the numbers of active players at the grassroots was in decline. An attempt to streamline the revised calendar for the ATP tour, in place since 2008, had not resolved a number of player grievances.

In 2011 anger peaked at the US Open. A record number of players withdrew with injuries. Torrential rain exposed problems in the court surface. The order of play was wrecked and this caused complaints about the crammed schedule and more generally that players were expected to appear at too many events. Flushing Meadow had always controversially insisted that both men's semi-finals be played on the Saturday, with the final the following day. This was clearly unfair to the second semi-finalist, but suited the television companies and their schedules. After five consecutive years in which rain continually interrupted play, the tournament organisers finally conceded that in 2013 the final was to be played on Monday, although this was not an ideal solution either, Monday being a working day with the consequent risk of smaller audiences.

Steve Tignor reported that 'players were so fed up with the way the game was run and the lack of revenue that was coming back to [most of] them that they talked openly of boycotting events and forming their own union'. The sport was 'divided and chaotic'.

Top players threatened strike action. The two Andys, Roddick and Murray, were particularly vocal. Nadal meanwhile criticised Roger Federer for not doing enough (as President of the Player Council) and eventually resigned from his role as Vice-President of the Council. He had wanted the rankings of top players to be protected for two years (as in golf) in cases of injury or illness. This would clearly have benefitted him and his chronic knee problems, but Federer opposed it as being unfair to lower-ranked players. A bigger problem was the unremitting length of the tournament calendar, giving players barely four weeks of rest at the end of the year and even less if they played in the Davis Cup – which was itself in trouble, 'on life support', McEnroe thought.

Negotiations led to the length of the tour being curtailed by one week; and from 2015 Wimbledon was to be put back by one week in order to give players more time to accustom themselves to grass (a need felt even more urgently after the record number of slips, falls and injuries during the 2013 Wimbledon).

Neil Harman mentioned the possibility that the grand slams might consider taking over the running of the game. In the meantime, in 2012 Brad Drewett was appointed head of the ATP. Steve Tignor had not had high hopes of Drewett, but before Drewett sadly and unexpectedly died of motor neurone-disease in 2013, he was able to negotiate a revised pay structure with the 'big four', the four top players. From 2013 this was to give at least some lower-ranked players better returns for their efforts.[3] At Wimbledon, for example, 'if Great Britain's Davis Cup hero, Dan Evans, ranked 318 in the world, were to get a wild card into the main draw ... and lost, he would go home with £23,000,' explained Kevin Mitchell of the *Guardian*. He contrasted this with what Evans might normally expect on the Futures circuit, 'where playing to near-empty stands ... he might earn as little as $200 (£131) at best, $1,300.'[4]

The yawning gap between the fabulously rich (or 'global properties' as Andrew Castle described them) at the top of the rankings, and players such as Evans, accurately reproduced the general pattern of capitalist development and the gap between rich and poor that had widened all over the world since the 1980s. The situation of Johnny Marray, co-winner of the Wimbledon men's doubles in 2012, baldly illustrated the difference. He lived from hand to mouth and at the age of nearly thirty, was renting a room in his sister's house. As he told Dave Walsh of the *Sunday Times*:

> Doubles money on the Challenger is pathetic... €650 for winning a tournament, but you've got your flight out of that and by the time you've paid for the new trainers you have to buy every three weeks and replaced the broken string on your racquet you'll be left with maybe €150 or €200 for your week's work.[5]

And this was not a regular income. You might not win another match, let alone a tournament, for some time. He acknowledged the help he obtained from the LTA but still knew he'd earn more as a barista. His joy at being a Wimbledon champion was ample reward for all the sacrifices, but few of those stuck on the Challenger circuit would ever win a Wimbledon, or possibly any title.

The economic inequalities within the game necessitated a frantic search for ranking points. Competition was ruthless.

Hordes of agents prowled the increasingly ferocious junior circuit. In the absence of linespersons at junior events it was always a temptation to cheat, while at the lower echelons of the Futures and Challengers circuits match fixing was known to occur. As Tracy Austin had said, back in the 1980s, you had to be completely self centred and selfish to get to the top.

Tennis seemed to be at some sort of crossroads. The game was targeting the huge potential Chinese market. Chinese star, Li Na, women's champion at Roland Garros in 2011, had a fan base of millions in her home country, but some believed that only a male Chinese champion would generate a quantum leap in interest. A discussion on the *Guardian* sports blog pointed out that the Shanghai Rolex Masters Tournament, an ATP 1000 event, held in October at a forbidding venue far outside the centre of the (huge) city, had yet to crack an audience. The big stars played (Federer possibly partly because of his sponsorship with Rolex) and the fans turned out for them, but this premier event was sometimes half empty during the early part of the week – part of the general effect of the huge celebrity of the top stars. When Serena Williams went out early at the 2013 Wimbledon, attendances dropped on the next day she had been expected to play.[6] It was noted, too, that at the July 2013 Hamburg tournament the arena was packed to the gills for Federer's matches; when both he and 'local boy' Tommy Haas failed to win through to the final, the auditorium was only half full for what turned out to be a thrilling encounter between an Argentinian qualifier, Delbonis, and Fabio Fognini.

Many followers of tennis were knowledgeable and played club tennis themselves. They knew the early rounds of a tournament were essential – to prove the worth of the best players, to facilitate upsets and often to generate great tennis – but the dominance of television generated a mass audience more interested in the stars than in the game itself.

In the United States the San Jose tournament, which had lasted for a hundred years, closed down in 2012; the Pacific

Southwestern tournament was long gone; the Los Angeles ATP tournament was sold and closed down; many other tournaments there and in Britain and Australia had disappeared. There was in 2013 no male American player in the top ten; aside from Andy Murray there was no British player inside the men's top 200. However well Wimbledon was marketed, this did not staunch the decline of the sport at the club or local level.[7] The gap between the television presence of a sport and active participants in the game widened in the nations – Australia, America, Britain – that were once its leaders. The number of active players in the UK, where the game was largely confined to private schools, halved in the first decade of the twenty-first century. During Wimbledon 2013 Judy Murray, Britain's Fed Cup captain (the Fed Cup being the equivalent for women of the Davis Cup) voiced her disappointment at the failure of the LTA to develop more free courts or move tennis away from its middle-class, elitist image, while Baroness Billingham, a former player, president of the Oxford LTA and a member of the House of Lords Olympic Legacy committee, was scathing about the failures of the LTA under the leadership of Roger Draper and described herself as proud of the successful five-year campaign to oust him. In Spain, France, Germany and Eastern Europe participation was more widely dispersed.

Philippe Chatrier's collegiate vision of tennis had produced a wonderful cohort of French players and although none had won a slam, they brought style, colour and glamour to a tour largely dominated by the monotone of angry power. Michael Llodra and Nicolas Mahut were Wimbledon doubles winners and looked in different ways like minor characters from a 1950s French thriller, each with strangely old-fashioned compelling looks. There was blond matinée idol, Julien Benneteau, who had been two points from beating Federer at Wimbledon in 2012; there was Jeremy Chardy, a combination of Heathcliff and Mr Darcy; and there was the rising star, Benoit Paire who looked like Jeremy Irons. And those weren't even the top players. Gael Monfils had a face like a

Benin bronze and an acrobat's movements; Richard Gasquet had a fluid game of captivating beauty and flair; Jo-Wilfried Tsonga was the French Muhammad Ali; Gilles Simon had vampire eyes and the most radiant smile and could outlast almost anyone on a tennis court.

It was all the more disappointing that in 2012 these last two revived familiar controversies by heaping scorn on the women's game. Simon argued that women shouldn't be paid as much as men, merely repeating a widely held view, and again, a statistical, numbers-related way of looking at the game; that because women played fewer sets they deserved less money. Tsonga retreated into the nineteenth century, maintaining that women couldn't play consistently on account of their hormones, deploying the hoary old argument of women's biology as destiny.

Daily Telegraph journalist, Oliver Brown, argued (whether seriously or not) that the answer was not for women to be paid less, but for them to play the same number of sets as men. 'Women's grand slam tennis is a nineteenth-century throwback,' he maintained, 'pleading for acceptance on a joint footing with the men's equivalent and yet recycling the original, outrageous myth that the ladies are too frail, too delicate to last five sets like the gentlemen.' He pointed out that for thirteen years the WTA year-end finals had gone to five sets and that Steffi Graf and her colleagues had managed to cope. Whether, with the way the women's game was currently played, there would be an audience for such matches was another matter.

From a feminist perspective Susan Ware questioned the priority given to certain specific qualities perceived as peculiarly manly. She challenged the way in which sports 'are divided by gender rather than ability, size or other factors'. She felt it was wrong that sports privileged 'male attributes of speed and strength rather than the endurance or agility more common to women', but she suggested that in any case the differences in athletic abilities between the sexes were exaggerated and that there might be more similarities than differences. She argued that the sporting culture did everything it possibly could to reinforce differences between the sexes and the belief that men were inherently stronger and faster than women. It was never questioned that women were unable to compete with men on an equal basis. Billie Jean King had made the same point back in 1984.[8]

Sport was the world headquarters of gender conservatism, rivalled only by the extremist arms of world religions. The obstinate belief in women's sporting inferiority and the unrelenting sexism of reportage was closely linked to the persistent fear of homosexuality that pervaded the sporting world. A handful of sportsmen had come out in recent years, but there were no out gays on the tennis circuit. The old 'sissy' slur might make it even more difficult than in other sports for a player to be open about his sexuality. But homosexuality in any sport runs up against the enduring image of the sporting hero.

Corporate conservatism supported and reinforced the dominant ideology of sport, yet the powers in tennis were more than ready to tinker with the game itself in the attempt to solve perceived problems. Laney had long ago warned that: 'A game as stylised as tennis should be treated with great restraint. One of the things wrong with it may be that so many people keep trying to alter it to suit other people who do not really play it.'[9] Conservatism in that sense was a force protective of the game and changes to the game might otherwise have been more drastic and more far reaching than had so far been the case. The brash event piloted in Houston had not won the day; but tennis had been coarsened.

The courts became slower and slower and this had to be defended by the creation of a myth: that in the 1990s men's tennis had been completely locked into a serving contest in which rallies had virtually ceased to exist. This was the exaggeration of a real problem and only a partial truth. Agassi and Michael Chang, for example, had not played that style of game. In retrospect the myth took hold, as myths do, partly because a younger generation (both players and spectators) who had no memory of that time was continually told that the so-called 'modern game' – not that there was anything particularly modern about interminable baseline rallies – was far superior to the serving contests of the nineties.

The 'modern game' brought its own problems, however. Sets that had once taken thirty minutes had now lengthened to an hour or more. (In the Australian Open semi-final of 2005, between Federer and Marat Safin, 395 points were played in 268 minutes; in 2012, Djokovic and Nadal played 369 points in 353 minutes.)[10]

However, instead of suggesting that a faster game might be at least part of the solution, further changes to the scoring system were suggested as ways of countering the problem resulting from the previous 'solution'. Perhaps five-set matches should be abandoned even at the slams – they already had been from the latter stages of the World Tour finals and ATP 1000 finals; or the 'let' when serving should be abolished.

Audiences didn't necessarily want to watch rallies that invariably went to twenty or thirty strokes (one point in the 2013 US Open final between Djokovic and Nadal lasted for fifty-four strokes) and contests that lasted five hours. These could be exciting at the very highest level – counter-punching building up like a house of cards – but could equally seem monotonous and repetitive. Frank Deford had once pointed out that in the 1920s 'each player grew up with his own style'. He quoted the Spanish player Manuel Alonso, who said: 'the beauty of that time was that each individual was a certain game … [whereas] these players today [the 1970s] all do the same thing against each other.' Individuality and eccentricity had not been wholly purged from the game, but the uniformity of surfaces and coaching left less room for the development of personality – for a player's style is his personality.

Although interminable matches caused problems for the TV schedules, no one seriously contemplated the reintroduction of faster courts. The French attempted it in 2010 at the winter indoor tournament at Bercy, Paris, and at Roland Garros (to a lesser extent) the following year, but in spite of the enthusiasm aroused, it was not repeated. There were powers behind the scenes determined to retain slow play.

It was a stunning irony that it was precisely this style of play for which women's tennis had long been condemned. As far back as 1933 the sports writer John Tunis had complained of the lack of variety in women's tennis. There was nothing but 'slug, slug, slug'. Similar complaints had echoed down the years.

The difference in 2010 when most of the top men were playing attritional baseline tennis was that this could now be reinterpreted as a wonderful example of endurance and muscle power. What had been unimaginative and deadly boring when women played from the baseline, became a macho triumph in men's singles.

Events leading up to Roland Garros and Wimbledon in 2013 suggested that players and spectators, commentators and officials, insiders and outsiders were longing for more variety. Commentators talked up a new generation of players who were trying to crack the dominance of those at the very top. They reported ecstatically at Wimbledon when a series of upsets by serve-and-volley players put out former champions: first the 2002 champion, Lleyton Hewitt was defeated by Dustin Brown, a startling all-court player with dreadlocks; Nadal was downed by Belgian Steve Darcis who camped at the net; and defending champion Federer fell to another serve volleyer, Sergiy Stakhovsky. Each of these giant killers lost in the next round, but there was unalloyed astonishment and delight that young players had found a way to transcend the technology that was supposed to have put an end forever to classic, old style net play. 'Tennis as it should be played' was the cry. That the tournament ended with the usual suspects squaring up didn't detract from the excitement produced by daring new talents. Spectators remembered – or learned for the first time – that attacking grass-court tennis was a thing of beauty and thrills. And indeed it seemed that players were trying to volley a bit more, Djokovic and Nadal quite capable of finishing off a point at the net.

The average age of the male player was rising. Longevity – possibly due to the increased attention to diet and fitness – was, in theory at least, welcomed, but managers, promoters and the commentariat were desperate for exciting new players to supplant those at the top.

The Italian Fabio Fognini and Frenchman Benoit Paire were not afraid to play tennis in new, daring and more eccentric fashion. Latvian Ernst Gulbis was gifted with outstanding talent and aggression. Considered most promising of all, Grigor Dimitrov of Bulgaria was hailed as the next rising star, an all-court player with every shot in the book. None, however, could find sufficient consistency to get to the top.

The tennis establishment criticised the rising cohort as insufficiently serious and dedicated. They clowned about, threw tantrums or played to the crowd. Erroll Flynn lookalike, Fognini, was an 'actor'; Dimitrov was too lightweight and better known for his romances with Sharapova and (possibly) Serena Williams than for winning titles. Gulbis was said to spend too much time in nightclubs instead of training in a boot camp. They earned too much money; ranked twenty-four in the world (and later inside the top twenty), Fognini had already earned three million dollars before he won a tournament.

To berate young players only just out of their teens for laziness, complacency and a failure to adhere to the Calvinist work ethic was completely to ignore the way in which once the sheen of celebrity had touched a player, it was bound, combined with the tantalising promise of so much gold at the end of the rainbow, to create a mirage world wholly at odds with the underlying reality: that the price for ultimate success was the renunciation of any sort of normal life.

The continual fight for survival on the circuit could also kill the joy of tennis. Jo-Wilfried Tsonga said: 'For me it's not just the top four [who have no personality]. It's all the players. But it's how the world goes now. Today you just go to the tournament and play. You share nothing.' He played without a coach for two years in order to reconnect with his love of the game and rather wistfully he recalled a Challenger tournament in Surbiton, where he won in 2007. There it was all so simple and unpretentious. He stayed in a small hotel and celebrated the win with a beer.

Now it seemed that the next generation simply baulked at the tour treadmill and the middle management pall that had seemed to have settled like frozen lava over the game. The surface was beginning to crack, like the courts at Flushing Meadow.

This was not a rebellion confined exclusively to tennis. In 2012 the Ukrainian male lead ballet star, Polunin, abruptly quit the Royal Ballet in London, claiming that he could no longer stand the unrelenting dedication required. He opened a tattooing parlour instead (but later did return to dancing with another company). An older colleague commented that Polunin might be doing 'too much too young' and that dancers were under greater pressure than in her youth.

All physical performers have to train; to excel in such fields does require dedication. But in the twenty-first century, in every field of endeavour – the professions, office work, call centres and the service sector – a long-hours culture demands an unrelenting commitment to work at all costs. Humankind is imprisoned in a science fiction future in which not to work was to become to all intents and purposes an enemy of the state. All must conform to a Gradgrind conception of hard work and making money as the chief purpose and virtue of life, work configured as the grim treadmill portrayed in Fritz Lang's *Metropolis*. In tennis, every time a player comes onto court the amount of money he has earned is displayed. When Andy Murray won the US Open the headline in the *Evening Standard* was not 'Murray is Champion' or similar, but 'Grand Slam Murray set to make £100M mint'.

The players at the top of the game no doubt enjoy their wealth, but they sometimes appear like King Croesus. Everything

Croesus touched turned to gold – but eventually, of course, he starved because his food, too, was converted into metal.

At the beginning of the French Open, Gulbis complained of the blandness of tennis and its personalities in an interview for the French sports magazine, *L'Équipe*. He blamed Roger Federer for being the 'perfect Swiss gentleman' – but it had all started long before Federer; when the promoters and sponsors had decided to clamp down on 'bad behaviour'. The threat of losing their clothing deals and other sponsorships kept the players in line. At the end of the twentieth century there certainly was a feeling that those who ran tennis required no controversy of any kind and the Tiger Woods debacle of 2009 made them even more hostile to the slightest whiff of deviant behaviour. Djokovic had reined in his 'clowning' and Andy Murray admitted that his press interviews were boring and dull because he was anxious to avoid saying anything at all controversial, while at the time of the strike threats in 2011 Federer had said he preferred not to discuss the issues in public, because it could lead to negative press. Gulbis was correct about the boredom, but possibly wrong in blaming, effectively, the messenger, when, to paraphrase Gloria Swanson in a different context, 'it was the game that got dull'.

Effectively the management wanted the impossible. They wanted a mass, popular, 'red blooded' sport, but they also wanted bland good behaviour. An example of how po-faced tennis had become was provided when Dimitrov beat Djokovic in Madrid. The crowd rooted noisily for the underdog, the Bulgarian, chanting his name and cheering him on. Commentator Mark Petchey prissily complained that they were showing insufficient 'respect' to the 'World Number One' as though Djokovic were the Pope or Nelson Mandela; a pompous attitude not even consistent with the description of sport as 'entertainment'.

Gulbis – supported predictably by McEnroe – wanted more controversy and revived the comparison with boxing, not the play itself, but the exchange of insults, the pre-match dramas and stand-offs. Honest antagonism might well be a welcome change from the clichés about how much the top players respect one another and how they are wonderful 'ambassadors' for the game. A game doesn't need ambassadors – another example of the pomposity of sport and its evangelists. Nations have ambassadors. No one discusses 'ambassadors' for the theatre or cinema. Ambassador in the context of tennis is a euphemism for PR, with stars essentially door-to-door salesmen, spreading the popularity of tennis. In itself that is a reasonable goal, but the language is absurdly pretentious.

Just as the grotesque financial inequalities in the game mimicked the inequalities of global capitalism, so Gulbis and his generation resembled youthful protesters throughout the world. From Egypt to Brazil they protested against the sclerosis of neo-liberal capitalism, the regime of middle-management politicians scurrying around at the behest of the IMF, and a repressive, conservative culture. It was particularly telling that street protests in Brazil were aimed at the vast sums to be spent on the 2016 Olympics when the populace believed that that money should have gone to improve welfare, housing and jobs. What the protestors lacked was an organised campaign and concentration of purpose. Meanwhile in tennis, the race for rankings, money and the exhaustion generated by moving from one tournament to the next made coherent demands for change difficult to even imagine, let alone carry out. So protest usually remained unorganised and fizzled out.

Gulbis evidently hit a nerve because his interview provoked much discussion. Many fans would prefer a game in which a one-sided insistence on fitness, endurance and the defensive game did not produce over-long matches consisting in interminable ground-stroke rallies. Personalities are not ultimately the issue; it is the personality of *the game itself* that television and corporate culture had flattened and subjected to 'McDonaldization'.

A critique of corporate culture and its philosophy of profit at all costs is not a nostalgic lament for the artless amateur tournaments of another time, of which Surbiton seemed like an echo. In tennis, as in everything else, change is continuous and inevitable, but it is legitimate to question its direction and extent. It is to be hoped, and must be assumed, that those involved in tennis and in positions of power in its running love the game, are protective of it and wish it to prosper, that they are not just killing the goose that laid the golden egg. There will always be some fans and players who prefer one type of tennis, and others who prefer the opposite. Ironically, what has been lost to tennis is variety – because if there was one thing that consumer society boasts it can produce it is precisely that: consumer choice, a cornucopia of different delights.

Money doesn't tell the whole story. It doesn't follow from a sell-out slam that those who bought tickets liked what they got. They lived in hope and memory and were often disappointed. Yet there are fashions in tennis as in everything else. Serve and volley went out of fashion, but sooner or later a different style from the so-called 'modern game' will emerge. Tennis will continue to evolve.

Indeed, lo and behold, at the start of 2014 came rumours that the courts at the Australian Open were faster – although the head groundsman denied this – and the balls a little lighter. Pat Cash, Wimbledon winner in 1987, thought the baseliners might not be happy to find the court surfaces at Melbourne Park 'quicker than they have been for many years. Attacking play will be rewarded, which I hope will revive something that's almost died in the modern game – variety'. He suggested that a decade ago some European players had threatened a boycott because of the extreme speed of the then popular surface, Rebound Ace, hence the turn to courts that became slower and slower. Now he was hoping for a change of direction. That Djokovic took on Boris Becker as his coach was seen as a move towards a more attacking game and a move away from those five-hour finals that, wrote Kevin Mitchell, might be fascinating to players and spectators who had known nothing else, but were 'anathema to romantics'. By romantic he may have implied that it is mere nostalgia to long for the all-court game, but a return to an airier and less muscle-bound tennis rather than a looking backwards, could herald a new dawn. Then tennis might cease to be the poor relation of boxing and recover its true self as that mixture of chess and dance, of intellectual geometry and aesthetic joy. Not for nothing was it known as the most glamorous of sports. 'Glamour' derives from an old word for witchcraft, so may tennis soon once more cast its spell as the magical points come one after another, like poetry on water, yet recurring over and over again.

BIBLIOGRAPHY

Books and journal articles

Tim Adams, *On Being John McEnroe*, London: Yellow Jersey Press, 2003.

Andre Agassi, *Open: An Autobiography*, London: Harper Collins, 2009.

Martin Amis, 'Tennis Personalities', in David Remnick, ed., *The Only Game in Town: Sports Writing from the New Yorker*, New York: Random House, 2010, pp 374–376.

Martin Amis, 'Tennis: The Women's Game' in *Visiting Mrs Nabokov and Other Excursions*, London: Penguin, 1993, pp 60–68.

Vijay Amritraj, with Richard Evans, *Vijay! From Madras to Hollywood via Wimbledon*, London: Libri Mundi, 1990.

David Andrews and Steven J Jackson, eds., *Sports Stars: The Cultural Politics of Sporting Celebrity*, London: Routledge, 2001.

Arthur Ashe, with Frank Deford, *Portrait in Motion*, Boston: Houghton Mifflin, 1975.

E Digby Baltzell, *Sporting Gentlemen: Men's Tennis from the Age of Honour to the Cult of the Superstar*, New York: The Free Press, 1995.

Charles Baudelaire, *The Mirror of Art: Critical Studies*, London: Phaidon, 1955.

Emmanuel Bayle, 'Le Dévelopment de la Féderation Française de Tennis sous la Présidence de Philippe Chatrier, 1975–1993, Un Modèle Stratégique pour le Mouvement Sportif et Olympique,' in Patrick Clastres et Paul Dietschy, eds., *Paume et Tennis en France XV–XX Siècle*, Paris: Nouveau Monde, 2009.

Cecil Beaton, *The Glass of Fashion*, New York: Doubleday & Co., 1954.

Boris Becker, with Robert Lübenoff and Helmut Sorge, *The Player: The Autobiography*, London: Bantam Books, 2005.

Derek Birley, *Land of Sport and Glory: Sport and British Society 1887–1910*, Manchester: Manchester University Press, 1995.

Mary Blume, *Côte d'Azur: Inventing the French Riviera*, London: Thames and Hudson, 1992.

Peter Bodo, *Courts of Babylon: Tales of Greed and Glory in the Harsh New World of Professional Tennis*, New York: Scribner, 1995.

Mihir Bose, *The Spirit of the Game: How Sport Made the Modern World*, London: Constable, 2011.

Dennis Brailsford, *British Sport: A Social History*, Cambridge: Lutterworth Press, 1992.

Mabel Brookes, *Crowded Galleries*, London: Heinemann, 1956.

Don Budge, *Don Budge: A Tennis Memoir*, New York: the Viking Press, 1969.

Herbert Chipp, *Recollections*, London: Merritt and Hatcher, 1898

Kenneth Clark, *Another Part of the Wood: A Self Portrait*, London: John Murray, 1974.

Patrick Clastres & Paul Dietschy, eds., *Paume et Tennis en France XV–XX Siècle*, Paris: Nouveau Monde, 2009.

Gianni Clerici, *Tennis*, London: Octopus Books,1976.

Gianni Clerici, *Divina Suzanne Lenglen, la Piu Grande Tennista del Mondo*, Roma: Fandango Libria, 2010.

Steven Connor, *A Philosophy of Sport*, London: Reaktion Books, 2011.

Allison Danzig and Peter Schwed, eds., *The Fireside Book of Tennis*, New York: Simon and Schuster, 1972.

Sue Davidson, *Changing the Game: The Stories of Tennis Champions Alice Marble and Althea Gibson*, Seattle: Seal Press, 1997.

Frank Deford, *Big Bill Tilden: The Triumphs and the Tragedy*, London: Victor Gollancz, 1977.

Sundiata Djata, *Blacks at the Net Vol I*, Syracuse: Syracuse University Press, 2006.

Alexandre Dumas, *The Three Musketeers*, London: Harper Collins, 2008.

Norbert Elias and Eric Dunning, *Quest for Excitement: Sport and Leisure in the Civilising Process*, Oxford: Basil Blackwell, 1986.

Larry Engelman, *The Goddess and the American Girl: The Story of Suzanne Lenglen and Helen Wills*, Oxford: Oxford University Press, 1988.

Dominic Erdozain, *The Problem of Pleasure: Sport, Recreation and the Crisis of Victorian Religion*, Woodbridge: Boydell Press, 2010.

Richard Evans, *McEnroe: A Rage for Perfection*, London: Sidgwick and Jackson, 1982.

Richard Evans, *Open Tennis: The First Twenty Years: The Players, the Politics, the Pressures, the Passion and the Great Matches*, London: Bloomsbury, 1988.

Karen Farrington, *Anna Kournikova*, London: Unanimous, 2001.

Yann le Faou, ' "Les Mousquetaires", Ambassadeurs de la France', in Patrick Clastres and Paul Dietschy, eds., *Paume et Tennis en France*, Paris Nouveau Monde 2009.

Jean Michel Faure, 'National Identity and the Sporting Champion: Jean Borotra and French History', *International Journal of the History of Sport*, volume 13, no. 1, 1996, pp. 86–100.

Marshall Jon Fisher, *A Terrible Splendour*, New York: Three Rivers Press, 2009.

Gordon Forbes, *A Handful of Summers*, London: Heinemann, 1978.

Paul Gallico, 'Funny Game', in Paul Gallico, *Farewell to Sport*, London: Simon and Schuster, 1988, pp. 137–150.

David Gautier, 'Tennis et Politique: l'example de Jean Borotra', in Patrick Clastres and Paul Dietschy, eds., *Paume et Tennis en France XV–XX Siècle*, Paris: Nouveau Monde, 2009.

Antoine (Coco) Gentien, *Aventures d'un Joueur de Tennis*, Paris-Genève: La Palatine, 1953.

Michael D Giardina, 'Global Hingis: flexible citizenship and the trans-national celebrity', in David L Andrews and Steven J Jackson, eds., pp. 201–217.

David Gilbert, 'The Vicar's Daughter and the Goddess of Tennis: Cultural Geographies of Sporting Femininity and Bodily Practices in Edwardian Suburbia', *Cultural Geographies*, vol. 18, no. 2, 2011, pp. 187–207.

Heiner Gillmeister, *Tennis: A Cultural History*, London: Leicester University Press, 1997.

Ricardo Pancho Gonzales, *Man with a Racket; The Autobiography of Pancho Gonzales as Told to Cy Rice*, London: Thomas Yozelof, 1959.

David Gray, *Shades of Gray: Tennis Writings of David Gray*, ed., Lance Tingay, London: Collins, 1988.

Pat Griffin, *Strong Women, Deep Closets: Lesbians and Homophobia in Sport*, Champagne, Ill: Human Kinetics, 1998.

Allen Guttmann, *From Ritual to Record: The Nature of Modern Sports*, New York: Columbia University Press, 1978.

Neil Harman, *Court Confidential: Inside the World of Tennis*, London: The Robson Press, 2013.

Dick Hebdige, *Subculture: The Meaning of Style*, London: Methuen, 1979.

Julius D. Heldman, 'The Style of Jack Kramer', in Allison Danzig and Peter Schwed, eds., *The Fireside Book of Tennis*, pp. 292–282.

Jon Henderson, *The Last Champion: The Life of Fred Perry*, London: Yellow Jersey Press, 2009.

David Hilliard, 'UnEnglish and Unmanly: Anglo-Catholicism and Homosexuality', *Victorian Studies*, Winter, 1982, pp. 181–210.

George Hillyard, *Forty Years of First Class Tennis*, London: Williams and Norgate, 1924.

Jane Hoffman, 'The Sutton Sisters', in Allison Danzig and Peter Schwed, eds., *The Fireside Book of Tennis*, New York: Simon & Schuster, 1972.

Catherine Horwood, 'Dressing Like a Champion: Women's Tennis Wear in Interwar England', in Christopher Breward, Becky Conekin and Caroline Cox., eds., *The Englishness of English Dress*, Oxford: Berg, 2002, pp. 45–60.

Johnette Howard, *The Rivals: Chris Evert vs Martina Navratilova: Their Epic Duels and Extraordinary Friendship*, London: Yellow Jersey Press, 2005.

Patrick Howarth, *When the Riviera Was Ours*, London: Routledge & Kegan Paul, 1977.

Johan Huizinga, *Homo Ludens: A Study of the Play Element in Culture*, London: Temple Smith, 1979 (1949).

Joe Humphreys, *Foul Play: What's Wrong With Sport*, Cambridge: Icon Books, 2008.

Helen Hull Jacobs, *Beyond the Game*, London: Methuen, 1950.

Eric N Jensen, *Body By Weimar: Athletes, Gender and German Modernity*, Oxford: Oxford University Press, 2010.

Donald Katz, *Just Do It: The Nike Spirit in the Corporate World*, New York: Random House, 1994.

Billie Jean King, with Frank Deford, *The Autobiography of Billie Jean King*, London: Granada, 1982.

Jack Kramer, with Frank Deford, *The Game: My Forty Years in Tennis*, London: André Deutsch, 1979.

Roman Krznaric, *The First Beautiful Game: Stories of Obsession in Real Tennis*, Oxford: Ronaldson, 2006.

Kyle Kusz, 'Andre Agassi and Generation X: Reading White Masculinity in 1990s America', in Andrews and Steven J Jackson, eds., *Sports Stars: The Cultural Politics of Sporting Celebrity*, London: Routledge, 2001, pp.

Robert Lake, *Social Exclusion in British Tennis: A History of Privilege and Prejudice*, unpublished PhD., Brunel University, 2008.

A L Laney, *Covering the Court: A Fifty Year Love Affair with the Game of Tennis*, New York: Simon and Schuster, 1968.

Jacques Henri Lartigue, *Mémoires Sans Mémoire*, Paris: Editions Laffont, 1975.

Stephen Liégeard, *La Côte d'Azur*, Paris: Maison Quintain, 1882.

Walter LaFeber, *Michael Jordan and the New Global Capitalism*, New York: W. W. Norton, 1999.

Tara Magdalinski, *Sport, Technology and the Body: The Nature of Performance*, London: Routledge, 2009.

Alice Marble with Dale Leatherman, *Courting Danger*, New York: St Martins Press, 1991.

Dan Maskell, *From Where I Sit*, London: Collins, 1988.

Peter Maxton, *From Palm to Power: The Evolution of the Racket*, London: Wimbledon Lawn Tennis Museum, 2008.

John McEnroe, with James Kaplan, *Serious: the Autobiography*, London: Time Warner, 2003.

Mandy Merck, 'Hard, Fast and Beautiful', in Mandy Merck, In *Your Face: 9 Sexual Studies*, New York: New York University Press, 2000, pp. 52–70.

Tatiana Metternicht, *Bericht eines Ungewöhnlichen Lebens*, München: Langen Müller, 1987.

Edward D Miller, *Tomboys, Pretty Boys and Outspoken Women*, Ann Arbour: University of Michigan Press, 2011.

A Wallis Myers, *Lawn Tennis at Home and Abroad*, London: George Newnes, 1903.

A Wallis Myers, *Memory's Parade*, London: Methuen, 1932.

Martina Navratilova, with George Vecsey, *Being Myself*, London: Harper Collins, 1985.

George Orwell, 'The Sporting Spirit', in George Orwell, *The Collected Essays, Journalism and Letters of George Orwell, Volume 4: In Front of Your Nose, 1945–1950*, Harmondsworth: Penguin, 1968.

Robert D Osborn, *Lawn Tennis: Its Players and How to Play*, London: Strahan and Company, 1881.

Jeffrey Pearson, *Lottie Dod: Champion of Champions: The Story of an Athlete*, Birkenhead: Countrywise Ltd., 1988.

Fred J Perry, *My Story*, London: Hutchinson and Co., n.d.,

Fred Perry, *Fred Perry: An Autobiography*, London: Hutchinson, 1984.

James W Pipkin, *Sporting Lives: Metaphor and Myth in American Sports Biographies*, Columbia: Missouri University Press, 2008.

Len and Shirley Richardson, *Anthony Wilding: A Sporting Life*, Canterbury: Canterbury University Press, 2005.

George Ritzer, *The McDonaldization of Society*, London: Sage, 2004.

Mary Roberts, 'Samson and Delilah Revisited: The Politics of Fashion in 1920s France', in Whitney Chadwick and Tirza True Latimer, eds., *The Modern Woman Revisited: Paris Between the Wars*, New Brunswick NJ: Rutgers University Press, 2003, pp. 65–94.

Raphael Samuel, *The Lost World of British Communism*, London: Verso, 2006.

Monica Seles, *Getting a Grip: On My Game, My Body, My Mind … Myself*, London: JR Books, 2009.

Kenneth Silver, *Making Paradise: Art, Modernity and the Myth of the French Riviera*, Cambridge, Ma: MIT Press, 2001.

Barry Smart, *The Sport Star: Modern Sport and the Cultural Economy of Sporting Celebrity*, London: Sage, 2005.

Nancy Spain, *"Teach" Tennant: The Story of Eleanor Tennant The Greatest Tennis Coach in the World*, London: Werner Laurie, 1953.

Kevin Starr, *Embattled Dreams: California in War and Peace: 1940–1950*, Oxford: Oxford University Press, 2003.

René Stauffer, *The Roger Federer Story: Quest for Perfection*, New York: New Chapter Press, 2006.

Egon Steinkampf, *Gottfried von Cramm: Der Tennis Baron*, München: Herbig, 1990.

William Talbert, *Playing For Life: Billy Talbert's Story*, London: Victor Gollancz, 1959.

Steve Tignor, *High Strung: Bjorn Borg, John McEnroe and the Untold Story of Tennis's Fiercest Rivalry*, London: Harper Collins, 2011.

Lance Tingay, *Tennis: A Pictorial History*, London: Collins, 1977.

Teddy Tinling, *Sixty Years in Tennis*, London: Sidgwick & Jackson, 1983.

T Todd, *The Tennis Players: From Pagan Rites to Strawberries and Cream*, Guernsey: Vallancey Press, 1979.

Neil Tranter, *Sport, Economy and Society in Britain, 1750–1914*, Cambridge: Cambridge University Press, 1998.

Thorstein Veblen, *The Theory of the Leisure Class*, London: George Allen and Unwin, 1949.

Sylvain Villaret et Philippe Tétart, 'Yannick Noah au Miroir des Médias', in Patrick Clastres & Paul Dietschy, *Paume et Tennis en France XV–XX Siècle*, Paris: Nouveau Monde, 2009.

Helen Walker, 'Tennis', in Tony Mason, ed., *Sport in Britain: A Social History*, Cambridge: Cambridge University Press, 1989.

David Foster Wallace, 'Federer Both Flesh and Not', in David Foster Wallace, *Both Flesh and Not: Essays*, London: Hamish Hamilton, 2012.

David Foster Wallace, 'Democracy and Commerce at the U S Open', in David Foster Wallace, *Both Flesh and Not: Essays*, London: Hamish Hamilton, 2012.

Susan Ware, *Game, Set, Match: Billie Jean King and the Revolution in Women's Sports*, Chapel Hill: University of North Carolina Press, 2011.

Patricia Campbell Warner, 'Taking up Tennis', in Patricia Campbell Warner, *When the Girls Came Out to Play: The Birth of American Sportswear*, Amherst: University of Massachusetts Press, 2008.

A M Waser, 'Tennis in France, 1880–1930', *International Journal of the History of Sport*, Volume 13, no.2, 1996, pp. 166–176, Volume 7, 2005.

Anthony Wilding, *On the Court and Off*, London: Methuen, 1912.

Helen Wills, *Fifteen Thirty*, New York: Scribner, 1937.

Elizabeth Wilson, *Bohemians: The Glamorous Outcasts*, London: I. B. Tauris, 2000.

Herbert Warren Wind, *Game Set and Match: The Tennis Boom of the Sixties and Seventies*, New York: C P Dutton, 1979.

Newspaper articles

Anon. 'La Face Obscure d'un Champion: Rafael Nadal, l'Ere du Soupçon', *L'illustré*, 2009, pp. 32–35.

Lynn Barber, 'Anyone for Tension?', *Sunday Times*, Magazine, 5 June, 2011.

Pat Cash, 'Pat Cash in Melbourne', *Sunday Times*, 12 January 2014, sports section p. 13.

Larry Elliot, 'What if this time, the party really is over?', *Guardian*, 6 May, 2013, p. 21.

Owen Gibson, 'Doping: now it's worse than it's ever been', *Guardian* sports section, 16 February, 2013.

Giles Hattersley, 'New Balls Please', *Sunday Times*, Style, 16 December, 2012, pp. 26–28.

Paul Hayward, 'Forget purity, sport has never been innocent', *Observer* sports section, 20 October, 2009.

Jon Henderson, 'Grisly, ghastly and gripping is just how Andy likes it', *Evening Standard*, 28 January, 2013, p. 59.

Stuart Jeffries, 'Is Germany too Powerful for Europe?', *Guardian*, G2, 1 April, 2013, p. 11.

Chris Jones, 'Nadal's London Calling', *Evening Standard*, 24 October 2013, World Tour finals supplement.

Elizabeth Kaye, 'The Power and the Glory', *Observer*, Magazine, 14 June, 2009.

Kevin Mitchell, 'You're going through so much pain, but you still enjoy it', *Guardian* Sport, 30 January, 2012, p. 3.

Kevin Mitchell, 'Extra Time for the Worshippers at the Church of Federer', *Guardian*, Sports Section, 12 January, 2013.

Kevin Mitchell, 'Wimbledon raises prize money to record levels for winners and losers', *Guardian*, 24 April, 2013, p. 43.

Kevin Mitchell, 'Djokovic hopes Becker's change of mindset can bring net gains', *Guardian*, 13 January, 2014, sports section, p. 8.

Peter Walker, 'Wimbledon Women's Quarter Final is Suddenly not the name of the Game', *Guardian*, 3 July, 2013.

David Walsh, 'Sponsorship? I get free contact lenses from my optician in Sheffield', *The Sunday Times*, 15 July, 2012.

Internet sites

Tim Adams, http://www.guardian.co.uk/sport/2009/jul05/monica-seles-interview accessed 12 March, 2013.

Peter Bodo, 'Sprezzatura', http://tennis.com/tennisworld/2009/ 06sprezzatura.html accessed 9 September, 2009.

S L Price, 'Boris Becker: Broken Promise', *Time*, http://www.time.com accessed 3 June, 2013.

Steve Tignor, 'The Rally: The Life and Legacy of Brad Drewett', http://www.tennis.com/ pro-game/2013/05/rally-life-and-legacy-brad/drewett/47346 accessed 5 June 2013.

REFERENCES

1 The game of love

1 Ricardo Pancho Gonzales, *Man With A Racket: The Autobiography of Pancho Gonzales*, as told to Cy Rice, London: Thomas Yozelof, 1959, p. 37.

2 Dan Maskell, *From Where I Sit*, London: Collins, 1988, p. 29.

3 A L Laney, *Covering the Court: A Fifty Year Love Affair with the Game of Tennis*, New York: Simon and Schuster, 1968, pp. 40–41.

4 Johnette Howard, *The Rivals: Chris Evert vs. Martina Navratilova: Their Epic Duels and Extraordinary Friendship*, London: Yellow Jersey Press, 2005, p. 129.

5 James W Pipkin, *Sporting Lives: Metaphor and Myth in American Sports Biographies*, Columbia: Missouri University Press, 2008, passim.

6 Frank Deford, *Big Bill Tilden: The Triumphs and the Tragedy*, London: Victor Gollancz, 1977, p. 76.

7 Helen Wills, *Fifteen–Thirty*, New York: Scribners, 1937, p. 194.

8 Gianni Clerici, *Tennis*, London: Octopus Books, 1976, p. 36.

2 Healthy excitement and scientific play

1 Roman Krznaric, *The First Beautiful Game: Stories of Obsession in Real Tennis*, Oxford: Ronaldson, 2006.

2 All quotes from Robert D Osborn, *Lawn Tennis: Its Players and How to Play*, London: Strahan and Company, 1881.

3 T Todd, *The Tennis Players: From Pagan Rites to Strawberries and Cream*, Guernsey: Vallancey Press, 1979, p. 38.

4 Helen Walker, 'Tennis', in Tony Mason, editor, *Sport in Britain: A Social History*, Cambridge: Cambridge University Press, 1989, p. 248.

5 This is recorded by Helen Wills in her autobiography, op. cit., and the conversation occurred when she unexpectedly encountered Maud Watson, while staying in her hotel in preparation for Wimbledon.

6 *See* Lance Tingay, *Tennis: A Pictorial History*, London: Collins, 1977, for an account of the early years of British tennis.

7 A M Waser, 'Tennis in France, 1880-1930', *International Journal of the History of Sport*, Volume 13, no. 2, 1996, pp. 166–176.

8   Antoine (Coco) Gentien, *Aventures d'un Jouer de Tennis*, Paris-Genève: La Palatine, 1953, p. 9.

9   E Digby Baltzell, *Sporting Gentlemen: Men's Tennis from the Age of Honour to the Cult of the Superstar*, New York: The Free Press, 1995, passim.

10 Anthony Wilding, *On The Court and Off*, London: Methuen, 1912, p. 205.

3   Real tennis and the scoring system

1   Heiner Gillmeister, *Tennis: A Cultural History*, London: Leicester University Press, 1997, passim. I have been reliant on Gillmeister's invaluable history throughout this chapter.

2   Krznarik, op. cit., p. 43.

3   Ibid.

4   Gillmeister, op. cit., p. 40.

5   Clerici, op. cit., p. 36.

6   Vijay Amritraj with Richard Evans, *Vijay! from Madras to Hollywood via Wimbledon*, London: Librir Mundi, 1990, p. 54.

7   Richard Evans, *Open Tennis The First Twenty Years: The Players, the Politics, the Pressures, the Passions and the Great Matches*, London: Bloomsbury, 1988, pp. 26–32.

4   The growth of a sporting culture

1   See Norbert Elias and Eric Dunning, *Quest for Excitement: Sport and Leisure in the Civilising Process*, Oxford: Basil Blackwell, 1986.

2   See Neil Tranter, *Sport, Economy and Society in Britain, 1750–1914*, Cambridge: Cambridge University Press, 1998, for an analytic summary of explanations for the growth of sport.

3   Dennis Brailsford, *British Sport: A Social History*, Cambridge: Lutterworth Press, 1992.

4   Steven Connor, *A Philosophy of Sport*, London: Reaktion Books, 2011, p. 22.

5   See Dominic Erdozain, *The Problem of Pleasure: Sport Recreation and the Crisis of Victorian Religion*, Woodbridge: Boydell Press, 2010 for a discussion of Victorian evangelicalism.

6   See David Hilliard, 'UnEnglish and Unmanly: Anglo-Catholicism and Homosexuality', *Victorian Studies*, Winter, 1982, pp. 181–210, and Nick Watson, Stuart Weir and Stephen Friend, 'The Development of Muscular Christianity in Victorian Britain and Beyond', *Journal of Religion and Society*, Volume 7, 2005, no page nos.

7   George Hillyard, *Forty Years of First Class Tennis*, London: Williams and Norgate, 1924, p. 143.

8   Len and Shelley Richardson, *Anthony Wilding: A Sporting Life*, Canterbury: Canterbury University Press, 2005, p. 157.

9   A Wallis Myers, *Memory's Parade*, London: Methuen, 1932.

10 Mabel Brookes, *Crowded Galleries*, London: Heinemann, 1956, p. 105.

5 On the Riviera

1   Mary Blume, *Côte d'Azur: Inventing the French Riviera*, London: Thames and Hudson, 1992, passim.

2   Kenneth Clark, *Another Part of the Wood: A Self Portrait*, London: John Murray, 1974, p. 1.

3   Stéphen Liégeard, *La Côte d'Azur*, Paris: Maison Quintain, 1882, p. 66.

4   Brookes, op. cit., pp. 62–5.

5   Gentien, op. cit., p. 39.

6   Kenneth Silver, *Making Paradise: Art, Modernity and the Myth of the French Riviera*, Cambridge: MIT Press, 2001, p. 49.

7   Patrick Howarth,*When the Riviera Was Ours*, London: Routledge & Kegan Paul, 1977, p. 45.

8   Quoted in Howarth, op. cit., p. 123.

9   Cecil Beaton, *The Glass of Fashion*, New York: Doubleday & Company, 1954, p. 166.

10 Jacques Henri Lartigue, *Mémoires sans Mémoire*, Paris: Editions Robert Laffont, 1975.

11 Helen Wills, *Fifteen–Thirty*, New York: Scribners, 1937, pp. 72–79.

12 Howarth, op. cit., p. 146.

13 Teddy Tinling, *Sixty Years in Tennis*, London: Sidgwick & Jackson, 1983, p. 40 et seq.

6 What's wrong with women?

1   Jeffrey Pearson, *Lottie Dod, Champion of Champions: The Story of an Athlete*, Birkenhead: Countrywise Ltd., 1988.

2   Patricia Campbell Warner, 'Taking up Tennis', in *When the Girls Came Out to Play: The Birth of American Sportswear*, Amherst: University of Massachusetts Press, 2008, p. 50, quoting Jeane Hoffman, 'The Sutton Sisters', in Allison Danzig and Patrick Schwed, eds., *The Fireside Book of Tennis*, New York: Simon & Schuster, 1972, p. 74.

3   Todd, op. cit., p. 129.

4   Ibid., quoting A Wallis Myers, *Lawn Tennis At Home and Abroad*, 1903.

5   Herbert Chipp, *Recollections*, London: Merritt and Hatcher, 1898, p. 57.

6   Laney, op. cit., p. 49.

7   Phyllis Satterthwaite was a beneficiary of the 'shamateurs' system on the Riviera, described in the previous chapter, being, according to Tinling, 'on the payroll of an important chain of Riviera hotels'. Tinling, op. cit. p. 40.

8   Helen Hull Jacobs, *Beyond the Game*, London: Marston, 1950, p. 95.

9   See David Gilbert, 'The Vicar's Daughter and the Goddess of Tennis: Cultural Geographies of Sporting Femininity and Bodily Practice in Edwardian Suburbia', *Cultural Geographies*, vol. 18, no. 2, 2011, pp. 187–207.

10 Mrs Larcombe, 'Chapter on Women's Tennis', in Wilding, op. cit., p. 236.

11 Gilbert, op. cit.

12 Tinling, op. cit., pp. 21–22.

13 *See* Gianni Clerici, *Divina Suzanne Lenglen, la Piu Grande Tennista del Mondo*, Roma: Fandango Libria, 2010, passim.

14 Mary Roberts, 'Samson and Delila Revisited: The Politics of Fashion in 1920s France', in Whitney Chadwick & Tirza True Latimer, eds., *The Modern Woman*

Revisited: Paris Between the Wars, New Brunswick, NJ: Rutgers University Press, 2003, pp. 65–94. Originally published in *American Historical Review*, 98, no.3 (June), 1993, pp. 657–683.

15 Tinling, op. cit., p. 25.

16 Ibid., pp. 34–5.

7 A match out of Henry James

1 The events are described in detail in Larry Engelmann, *The Goddess and the American Girl:the Story of Suzanne Lenglen and Helen Wills*, Oxford: Oxford University Press, 1988; and also by numerous other writers, including Teddy Tinling and A L Laney.

2 Dan Maskell, op. cit., pp. 58–9.

3 Helen Wills, op. cit., p. 21.

4 Helen Wills, op. cit., p. 192.

5 Catherine Horwood, 'Dressing Like a Champion: Women's Tennis Wear in Interwar England', in Christopher Breward, Becky Conekin and Caroline Cox, eds., *The Englishness of English Dress*, Oxford: Berg, 2002, p. 54.

6 Ibid., pp. 45–60.

7 Engelmann, op. cit. pp. 328–9.

8 The lonely American

1 Frank Deford, *Big Bill Tilden: The Triumphs and the Tragedy*, London: Victor Gollancz, 1977. I have been extensively reliant on Deford's biography in this chapter.

2 Dan Maskell, op. cit., p. 251.

3 A L Laney, op. cit. p. 42, 43.

4 Gentien, op. cit., p. 66.

5 Deford, op. cit. p. 60.

9 The Four Musketeers

1 Alexandre Dumas, *The Three Musketeers*, London: Harper Collins, 2008, p. 15.

2 Yann Le Faou, 'Les "Mousquetaires", Ambassadeurs de la France', in Patrick Clastres and Paul Dietschy, eds., *Paume et Tennis en France XV–XX Siècle*, Paris: Nouveau Monde, 2009.

3 Jean Michel Faure, 'National Identity and the Sporting Champion: Jean Borotra and French History', *International Journal of the History of Sport*, vol. 13, no. 1, 1996, pp. 86–100.

4 Laney, op. cit.

5 *See* David Gautier, 'Tennis et Politique: l'example de Jean Borotin', in Clastres and Dietschy, op. cit.

10 Working-class heroes

1 *See* Dan Maskell, op. cit., passim.

2 Ibid., p. 71.

3   Fred Perry, *Fred Perry: An Autobiography*, London: Hutchinson, 1984, p. 9. *See also,*
    Jon Henderson, The Last Champion: the Life of Fred Perry, London: Yellow Jersey Press,
    2009.

4   Fred J Perry, *My Story*, London: Hutchinson & Co., n.d., Chapter XXV 'Fred' – by
    his father (Mr S F Perry fills in some gaps in his son's story).

5   Perry, op. cit., 1984, pp. 63, 59.

6   Perry, op. cit., 1984, p. 42.

7   Ibid., p. 44.

8   Ibid., p. 45.

9   Ibid., p. 85.

11 Tennis in Weimar – and after

1   Deford, interview with Gottfried von Cramm, op. cit., p. 160.

2   Erik N Jensen, *Body by Weimar: Athletes, Gender and German Modernity*, Oxford:
    Oxford University Press, 2010, p. 22.

3   *See* throughout this chapter, Egon Steinkampf, *Gottfried von Cramm: Der Tennis*
    Baron, München: Herbig, 1990.

4   Allison Danzig and Peter Schwed, eds., *The Fireside Book of Tennis*, New York: Simon
    and Schuster, 1972, p. 655.

5   Don Budge, *Don Budge: A Tennis Memoir*, New York: The Viking Press, 1969, p. 89.

6   Tatiana Metternich, *Bericht eines Ungewöhnlichen Lebens*, München: Langen Müller,
    1987.

7   Budge, op. cit., p. 7; Steinkampf, op. cit. Marshall Jon Fisher,
    A Terrible Splendor, New York: Three Rivers Press, 2009.

12 As a man grows older

1   Paul Gallico, 'Funny Game', in *A Farewell to Sport*, London: Simon & Schuster, 1988,
    pp. 137–150.

2   Steve Tignor, *High Strung: Bjorn Borg, John McEnroe, and the Untold Story of Tennis's*
    Fiercest Rivalry, London: Harper Collins, 2011, p. 48.

3   *See* Elizabeth Wilson, *Bohemians: The Glamorous Outcasts*, London: IB Tauris, 2000.

4   Deford, op. cit., p. 60.

5   Bill Tilden, a descendant, (his great grandfather was the brother of Tilden's
    grandfather) told me that the tennis player's name was never mentioned in the
    family.

13 Three women

1   Nancy Spain, *"Teach" Tennant: The Story of Eleanor Tennant, The Greatest Tennis*
    Coach in the World, London: Werner Laurie, 1953. I have made extensive use of the
    biography throughout this chapter.

2   Alice Marble with Dale Leatherman, *Courting Danger*, New York: St Martins Press,
    1991, passim; Sue Davidson, *Changing the Game: The Stories of Tennis Champions Alice*
    Marble and Althea Gibson, Seattle: Seal Press, 1997, passim.

14 Home from the war

1   Raphael Samuel, *The Lost World of British Communism*, London: Verso, 2006, p. 9.

2   Baltzell, op. cit., Chapter 15, 'Indian Summer of a Golden Age: Riggs, Kramer, Gonzales and the Pro Tour', pp. 303–322.

3   Ibid., p. 307, quoting Bobby Riggs (with George McGann), *Court Hustler*, New York, Lipppincott, 1973.

4   Jack Kramer with Frank Deford, *The Game: My Forty Years in Tennis*, London: André Deutsch, 1979, p. 64.

5   William Talbert, *Playing For Life: Billy Talbert's Story*, London: Victor Gollancz, 1959.

6   The obituary, by Jim Murray for the *Los Angeles Times*, is reprinted in Baltzell, op. cit., p. 242.

7   Kramer, op. cit., p. 36. *See also* Julius D Heldman, 'The Style of Jack Kramer', in Danzig and Schwed, eds., op. cit., pp. 279–282.

8   Laney, op. cit., p. 248.

9   Quoted in Kramer, op. cit.

15 Gorgeous girls

1   Kevin Starr, *Embattled Dreams: California in War and Peace: 1940-1950*,Oxford: Oxford University Press, 2002, p. 127.

2   Although Blunt's involvement only became public knowledge in the late 1970s.

3   Tinling, op.cit., p. 126.

4   Ibid., p 119.

5   See Tinling, op. cit., chapters 16 and 17, for his account of this episode.

6   Mandy Merck, 'Hard Fast and Beautiful', in *Mandy Merck, In Your Face: 9 Sexual Studies*, New York: New York University Press, 2000, pp. 52–70.

7   My thanks to Mandy Merck for this information. In Patricia Highsmith's novel Guy Haines is an architect, slowly corrupted and destroyed by the relationship with Bruno. Hitchcock altered the plot to create a happy ending, positioning Haines more as a victim. The decision to make him a tennis player – a simple sportsman – references his naivety, but in choosing the 'sissy' game Hitchcock also slyly underlines the 'queer' undertones of the tale.

16 Opening play

1   David Gray, *Shades of Gray: Tennis Writings of David Gray*, ed., Lance Tingay, London: Collins, 1988, p. 32.

2   Ibid., p. 140. The events surrounding the coming of open tennis are covered in detail both by Gray and by Richard Evans op. cit.

3   Ibid., p. 68.

4   Gordon Forbes, *A Handful of Summers*, London: Heinemann, 1978, p. 29.

17 Those also excluded

1   Sundiata Djata, *Blacks at the Net Vol. I*, Syracuse: Syracuse University Press, 2006, to which I am indebted throughout this chapter.

2   Ibid., p. 8.

3   Ibid., p. 18.

4   Ibid., pp. 25–27.

5   Ibid., p. 30.

6   Davidson, op. cit., p. 131.

7   Herbert Warren Wind, *Game Set and Match: The Tennis Boom of the Sixties and Seventies*, New York: C P Dutton, 1979, p. 126.

8   Peter Bodo, *Courts of Babylon: Tales of Greed and Glory in the Harsh New World of Professional Tennis*, New York: Scribner, 1995, pp. 259–271.

9   Until Kim Clijsters won the US Open in 2010 and the Australian Open in 2011.

10   Amritraj, op. cit., p. 24.

11   Ibid., p. 77.

12   Ibid., p. 164 et. seq.

18 Tennis meets feminism

1   *See* Susan Ware, *Game, Set, Match: Billie Jean King and the Revolution in Women's Sports*, Chapel Hill: University of North Carolina Press, 2011.

2   Billie Jean King with Frank Deford, *The Autobiography of Billie Jean King*, London: Granada, 1982, pp. 146–148.

3   Quoted in Susan Ware, op cit., p. 25.

4   Kramer, op. cit.

5   Howard, op. cit., p. 38.

6   Warren Wind, op. cit., 'Texas and the New Entrepreneurs', pp. 60–70.

7   There are many accounts of this event as all the tennis correspondents covered it. For an insightful recent interpretation see Edward D Miller, 'Billie Jean King: the Tomboy versus the Nerd-Jock', in *Tomboys, Pretty Boys and Outspoken Women*, Ann Arbor: University of Michigan Press, 2011. *See also* Susan Ware, op. cit.; and Warren Wind, 'Mrs King Versus Mr Riggs', in *Warren Wind*, op cit., pp. 114–120.

8   Pearson, op. cit., p. 51.

9   Gentien, op. cit.

10   Pat Griffin, *Strong Women, Deep Closets: Lesbians and Homophobia in Sport*, Champagne, Ill: Human Kinetics, 1998, p. 17.

11   Bodo, op. cit., pp. 280–281.

12   Ware, op. cit.

19 Bad behaviour

1   *See* Warren Wind, op cit., 'The Tennis Explosion', pp. 181–197, for an account of the tennis boom.

2   Tim Adams, *On Being John McEnroe*, London: Yellow Jersey Press, 2003, p. 66.

3   Bodo, op. cit., p. 262.

4   Hitchcock created a murderous tennis star in *Dial M for Murder*, as well as associating tennis and murder in *Strangers on a Train*. The murderer in Woody Allen's *Match Point* is also an (ex) tennis pro. However, in spite of the crime fiction

association between the two, only one real life tennis player has ever been convicted of murder: In 1908 Vere St Thomas Leger Gould was convicted in France, with his wife, of the murder of Emma Levin. He committed suicide in prison on Devil's Island a year later.

5   Ibid., Bodo, op. cit., p. 19.

6   Amritraj, op. cit., pp. 97–98.

7   Bodo., op. cit., p. 385.

8   Dick Hebdige, *Subculture: The Meaning of Style*, London: Methuen, 1979, p. 107.

9   Evans, op. cit., p. 188.

10 Quoted in Tim Adams, op. cit., p. 39.

11 Steve Tignor, op. cit., p. 2.

12 David Foster Wallace, 'Democracy and Commerce at the U S Open', in *David Foster Wallace, Both Flesh and Not: Essays*, London: Hamish Hamilton, 2012, pp. 127–162. (orig. publ. 1996).

20 Corporate tennis

1   Donald Katz, *Just Do It: The Nike Spirit in the Corporate World*, New York: Random House, 1994, p. 7.

2   Ibid., p. 11.

3   Walter Lefeber, *Michael Jordan and the New Global Capitalism*, New York: WW Norton, 1999, p. 50 et. seq.

4   Emmanuel Bayle, 'Le Dévelopment de la Féderation Française de Tennis Sous la Présidence de Philippe Chatrier, 1975–1993: Un Modèle Stratégique pour le Mouvement Sportif et Olympique, in Clastres & Dietschy, op. cit., pp. 219–248.

5   Amritraj, op. cit., p. 204.

6   Tim Adams, op. cit., p. 98.

7   Richard Evans, *McEnroe: A Rage for Perfection*, London: Sidgwick and Jackson, 1982, p. 36.

8   Arthur Ashe, *Portrait in Motion*, Boston: Houghton Mifflin, 1975.

9   Allen Guttmann, *From Ritual to Record: The Nature of Modern Sports*, New York: Columbia University Press, 1978.

10 George Ritzer, *The McDonaldization of Society*, London: Sage, 2004.

21 Women's power

1   Howard, op. cit., p. 28.

2   Ibid.

3   Ibid, p. 55.

4   Martina Navratilova with George Vecsey, *Being Myself*, London: Harper Collins, 1985.

5   Bodo, op. cit., p. 185.

6   Martin Amis, 'Tennis: The Women's Game', in *Visiting Mrs Nabokov and Other Excursions*, London: Cape, 1993, pp. 60–68.

22 Vorsprung durch Technik

1   *See* Barry Smart, *The Sport Star: Modern Sport and the Cultural Economy of Sporting Celebrity*, London: Sage, 2005.

2   Peter Maxton, *From Palm to Power: The Evolution of the Racket*, London: Wimbledon Lawn Tennis Museum, 2008, p. 34.

3   Ibid., p. 37.

4   Ibid., p. 57.

5   Bodo, op. cit., p. 37.

6   Warren Wind, op. cit., pp. 202–203.

7   Chris Jones, 'Nadal's London Calling', *Evening Standard*, 24 October, 2013, World Tour Finals supplement, p. 3.

8   Anon., 'La face obscure d'un champion: Rafael Nadal, l'ère du soupçon', *L'illustré*, July, 2009, pp. 32–35.

9   Paul Hayward, 'Forget purity, sport has never been innocent', *Observer*, sports section, 20 October, 2009, p. 11.

10 Owen Gibson, 'Doping: now it's worse than it's ever been', *Guardian*, sports section, 16 February, 2013, pp. 1–4.

23 Celebrity stars

1   Thorstein Veblen, *The Theory of the Leisure Class*, London: George Allen and Unwin, 1949, Chapter x. (Originally published 1899.)

2   George Orwell, 'The Sporting Spirit', 1945, in George Orwell, *The Collected Essays, Journalism and Letters of George Orwell, Volume 4: In Front of Your Nose, 1945–1950*, Harmonsdworth: Penguin, 1968, pp. 61–62.

3   Steven Connor, op. cit., p. 33.

4   Sylvain Villaret and Philippe Tétart, 'Yannick Noah au Miroir des Médias', in Clastres and Dietschy, pp. 249–270.

5   *See* Boris Becker with Robert Lübenoff and Helmut Sorge, *The Player: The Autobiography*, London: Bantam Books, 2005.

6   S L Price, 'Boris Becker: Broken Promise', *Time*, http://www.time.com, accessed 3 June, 2013.

7   Andrews and Jackson, eds., *Sports Stars: The Cultural Politics of Sporting Celebrity*, London: Routledge, 2001, pp. 7–8. *See also* Barry Smart, op. cit.

8   Smart, op. cit., p 82.

9   Andre Agassi, *Open: An Autobiography*, London: Harper Collins, 2009, passim. In his acknowledgements, Agassi writes of the help he was given in the writing by J R Moehringer; and James W Pipkin devotes a section of his book to the very real but often despised skill of the 'ghost' writer, as a genuine craftsman.

10 Kyle W Kusz, 'Andre Agassi and Generation X: Reading White Masculinity in 1992 America', in Andrews and Jackson, eds., op. cit., pp. 51–69.

11 Agassi, p. 152.

12 Ibid., p. 168.

13 *See* Pipkin, op. cit., who writes insightfully of this 'sense of an ending'.

14 Personal communication, Tariq Ali.

15 Monica Seles, *Getting a Grip: On My Game, My Body, My Mind … Myself*, London: JR Books, 2009. *See also*, Tim Adams, http://www.guardian.co.uk/sport//2009/jul05/monica-seles-interview. Accessed 12 March, 2013.

16 Karen Farrington, *Anna Kournikova*, London: Unanimous, 2001, p. 7.

17 Ibid., p. 23.

18 Michael D Giardina, 'Global Hingis: flexible citizenship and the transnational celebrity', in David L Andrews and Steven J Jackson, op. cit., pp. 201–217.

24 Millennium tennis

1 Derek Birley, *Land of Sport and Glory: Sport and British Society 1887–1910*, Manchester: Manchester University Press, 1995.

2 By 2013 Novak Djokovic was clad in subtler and closer fitting outfits by the Japanese mass fashion company, Uniqlo; Tomas Berdych was dressed by the Swedish fast fashion firm, H & M.

3 John McEnroe with James Kaplan, *Serious: The Autobiography*, London: Time Warner, 2003, p. 87.

4 Peter Bodo, 'Sprezzatura', http://tennis.com/tennisworld/2009/06/sprezzatura.html; accessed 9 September, 2009.

5 René Stauffer, *The Roger Federer Story: Question for Perfection*, New York: New Chapter Press, 2006, p. 194.

6 Bodo, op. cit. 2009.

7 David Foster Wallace, 'Federer Both Flesh and Not', in Foster Wallace, op. cit., pp. 7–33.

8 Charles Baudelaire, 'Landscape', in *The Mirror of Art: Critical Studies*, London: Phaidon, 1955, p. 276.

9 Lynn Barber, 'Anyone for Tension?', *Sunday Times*, Magazine, 5 June, 2011, pp. 14–20.

10 Giles Hattersley, 'New Balls Please', *Sunday Times*, Style, 16 December, 2012, pp. 26–28.

11 Jon Henderson, 'Grisly, ghastly and gripping is just how Andy likes it', *Evening Standard*, 28 January, 2013, p. 59.

12 Gonzales, op. cit., p. 40.

13 Kevin Mitchell, 'You're going through so much pain, but you still enjoy it', *Guardian*, Sport, 30 January, 2012, p. 3.

14 Elizabeth Kaye, 'The Power and the Glory', *Observer*, Magazine, June, 2009.

15 Stuart Jeffries, 'Is Germany too Powerful for Europe?', *Guardian*, G2, 1 April, 2013, p. 11.

16 Martin Amis, 'Tennis Personalities', in David Remnick, ed., *The Only Game in Town… Sports Writing from the New Yorker*, NY: Random House, 2010, pp. 374–376, orig. pub. 1994.

25 The rhetoric of sport

1 McEnroe, op. cit., p. 126.

2 Neil Harman, Court Confidential: Inside the World of Tennis, London: The Robson Press, 2013, pp. xi–xii.

3   Howard, op. cit., p. 78.

4   Tara Magdalinski, *Sport, Technology and the Body: The Nature of Performance*, London: Routledge, 2009.

5   Laney, op. cit., p. 251.

6   Mihir Bose, *The Spirit of the Game: How Sport Made the Modern World*, London: Constable, 2011, p. 565.

7   Ibid., p. 564.

8   Joe Humphreys, *Foul Play: What's Wrong With Sport*, Cambridge: Icon Books, 2008, pp. 231–232.

9   Johan Huizinga, *Homo Ludens: A Study of the Play Element in Culture*, London: Temple Smith, 1970, (1949), passim.

26 Back to the future

1   Larry Elliot, 'What if, this time, the party really is over?', *Guardian*, 6 May, 2013, p. 21.

2   Harman, op. cit., p. xix.

3   Steve Tignor, 'The Rally: The Life and Legacy of Brad Drewett', http://www.tennis.com/pro-game//2013/05/rally-life-and-legacy-brad/drewett/47346, accessed 5 June, 2013.

4   Kevin Mitchell, 'Wimbledon raises prize money to record levels for winners and losers', *Guardian*, 24 April, 2013, p. 43.

5   David Walsh, 'Sponsorship? I get free contact lenses from my optician in Sheffield', *The Sunday Times*, 15 July, 2012, p. 13.

6   Peter Walker, 'Wimbledon women's Quarter-final is Suddenly Not the Name of the Game', *Guardian*, 3 July, 2013, p. 6.

7   *See* Robert Lake, *Social Exclusion in British Tennis: A History of Privilege and Prejudice*, unpublished PhD., Brunel University, 2008.

8   Ware, op. cit., pp. 171–172.

9   Laney, op. cit., p. 269.

10   Harman, op. cit., p. 49.

11   Pat Cash, 'Pat Cash in Melbourne', *Sunday Times*, 12 January, 2014, sports section, p. 13.

12   Kevin Mitchell, 'Djokovic hopes Becker's change of mindset can bring net gains', in *Guardian*, 13 January, 2014, sports section, p. 8.

ACKNOWLEDGEMENTS

The creation of a book is a collective enterprise and, although it is the author's name on the cover, it could not have been created without the publisher, editors, designer, printer, and others who produced it. I should therefore like to thank everyone at Profile Books/Serpent's Tail for their enthusiasm and support and especially Pete Ayrton and Ruthie Petrie; Cecilia Mackay for her picture research, and Sue Lamble for the design.

Although they are unaware of the help they have given me, I should also like to thank the two best television commentators, Mats Wilander and Frew McMillan for their thoughtful and genial insights.

PHOTO CREDITS

INDEX